Studies in Contemporary Economics

Wolfgang Gebauer (Ed.)

Foundations of European Central Bank Policy

With 36 Figures

Springer-Verlag Berlin Heidelberg GmbH

Professor Dr. Wolfgang Gebauer
Johann Wolfgang Goethe-Universität
Professur für Geld und Währung
Zeppelinallee 29
D-60325 Frankfurt/Main, FRG

Die Deutsche Bibliothek - CIP-Einheitsaufnahme
Foundations of European central bank policy/
Wolfgang Gebauer (ed.). - Heidelberg : Physica-Verl., 1993
(Studies in contemporary economics)
ISBN 978-3-7908-0690-8 ISBN 978-3-642-50302-3 (eBook)
DOI 10.1007/978-3-642-50302-3

NE: Gebauer, Wolfgang [Hrsg.]

Originally published by Physica-Verlag Heidelberg in 1993.

88/7130-543210 - Printed on acid-free paper

Table of Contents

Introduction

European central bank policy is already taking place today in an informal way. It comprises, in short, European exchange rate management and interest rate policy decisions within and without the European Monetary System (EMS). A focal point of such policy actions are the money market operating targets of European Central Banks. Those central bank policies appear to be dominated, however, by the Deutsche Bundesbank. This has caused recurring critical discussion of European asymmetries and German leadership in monetary stabilization policies, before and after the EMS turbulences of September 1992. However, it should be pointed out that German dominance has increasingly evolved in a cooperative way, ever since the Committee of European Central Bank Governors began to meet regularly in 1964; the Basle-Nyborg accord of 1987 formed a further stage of cooperative efforts within the EMS.

Presently, a small group of countries (including Benelux and Austria) generally follows, after prior 'concertation', German monetary policy patterns. In this narrow sense, there exists a European central bank policy within a "Deutsche-Mark-Zone". In a broader sense, European central bank policy is shaped, after proper consultation, by monetary cooperation between the larger EMS countries, but once again dominantly influenced by Germany; recent problems of high interest rates in France and elsewhere due to (relative) restrictive German monetary policies are striking examples.

German monetary dominance, in the narrow or broad sense, obviously creates, in the long-run, an untenable situation in the eyes of European partner countries. And this is precisely where the main argument for implementation of the Maastricht treaty comes in: it provides a scheme for balanced cooperation between European countries by explicitly sharing responsibilities and progressing towards monetary and economic union. Indeed, it should be envisaged that the second stage of this integration process will begin in January 1994, as originally planned. We shall witness, in particular, a "mutation" of the old Basle Committee of European Central Bank Governors into a European Monetary Institute (EMI), laying the ground for a future European Central Bank System.

However, the analytical foundations of future European Central Bank policies are seriously incomplete, to say the least. Most important, the main theoretical and empirical foundations of monetary targeting have been progressively crumbling away during the last decade. Given the international evidence of downgrading or de facto abandoning of monetary targeting, traditional monetarist views on a basic central bank policy design are to be seriously questioned. In addition, the implementation of future European central bank policies faces many unresolved instrumental, operational and institutional issues. Finally, open analytical and conceptual questions exist with countries outside the forthcoming European monetary union (EMU) - including those countries that are presently member of the EMS but might not qualify for EMU.

The present volume tries to tackle these issues in a selective way; there can be, of course, no attempt to treat all - so far missing or controversial - foundations of European central bank policy in a comprehensive way. In Part I, the basic, century-old issue of the exogeneity of money is addressed. Thereafter, operational and institutional problems of an optimal European policy design are dealt with, including the Ecu. In a final third part, selected external issues are taken up. Except for two contributed articles, all papers were presented, in a preliminary way, at an international workshop on "Foundations of European Central Bank Policy", held at the European University Institute (EUI) in Florence in June 1992. The present volume summarizes in selected articles the topics that have been discussed.

The *first part* opens with an empirical study of **Manfred Willms** (University of Kiel) in which the author claims the German money stock, narrowly defined as M1, to be controllable by the Deutsche Bundesbank. But broadly defined monetary aggregates, such as M3, are not dominantly influenced by monetary base control, as variations in the relevant money multiplier are too large. Since these variations consist of unpredictable changes in the coefficients of the multiplier coefficients, they can in fact not sufficiently be anticipated. Willms concludes that the German monetary base is endogenously determined by the multiplier in so far as the Bundesbank uses M3 as monetary target variable.

The money-supply approach in general is critizised by **Matthias Müller** (University of Frankfurt/Main) who - pointing at the institutional factors of the money creation process and the refinancing mechanism in Germany - stresses that the Bundesbank has too often failed to hit its monetary targets in the past. He considers the money stock being determined by real factors, i.e. fiscal policy or real wages. For that reason Müller supports a concept of "endogenous money" and abandons the often used idea of an exogenous money supply. The seemingly high success of the Bundesbank in keeping inflation rates low in a European comparison is only due, in his view, to the high degree of credibility of the Bundesbank which leads the markets to perform 'self-fulfilling expectations' on the effectiveness of monetary policy instruments with respect to a pre-announced anti-inflationary monetary policy.

The critique on the concept of exogenous money supply is strengthened by **Andreas Beyer** (University of Frankfurt/Main) who examines several concepts of exogeneity and causality and finds that the result of empirical work on the exogeneity of money is closely related with the used definition of exogeneity and causality, respectively. After showing that the definition of causality by Granger and the empirical work of Sims based on testing Granger-causality is insufficient with respect to identification restrictions and the completeness of the model ("Lucas-critique"), Bayer introduces the three concepts of exogeneity established by Engle/Hendry/Richard (weak, strong and super exogeneity). Super exogeneity in the sense of Engle/Hendry/Richard includes the structural invariance of the model with respect to the parameters of interest and therefore takes account of the Lucas-critique. Bayer concludes that super-exogeneity cannot be found for the money stock. It follows that - in contrast to a monetarist point of view - the money supply is potentially determined by the price level, and not vice versa.

From this point of view a monopoly on central bank money is not necessary for the functioning of the monetary and financial system. **Stefan Kalb** (EUI, Florence) analyzes the working of "currency competition" by looking closely on the historic example of the "Suffolk System" in New-England, 1824. He comes to the result that such a liberal form of money-"supply" may on the one hand enhance welfare by making the financial system more effective but on the other hand does not necessarily imply danger for price stability. According to its endogenous character, money can only be expanded by an enhanced money demand of the public which itself does not bear inflationary pressure.

The *second part* begins with a paper by **Francesco Papadia and Ciro Schioppa** (Banca d'Italia, Rome) analyzing the improvement in the process of economic convergence to enter the final phase of the European Monetary Union. A comparison between the progress still to be made by the member countries and the development of the convergence criteria variables from 1979 to mid-1992, leads the authors to the result that reaching the convergence criteria of the Maastricht treaty until 1996 is still possible for all EC member states except Greece, if the positive development of the respective variables can be assumed to continue in the future.

This optimistic view is not shared by **Hans-Jürgen Treutler** (Hessische Landeszentralbank, Frankfurt/Main) who misses necessary institutional patterns for a successful stabilization policy and a sufficient social consensus on a strong anti-inflationary monetary policy in some European member states. He claims a considerable part of the success of some countries not to result from their own stabilization policy but from pegging their currency to the D-Mark. Nevertheless, the convergence criteria written down in the Maastricht treaty can be interpreted, in his view, as a sign for the willingness to perform stabilization policies in all relevant countries. However, the obvious impossibility of some member states to fulfil the criteria may carry the danger that in the end the criteria will not be taken too serious. Expecting this, Treutler fears that many countries might reduce their efforts, thus endangering the whole project. In his view, it is necessary to gain credibility for the unification process as a whole and for monetary policy in special. To achieve the latter, monetary targeting should be continued, as it has performed, according to Treutler, adequately in terms of anti-inflationary policy in the past.

The organization of monetary policy in the transition to EMU, i.e. in phase II of the Delors report, is analyzed in a contributed paper by **Daniel Gros** (CEPS, Bruxelles). In phase II the European Monetary Institute will begin to implement European monetary policy actions, whereas the ultimate responsibility for monetary policy remains in the hands of the national central banks and governments. The question therefore is how to control overall European monetary expansion, given a continued high degree of autonomy for the national central banks. Gros argues that control of the money stock cannot be technically executed via a clearing system, because the EMI will not be able to rely on a stable demand for clearing balances by commercial banks, since clearing will be mainly done at the national level in national currencies, nor through control of the demand of the public for currency in circulation, since the common single currency will be introduced only in the final stage of EMU. For that reason Gros proposes a uniform community-wide reserve requirement system to put an upper limit on total monetary expansion during the transition period. Nevertheless, because of its 'tax-on-deposits' character, reserve requirements are not seen to be an ideal instrument of monetary policy in general.

Pompeo Della Posta (EUI, Florence) examines the reasons in favour of coordination, autonomy or discipline of fiscal policies in the European Union against the background of the convergence criteria. Before analyzing strategic games between a domestic treasury and different players (national central bank, European central bank, foreign treasury, private sector) he first presents the main arguments for the three fiscal policy regimes. Della Posta fears that countries that are well within the limits imposed by the Maastricht treaty probably feel authorized to run expansionary fiscal policies such that there might be a tendency in some countries to exploit the "room of manoeuvre" left in the treaty.

The possibility of using the term structure of interest rates (yield curve) to predict business cycles is discussed in a paper by **Klaus Schmidt** (University of Frankfurt/Main). By using LSE-estimation techniques, he finds the spread (the difference between a long- and a short-term interest rate, indicating the slope - not the level - of the yield curve) to have predictive power for growth rates of German real GNP up to 1.5 years into the future. According to his results, an inverse yield curve (with higher short-term rates than long-term rates) indicates a forthcoming decline in the growth rates of real GNP and vice versa. However, a satisfying theoretical background for this empirical phenomenon is still missing. A close relationship between the spread and several components of GNP (consumption, investment in buildings and investment in equipment) can nevertheless be claimed. The possibility remains to use the spread in order to forecast real GNP growth. If the spread would reflect central bank policy in a consistent and symmetric way, the term structure of interest rates could be seen as a serious candidate for an indicator on a European level.

Alfred Steinherr (EIB, Luxemburg) concentrates, in a contributed article, on the role of the Ecu. The Ecu is described as a complicated weighted currency basket based on the 12 community currencies, its weights being a function of current exchange rates which themselves are a function of the particular international interest rate differentials. Steinherr points out that the Ecu as a weighted basket (resp. as a diversified portfolio) and the Ecu as a currency are two different subjects: there is no risk-free arbitrage forcing returns of both to equilibriate even if transaction costs are considered. As a result, the Ecu can be regarded independent of the basket. Steinherr defines the *official Ecu* as being created by the EMS treaty and used for certain official transactions and by the central banks. In contrast, the *private Ecu* has developed in the markets as a financial innovation, with the contracting parties denominating payment obligations in Ecu, thereby accepting its official definition. The *abstract Ecu* is conceived by Steinherr as the future single European currency that will be established according to the Maastricht treaty, independent of the basket definition. The advantage of the private Ecu prior to the establishment of EMU and one of the major reasons for its success (besides the diversifaction argument) is seen against this 'abstract' function - i.e. that Ecu will be the single European currency in stage III. For this reason, Steinherr anticipates that the private Ecu will perform a considerable growth phase, prior to stage III of EMU, indicating that the public intends to exploit the advantages of the forthcoming larger European financial markets.

The *third part* of the volume considers external issues and starts with a paper by **Stefan Collignon** (AUME, Paris) analyzing the possibilities of integrating the Central and Eastern European countries to EMU. To reduce inflation and to render money scarce, i.e. to establish the main precondition to regain the store of value function of money, several tasks of systemic transformation are identified: privatization to clarify property rights and to enable economic decision making, price liberalization to give companies the autonomy to manage resources and production in accordance with money market signals, currency convertibility in internal and external markets to make integration into world markets feasible, stabilization of public finance to reduce budget deficits and to build up an efficient tax system, and appropriate income and exchange rate policies. According to Collignon, the EC should furnish external support to reach these aims by accepting Association Agreements in the short-run and by installing an Ecu-Zone consisting of an Ecu-Zone Surveillance Board, a Reserve Pool & Stabilization Fund and an Exchange Rate Mechanism in the long-run. Such arrangements might provide greater confidence in the economic development of the Eastern and Central European countries, thus encouraging potential investors.

Akos Valentinyi (Institute for Economic and Market Research, Budapest) uses the example of Hungary to describe the problems of Eastern European countries in achieving currency convertibility on the way to a market oriented economy. After analyzing several different definitions for currency convertibility, the conditions for its introduction are examined. Valentinyi finds that the benefits and costs of currency convertibility depend crucially on the manner of its introduction: a fast liberalization probably leads early to the benefits of currency convertibility - sharper competition in the domestic market, rapid development of the new price system expressing relative scarcities, better adjustment capability of the economy, increase in investment propensity of non-residents - but might enhance the danger of higher inflation; a slow liberalization may avoid this danger but instead lead to a severe recession. After introduction of currency convertibility, its sustainability must be confirmed. To achieve this aim, Valentinyi points out several central factors, such as the tax system, the budget deficit, the institutional aspects of the monetary system and the exchange rate regime that have to be taken into account. Being aware of this broad field of problems and the lack of information about the reactions of the economic agents during the transition period, Valentinyi concludes that liberalization and introduction of currency convertibility should be carried out carefully and stepwise, as the existing policy instruments cannot cope with possibly upcoming shocks.

Not only the Central and Eastern European countries, but also the Nordic countries try to establish tighter relations to the European Community. One of the obvious signs of this development has been the exchange rate pegging of the currencies of Norway, Sweden and Finland to the Ecu. This pegging is analyzed by **Sinimaaria Ranki** (Swedish School of Economics and Business Administration, Helsinki) from the Nordic point of view. She stresses that the composition of the Ecu basket does not correspond to the composition of the foreign trade relations between the Nordic countries and the EC member countries. If the pegging will be sustained, an adaptation of the foreign trade relations to the structure of the Ecu can be expected which will intensify the relations of the EC to the Nordic countries towards a full membership. Therefore, the Ecu-pegging is justified more in political than in economic terms; a strategy of adapting the foreign trade structure might lead to a recession due to a fall in foreign demand which can already be observed in Finland, as the empirical part of Ranki's paper shows. She concludes that it was only a short-term gain in credibility being bought by Ecu-pegging. The positive short-run effect was turned around by strong economic imbalances, leading to devaluation. It follows that a politically optimal but economically suboptimal exchange rate commitment should be sufficiently credible to signal strong anti-inflationary stabilization policies.

In retrospect, the workshop proved to be a unique and truly international event - conceived at Frankfurt University, conducted at the premises of the European University Institute in Florence, and attended by scholars from ten countries. The selected contributions assembled in this volume reflect such wide-ranging participation. Indeed, it was precisely international scientific cooperation which made the event a successful one. Recent, most deplorable developments as regards "foreigners" in Germany are forcing me to state such a truism explicitly.

Finally, it should be emphasized that the workshop could not have taken place without many helping hands. Most importantly, I would like to express my gratitude and esteem to Secretary General Dr. Buzzonetti of the European University Institute in Florence for his generous and decisive backing of the workshop idea right from the beginning, despite some initial obstacles. I am indebted to some of his collaborators as well, in particular to Mrs. Pascucci, who provided the necessary organizational logistics, and to Mr. Hulley and Mr. Di Tommaso, who helped in solving the housing problem resp. in providing a perfect conference room and cafeteria facilities. Not to forget, my thoughts of gratitude are with those members of the EUI Economics Department, who in various ways supported the workshop in an European spirit.

As regards helping hands "at home", generous financial support by the Bankenverband Hessen and the Landeszentralbank in Hessen is gratefully acknowledged. Explicit thanks are going as well to my Frankfurt collaborators, who demonstrated an impressing motivation and capability in scientific and organizational terms. Matthias Müller and Elisabeth Walch perfectly settled the task of bringing the manuscripts into their final shape. Last not least, I am indebted to all participants and collaborators for their willingness to invest time and energy, thus contributing to a most stimulating workshop.

Frankfurt, February 1993 Wolfgang Gebauer

Part I

Endogenous Money

The Money Supply Approach: Empirical Evidence for Germany

Manfred Willms
University of Kiel

1 Introduction

In the post-war period, Germany has experienced the lowest inflation rate of all industrial countries. The moderate and relatively stable inflation rate reduced price uncertainty and contributed to economic growth, since real interest rates could be kept on a longrun low level and inflationary expectations did not induce severe disturbances to the economy.

The reasons for this record are threefold: First, the Bundesbank enjoys a high degree of independence. An accomodation of the government's short-sighted employment oriented budgetary policies has been carefully avoided. Second, the Bundesbank is primarily committed to the achievement of price level stability. The Bundesbank act requires the Bank to support the general course of economic policy only as long as the achievement of price level stability is not endangered. Third, the Bundesbank views price level stability and inflation, at least over longer time horizons, as monetary phenomena. The Bank, therefore, pays special attention to the evolution of monetary aggregates.[1]

This paper analyzes the money supply process in Germany over the last three decades. Section 2 outlines the basic approach of money stock control of the Deutsche Bundesbank. Section 3 shows the impact of policy instruments on the stock of high powered money (the monetary base) and the change in monetary instruments over time. Section 4 investigates the interrelationship between the monetary base and the monetary aggregates M1 and M3 by applying the cointegration technique. This section examines whether a tendency towards a long-run equilibrium exists between the monetary base and the money stocks. Finally, section 5 describes the behavior of the money multiplier for M3 and its components.

2 Money Stock Control Procedure of the Bundesbank

Although controlling the money supply has always been in the center of the monetary policy of the Bundesbank, the explicit formulation and announcement

[1] For empirical evidence on the relationship between the growth of the money stock and inflation see Deutsche Bundesbank (1992).

of a target rate for the growth of a monetary aggregate was first introduced for the year 1975.[2] Until 1987, the target aggregate has been the "Central Bank Money Stock". This aggregate, a sum of currency in the hands of the public and demand, time, and savings deposits weighted by their 1974 required reserve ratios, is a reduced form of the money stock M3. It differs from M3 by the weights associated with the various types of deposits. In M3 these weights are unity. Since 1988, the Bundesbank uses the money stock M3 itself as a target variable, defined as the sum of currency in the hands of the public, demand deposits, time deposits plus funds borrowed by banks for less than 4 years and savings deposits at statutory notice. The Bundesbank justifies the application of wider monetary aggregates as target variable instead of M1 by its empirically observed close relationship to the price level and by its relatively reliable reaction to changes in monetary policy.[3]

The Bundesbank utilizes either straight growth rates or a range of growth rates of its chosen target variable. The growth rates or ranges are announced at the end of a year for the year ahead. They are calculated by considering the expected growth rate of potential output $\hat{y}^e$, a target rate of inflation $\hat{P}^*$ (since 1985 2 per cent) and the expected trend rate of velocity $\hat{V}^e$. Thus, the target rate of the money stock M^* is determined by applying the following quantity theory equation:

$$\hat{M}^* = \hat{y}^e + \hat{P}^* - \hat{V}^e \tag{2}$$

The chosen target variable is jointly determined by the behavior of the Bundesbank, the commercial banks, and the public. Therefore, the target variable is not under the Bundesbank's direct control. The Bundesbank can directly control only the stock of high powered money (the monetary base) which it supplies as a monopolist. This aggregate can be controlled by fixing either the quantity or the price. If the quantity is fixed, the price will be an endogenous variable, and if the price is fixed, the quantity will be endogenous. Principally, the Bundesbank applies the second concept. All policy instruments are aimed at the supply price of the monetary base.[4] However, the supply price is not directly observable. The variable which best reflects the supply price is the call-money rate in the Frankfurt interbank market. This is the rate at which banks borrow very short-term funds from each other. The stock of base money is affected whenever the Bundesbank offers rates that deviate from the call-money rate. If the Bundesbank offers higher rates, banks will channel funds to the Bundesbank, thus contracting the volume of base money. If lower rates are offered, the monetary base expands. Arbitrage ensures that the call-money rate immediately reacts to changes in the Bundesbank's policy instruments. Consequently, the call-money rate can be

---

[2] On the reasons for introducing a money stock target see Schlesinger (1985), pp 124 - 131.

[3] See Issing (1992), p 4.

[4] For an excellent discussion of this approach see Neumann, von Hagen (1992).

interpreted as the Bundesbank's operational target variable.[5]

The supply price of base money together with the public's and the banks' demand for base money determines the equilibrium money stock. The demand for and the allocation of base money between currency and reserves depend on portfolio decisions in both sectors, especially on the size and structure of deposits. The Bundesbank calls this money stock control procedure "control via money market conditions". Thus:

> "The Bundesbank uses its instruments to control the supply price of base money such that the equilibrium quantity, together with the equilibrium portfolio allocations of banks and non-banks, results in the desired money supply".[6]

A schema of the money stock control process is presented in Figure 1. By aiming at the interbank call-money rate, the Bundesbank tries to generate a predictable impact on those interest rates which are not under its direct control (bank deposit, bond market, and bank lending rates). These interest rates, in turn, determine the demand for bank credits and bank deposits and thus for M3.[7]

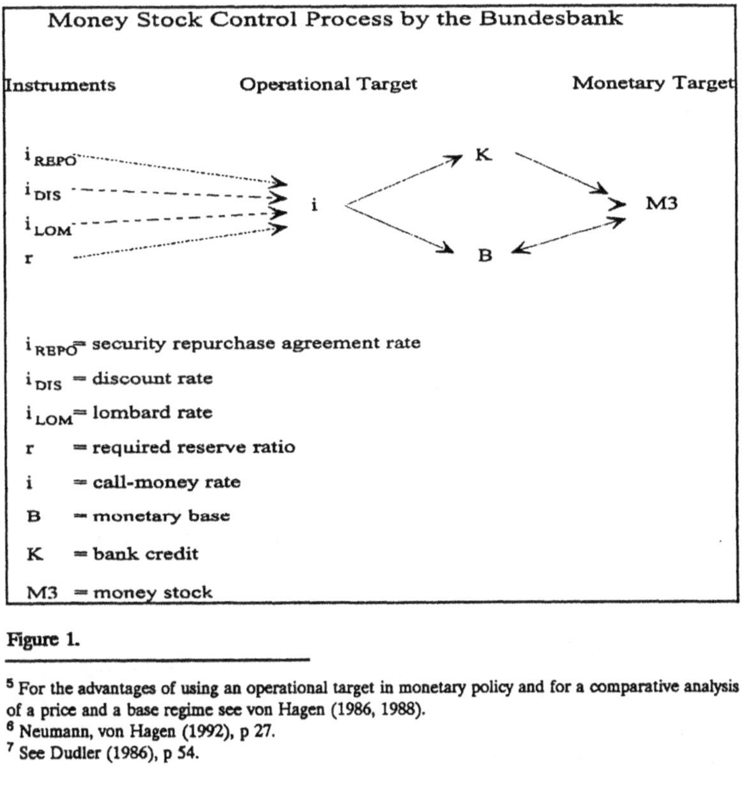

Figure 1.

[5] For the advantages of using an operational target in monetary policy and for a comparative analysis of a price and a base regime see von Hagen (1986, 1988).
[6] Neumann, von Hagen (1992), p 27.
[7] See Dudler (1986), p 54.

By influencing the call-money rate and by quantity restrictions the Bundesbank supplies that volume of base money which it considers to be consistent with the desired expansion of M3. Experience shows that changes in policy instruments generate the expected impact on M3 by a time lag of one to two quarters.[8]

3 Policy Instruments and their Impact on the Monetary Base

Although the Bundesbank controls the money stock via money market conditions and does not directly focus on controlling the monetary base, the effects of the policy instruments show up in this variable. It is the monetary base and not M3 which directly reflects the course of monetary policy.[9]

Figure 2 illustrates the development of the monetary base adjusted for the impact of changes of required reserves and its source components for the period 1960:1 to 1989:12. The adjustment has been carried out by the multiplicative method applied by the Sachverständigenrat.[10] The multiplicatively adjusted monetary base is defined as

(3.1)
$$B^a = B \cdot KF,$$

with

(3.2)
$$KF = \prod_{\tau=t_0}^{t} \frac{B_\tau + \sum_{i=1}^{n} (r_{i,\tau-1} - r_{i,\tau}) D_{i,\tau-1}}{B_\tau}$$

B^a = multiplicatively adjusted monetary base
B = ordinary monetary base
KF = correction factor
D = deposits
r = required reserve ratio
i = type of deposit

During the period under consideration, the Bundesbank conducted monetary policy under exchange rate constraints.[11] Until 1973 policy was restricted by the Bretton Woods System and after that by the European Currency Snake.

[8] Deutsche Bundesbank (1985), p 23; Jahnke (1991).

[9] For this reason, since years, the German Council of Economic Experts (Sachverständigenrat) favors the use of central bank money instead of M3 as target variable of monetary policy.

[10] Sachverständigenrat (1991), pp 271 ff.

[11] For a detailed analysis of the Bundesbank operations under exchange rate constraints see von Hagen (1989) and Neumann, von Hagen (1992).

Figure 2:

Development of Multiplicatively Adjusted Monetary Base and its Components 1960,1 - 1989,12

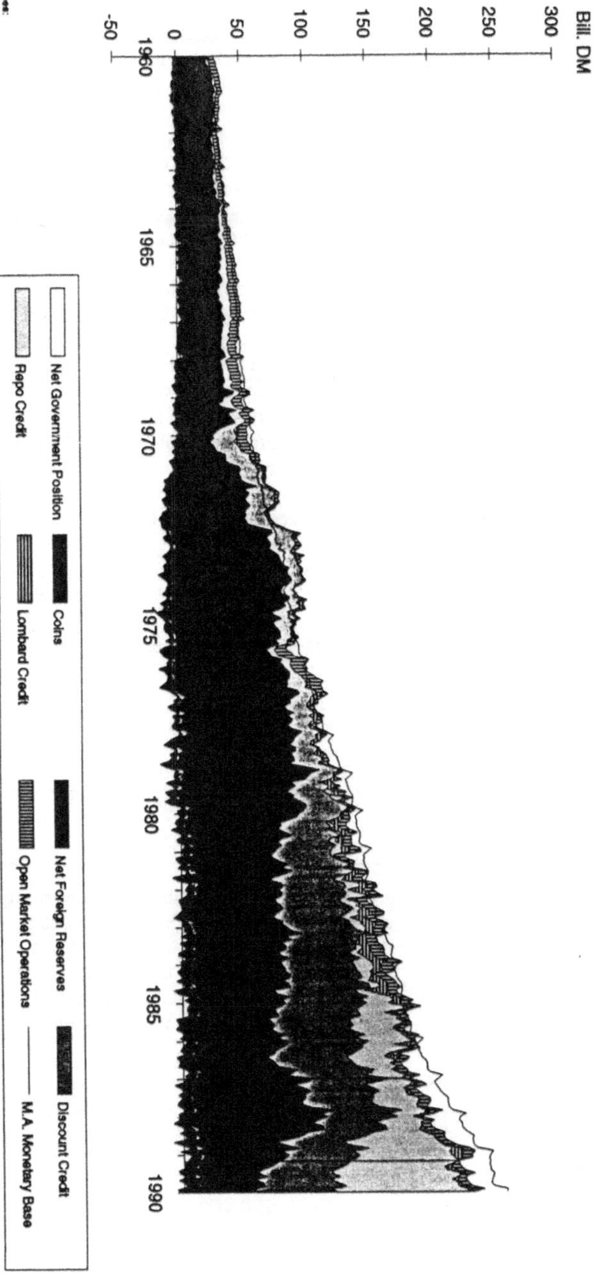

Sources:
Multiplicatively Adjusted Monetary Base: Sachverständigenrat
Components: Monthly Reports of the Deutsche Bundesbank

Since 1979 monetary policy is confronted with the exchange rate constraints set by the European Monetary System (EMS). While these constraints are due to government decisions, the Bundesbank voluntarily adopted a self-imposed restriction by trying to smooth DM/Dollar exchange rate fluctuations after the breakdown of the Bretton Woods System.

The Bundesbank always took great efforts to sterilize the impact of exchange market interventions on the monetary base. In the Bretton Woods era the sterilization was accomplished solely by counteracting operations in the domestic components. In the EMS era sterilization can also take place by offsetting interventions in different exchange markets, i.e., the purchase of EMS currencies and the sale of Dollars by a similar amount.

The central question is to what extent the Bundesbank was able to sterilize the influence of foreign reserve inflows on the monetary base. Obviously, for most of the period from 1960:1 to 1989:12 foreign reserves did not cause severe problems with respect to money stock control.[12] This was either due to the fact that no disturbances occurred within the international monetary system or that they have been eliminated by exchange rate adjustments. Accordingly, a number of empirical studies conclude that the Bundesbank could almost completely sterilize foreign exchange market interventions and that exchange rate constraints did not substantially interfere with money stock control.[13]

There were only a few periods in which pressures from the foreign exchange market made complete sterilization impossible so that interventions caused growth rates of the monetary base far above the long-run average. This was particularly the case from 1970:9 to 1973:7 and from 1986:5 to 1988:4 (Table 1).

Table 1. Average Annual Growth Rates of the Monetary Base and Growth Contributions of the Foreign and Domestic Component - per cent -

		Contribution of	
Period	B^a	Foreign Component	Domestic Component
1970:9 - 1973:7	10.40	18.85	- 8.45
1986:5 - 1988:4	8.11	7.52	0.59

During the first period the high growth rates of the monetary base were due to the substantial interventions within the final stage of the Bretton Woods System. In the second period the interventions were related to the Bundesbank's efforts to dampen the depreciation of the Dollar. As a result, during this period the actual growth rates of Central Bank Money (1986 and 1987) and of M3 (1988) exceeded their target rates considerably. For most other periods of excessive

[12] Figure 2 shows that net foreign reserves substantially increased only during relatively short periods while they were stable or even declining during much longer periods.

[13] See for example Willms (1971); Obstfeld (1983); Mastropasqua, Micossi, Rinaldi (1988); Bofinger (1988).

growth of the monetary base, a systematic impact of the foreign component could not be observed.

A more detailed analysis of Bundesbank behavior under exchange rate constraints presents von Hagen (1989). By investigating the period from 1979 to 1987, von Hagen distinguished between short-run and long-run sterilization effects and separates periods of offsetting and non-offsetting exchange market interventions. One of his findings is that the Bundesbank has always been able to fully sterilize the short-run impact of interventions by counteracting money market and lombard credit operations. With respect to the long-run effect on the monetary base the conclusion is that the Bundesbank can successfully sterilize in periods of offsetting interventions but has been less successful in periods of non-offsetting interventions (1986 and 1987). Offsetting interventions have been carried out in periods in which the DM was weak in one market but strong in another. Such interventions were impossible when the DM was strong both vis-a-vis the Dollar and the EMS-currencies.

In addition to Figure 2 where the absolute importance of foreign reserves and the various instruments of monetary policy is illustrated, Table 2 provides a long-run overview of the relative importance of foreign reserves and the application of the various instruments of monetary policy. Remarkably, foreign reserves sometimes contributed more than 90 per cent to the monetary base. This contribution had declined to less than 20 per cent by the end of 1989.

The substantial changes in the stock of foreign reserves made a flexible use of those instruments necessary that determine the domestic component of the monetary base. For a long time, discount credits have been the most important instrument for smoothing the impact of changes of foreign reserves on the monetary base. When foreign reserves increased, discount credits have been reduced, and they have been expanded when foreign reserves declined. For similar purposes the net government position and required reserve policy have been utilized. Their contribution to the monetary base was sometimes positive and sometimes negative. Changes in the net government position reflect the Bundesbank's efforts to channel government deposits from central bank accounts to the banking sector or vice versa, depending on the inflow or outflow of foreign reserves. Sterilisation effects, by required reserves, have not only been obtained by increases of required reserve ratios on deposits of residents, but also by special ratios for non-residents. In some periods reserve ratios of 80 per cent were imposed on the growth of non-residents' deposits. However, since the late 1970s the Bundesbank has considerably reduced the burden on the banking sector with respect to required reserves. The average reserve ratio went down from 7.93 per cent in 1975 to 4.86 per cent in 1989. As a result, by the end of 1989 required reserve policy contributed 16.74 per cent to the adjusted monetary base.

Lombard credits have never played an important role in determining the monetary base. With a few exceptions their contribution has been negligible.

The most obvious change occurred with respect to open market operations. While in the 1960s their contribution to the monetary base was much greater than that of the discount credits, their influence has declined dramatically since the early 1970s. Within the legal framework of open market operations, in 1980 the

Bundesbank introduced a new instrument, security-based repurchase agreements (REPOs). In the meantime, REPOs became the most important instrument of monetary policy. At the end of 1989 their contribution to the monetary base reached 41 per cent.

Table 2. Multiplicatively Adjusted Monetary Base and its Main Components - End of Year Data -

	B^a Bill. DM	Contribution of Components in per cent						
		Net Foreign Reserves	Discount Credit	Open Market Operations	Lombard Credit	Required Reserves	Net Government Position	Repo Credit
1960	26,55	90,88	5,63	20,03	0,50	- 4,67	- 9,33	0,00
1965	41,88	74,89	9,81	14,39	0,05	- 1,31	1,58	0,00
1970	58,61	44,53	32,24	12,85	2,63	8,01	- 2,16	0,00
1975	90,44	90,76	17,40	1,62	0,30	- 11,53	- 13,27	0,00
1980	140,91	63,30	23,60	3,16	1,68	1,80	- 1,87	0,00
1985	179,78	37,11	35,86	4,07	5,11	12,42	3,14	10,25
1989	258,03	19,27	24,44	1,21	0,05	16,74	- 0,78	41,20

Sources: Adjusted Monetary Base: Sachverständigenrat. Components: Monthly Reports of the Deutsche Bundesbank

The substantial change in the structure of the domestic components of the monetary base indicates a considerable shift in the Bundesbank's control procedure especially after the breakdown of the Bretton Woods System. Although the Bundesbank did not give up its basic philosophy of money stock control via the control of money market conditions it tightened the application of the directly interest rate-affecting instruments.

Until mid-1973, the initiative to create reserves was to a large extent in the hands of commercial banks. At the given discount or open market rate private banks could borrow through the discount window or by open market operations as long as they had adequate securities and their rediscount quota was not fully used up. During this time, commercial banks held stocks of papers which they could liquidate at the Bundesbank at any time, they held excess reserves, and they had unused rediscount quota at their disposal. Since the mid 1970s the Bundesbank systematically fixes the discount rate below the call-money rate so that borrowing through the discount window became the least expensive source of refinancing. Accordingly, the banks fully exploit their rediscount quota and hold negligible amounts of excess reserves.

On the other hand, commercial banks have free access to Lombard borrowing. However, since the Lombard rate is normally fixed above the call-money rate, this is the most expensive source of refinancing from the Bundesbank. Therefore, banks use this form of borrowing only during short periods of extreme reserve demand. If necessary, the Bundesbank can restrict excessive Lombard borrowing by introducing Lombard quotas or by making Lombard loans subject to daily cancellation.

Whereas the discount rate and the Lombard rate, due to their signalling function, are not frequently changed, security repurchase agreements allow for a flexible adjustment of money market conditions. Within this instrument the Bundesbank offers volume tenders and interest tenders. In the case of volume tenders the Bundesbank announces the interest rate at which the banks can make bids. The Bundesbank then allocates a limited volume at a constant share according to the amount requested by the individual bank. With respect to interest tenders the Bundesbank asks for quantity and interest rate bids and allocates the volume to the banks which offer the highest interest rates. Since tenders have a short maturity between three days and two months and since several tenders with different expiration dates are in the market, the Bundesbank can continuously decide on new volumes and new conditions. Therefore, repurchase agreements are an optimal instrument, both for short-run and long-run base money control.

The interrelationship between the discount rate, the Lombard rate and the call-money rate is illustrated in the upper section of Figure 3. Until the mid 1970s, compared to the subsequent period, the call-money rate fluctuated much more and was more frequently outside the range determined by the discount rate and the Lombard rate. Obviously, the change in the application of policy instruments after the breakdown of the Bretton Woods System led to a stabilization of the call-money rate and enabled the Bundesbank better to keep it within the range of the other rates. Periods in which the call-money rate was above the Lombard rate, i.e., when Lombard borrowing was more attractive than borrowing in the interbank market, the Bundesbank made use of the restrictions described before. As a result, the combination of interest policy and quantity constraints by rediscount quota, Lombard quota, and reserve requirements allowed the Bundesbank closely to control the monetary base. Accordingly, the growth rates of the multiplicatively adjusted monetary base (lower section of Figure 3) systematically move in the opposite direction as the interest rates.

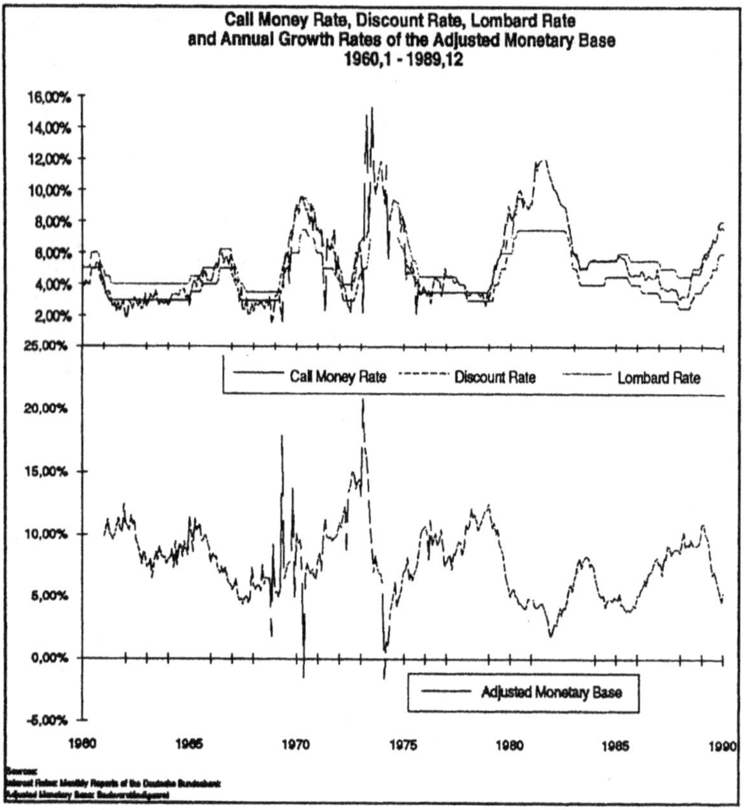

Figure 3.

4 Relationship between the Monetary Base and the Money Stock

Independent of the specific control regime, the monetary base plays a central role within the money supply process of each country. In the long run, an expansion of other monetary aggregates is not possible without the expansion of the monetary base. With respect to the relationship between the monetary base and monetary aggregates the following questions arise:

- What is the relative importance of the monetary base and of other variables to the growth of monetary aggregates?
- Does a long-run equilibrium exist between the various monetary aggregates and the monetary base, and how fast does the adjustment toward equilibrium take place?
- What are the short-run and long-run elasticities of these aggregates with respect to the monetary base?

Turning to the first question, the multiplier approach will be applied where a certain monetary aggregate M is the product of the multiplicatively adjusted monetary base B^a and the multiplier m:[14]

$$M = m \cdot B^a \tag{4.1}$$

The multiplier mainly reflects the influence of public behavior on the money stock. Taking logarithms, the growth of the money stock can be subdivided into the growth of the monetary base and the growth of the multiplier according to the following formula:

$$\frac{d\ln M}{dt} = \frac{d\ln B^a}{dt} + \frac{d\ln m}{dt} + \frac{d\ln B^a}{dt} \cdot \frac{d\ln m}{dt} \tag{4.2}$$

The correction term $d\ln B^a/dt \cdot d\ln m/dt$ adjusts for the difference between the actual growth of the money stock and the growth of the logarithmized values.

The following analysis concentrates on M1 and M3 as monetary aggregates. M3 has been chosen because it is the target variable of the Bundesbank, and M1 because it directly reflects the public's purchasing power and thus plays an important role in the evaluation of monetary policy.

The annual growth rates of M1, M3, and the multiplicatively adjusted monetary base are illustrated in Figure 4. The growth rates of the money stocks move closely together with those of the monetary base. However, while the growth rates of M1 typically overshoot or undershoot the corresponding rates of the monetary base, the pattern between M3 and the base is not systematic.

On average, over the 30 years from 1960:1 to 1989:12 M1 grew by an annual rate of 7.79 per cent and M3 by 8.91 per cent (Table 3). The monetary base, adjusted for changes in reserve requirements via the multiplicative procedure, increased by an average annual rate of 7.83 per cent, while the multiplier m1 declined by 0.04 per cent and the multiplier m3 grew by 1.08 per cent.
Accordingly, the base contributed on average 100.5 per cent to the growth of M1 and to 87.9 per cent M3. Thus, the contribution of the multiplier m1 amounted to -0.5 per cent and that of the m3 multiplier to 12.1 per cent.

---

[14] For an earlier application of this approach to Germany see Siebke, Willms (1970); Siebke (1972) and Neumann (1977).

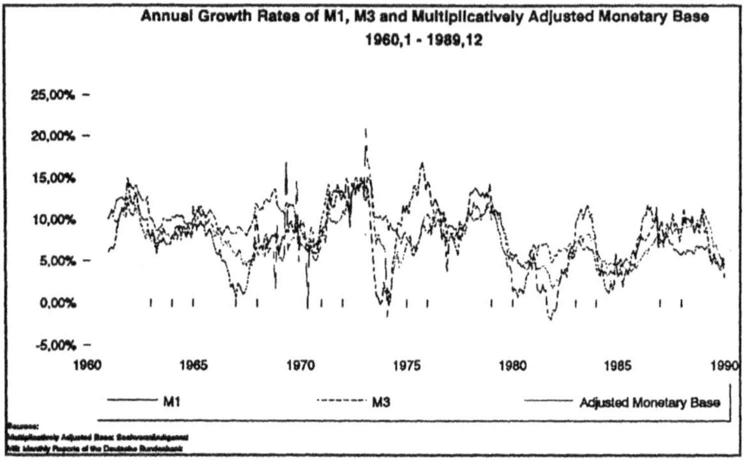

Figure 4.

Table 3. Average Annual Growth Rates of M1 and M3 and Growth Contributions of the Adjusted Monetary Base and the Multiplier - per cent -

Period	M1	M3	B^a	m1	m3
1961:1-1989:12	7.79	8.91	7.83	-0.04	1.08
1961:1-1973:12	8.18	10.92	8.80	-0.62	2.12
1974:1-1989:12	7.48	7.27	7.05	0.43	0.22

During the Bretton Woods era the contribution of the M1 multiplier was much more negative and that for M3 much more positive than in the total period (1960-1989). In the post-Bretton Woods era, both the growth rates of M1 and of M3 have been positively affected by the corresponding multipliers. However, during this period the contribution of m3 became even smaller than that of m1, indicating on average a narrowing between the growth rates of B^a and M3.

Concerning the second question, the nature of the long-run equilibrium relationship and the adjustment mechanism between the monetary base, M1 and M3 can be examined by applying the cointegration and error correction technique developed by Engle/Granger (1987) and further advanced by Kremers/Ericsson/Dolado (1992). The application of this method requires the time series to be stationary after first differencing. Intuitively, stationarity simply means that the time series will converge to some average value over time. Otherwise, the move from one period to the following period is dominated by random shocks, so that the time series exhibits a random walk.

The stationarity of the variables in question has been tested by applying the augmented Dickey-Fuller test. This test consists of regressing the first difference of the variable in question on its lagged level plus a constant and lagged first differences as appropriate:

$$\Delta y_t = a_0 + a_1 y_{t-1} + \sum_{i=1}^{n} b_i \Delta y_{t-i} \qquad (4.3)$$

If the time series is stationary, the coefficient on the lagged level should be negative and significantly different from zero. If the time series is not stationary, the test is repeated after the time series has been differenced again.

The results of the augmented Dickey-Fuller tests as presented in Table 4 show that all variables were non-stationary at their levels and stationary after first differencing. Therefore, cointegration regressions between the variables in question can be carried out. Testing for cointegration determines whether those disturbances that cause non-stationary behavior in M1 or M3 are of the same type as those causing non-stationarity in the monetary base. If non-stationarity in the variables arises from different sources, the money stock and the monetary base will drift away from each other. In that case no long-run equilibrium exists.

Table 4a. Test for Stationarity[a]; Test for Levels of Variables[b]

Period		B[a]	M1	M3
1960:12-1989:12	Constant	0.45 (1.39)	0.55 (1.86)	0.04 (0.44)
	Lagged level	-0.02 (-1.38)	-0.02 (-1.79)	-0.00 (-0.39)
1961:1 -1973:12	Constant	2.04 (1.87)	1.43 (2.26)	1.44 (2.02)
	Lagged level	-0.08 (-1.87)	-0.06 (-2.18)	-0.06 (-1.99)
1974:1 -1989:12	Constant	0.47 (1.81)	1.01 (2.50)	0.51 (1.65)
	Lagged level	-0.02 (-1.76)	-0.04 (-2.30)	-0.02 (-1.55)
1980:1 -1989:12	Constant	0.78 (1.99)	1.69 (2.32)	3.06 (2.76)
	Lagged level	-0.03 (-1.99)	-0.06 (-2.23)	-0.12 (-2.74)

Table 4b. Test for Differences of Variables[2]

Period		B[a]	M1	M3
1960:12-1989:12	Constant	0.005 (2.33)	0.06 (27.6)	0.02 (18.4)
	Lagged level	-1.52 (-16.90)	-1.19 (-23.20)	-0.86 (-16.00)
1961:1 -1973:12	Constant	0.00 (0.07)	0.05 (16.1)	0.02 (11.06)
	Lagged level	-2.04 (-9.84)	-1.01 (-13.30)	-0.90 (-16.70)
1974:1 -1989:12	Constant	0.01 (7.51)	0.08 (27.7)	0.03 (16.8)
	Lagged level	-0.69 (-5.72)	-1.00 (-6.78)	-1.04 (-14.20)
1980:1 -1989:12	Constant	0.01 (7.09)	0.08 (22.2)	0.04 (12.3)
	Lagged level	-0.63 (-4.29)	-1.02 (-5.09)	-1.15 (12.10)

[a] Regressions were estimated after taking logs of all series. Each regression contains six lags of the first difference of the dependent variable among which the significant ones were selected using the stepwise procedure in RATS.
[b] t-statistics are in parenthesis. In an augmented Dickey-Fuller test (ADF) the coefficient on the lagged level is statistically significant, if the t-statistic is greater than -3.

The test for cointegration requires the following regression:

$$(4.4) \qquad M_{it} = \alpha_i + \beta_i B_t^a + u_{it} \qquad (i=1,3)$$

Money stock and monetary base are cointegrated, if the residuals u_{it} are stationary. This can be examined by an augmented Dickey-Fuller test (ADF).

The results are presented in Table 5. For the 30 years period the multiplicatively adjusted base is cointegrated with M1 at the 10 per cent level of significance. However, splitting the sample into the Bretton Woods era and thereafter, cointegration can only be found in the latter period. In contrast, M3 is not cointegrated with the monetary base in any of the periods considered. Apparently, M3 and the monetary base drift away from each other in the long run.

Table 5. Test for Cointegration[a]

Period		M1	M3
	B[a]	1.0	1.15
1960:12-1989:12		(42.07)	(299.4)
	ADF	-2.87	-0.54
	B[a]	0.94	1.28
1961:1 -1973:12		(155.3)	(164.9)
	ADF	-2.26	-2.38
	B[a]	0.99	1.03
1974:1 -1989:12		(160.6)	(214.9)
	ADF	-2.88	-1.51
	B[a]	1.06	0.97
1980:1 -1989:12		(121.8)	(89.8)
	ADF	-3.06	-2.02

[a] t-statistics are in parenthesis

The cointegration properties for M1 allow an error correction model to be estimated. This model implies a gradual adjustment towards the cointegration relationship in the long run. The estimated equation has the following form:

$$(4.5) \qquad \Delta M_1 = \beta_0 + \beta_1 \, \Delta B^a + \beta_2 EC_{t-1},$$

where the error correction term EC represents the estimated residual of equation (4.4). The first term captures the short-run effect of the monetary base on the money stock, while the error correction term reflects the adjustment towards long-run equilibrium.

The results are presented in Table 6, where only for reasons of comparison the error correction estimates for M3 have been added. They show that the short-run impact of the monetary base on M1 is always statistically significant and has continuously increased over the subperiods. The effect of the shift in the policy strategy after the breakdown of the Bretton Woods System becomes visible in the substantial rise of the impact coefficient from 0.204 in the period 1961/73 to 0.685 in the period 1974/89. Considering only the 1980s, this variable even increased further to a value of 0.824. A continuous rise, especially in the latter period, can also be observed for the error correction term of M1. This indicates that the speed of adjustment has increased over time.

In the case of M3 the short-run impact of the monetary base is substantially smaller and has not consistently risen over time. Apart from that, the error correction terms are never statistically significant. This corresponds to the finding of the cointegration test.

Table 6. Error Correction Specification between the Adjusted Monetary Base and the Money Stocks[a]

Period	ΔB^a	EC_{t-1}
Dependent Variable: $\Delta M1$		
1961:1 - 1989:12	0.303 (5.60)	-0.06 (-2.54)
1961:1 - 1973:12	0.204 (3.67)	-0.08 (-1.81)
1974:1 - 1989:12	0.685 (3.86)	-0.10 (-2.80)
1980:1 - 1989:12	0.824 (2.92)	-0.235 (-3.36)
Dependent Variable: $\Delta M3$		
1961:1 - 1989:12	0.122 (4.84)	0.006 (0.09)
1961:1 - 1973:12	0.073 (2.54)	-0.01 (-0.57)
1974:1 - 1989:12	0.330 (4.33)	-0.02 (-1.18)
1980:1 - 1989:12	0.213 (0.08)	-0.02 (-0.49)

[a] t-statistics are in parenthesis.

Turning to the question of the elasticity relationship between the monetary aggregates and the monetary base, estimates of equations (4.4) and (4.5) can be utilized. For the 30 years period, the long-run elasticity for M1 is 1.0 and for M3 1.15. The coefficient on the differenced value of the monetary base in the error correction model can be interpreted as a short-run elasticity. For the total period, with 0.303 for M1 and 0.122 for M3, their magnitudes are rather small. However, as shown before, there has been a tendency towards a considerable increase of these values since the mid-1970s.

The outcome of the cointegration and error correction analysis can be summarized as follows:

- The multiplicatively adjusted monetary base and M1 are cointegrated. Thus a stable long-run equilibrium relationship exists between these variables.
- The short-run relationship between B^a and M1 as well as the adjustment towards long-run equilibrium, has increased considerably over time.
- A cointegration relationship between B^a and M3 could not be confirmed.

The last result indicates that the time series of B^a and M3 drift away from each other. If this is the case, the multiplier m3 should reflect trend movements. Therefore, the development of the multiplier for M3 and the behavior of its components are examined in the next section.

5 Money Multiplier and its Components

While the monetary base, especially since the mid-1970s, dominantly reflects the behavior of the Bundesbank, the money multiplier measures the contribution of the portfolio behavior of the public and the commercial banks to the development of the money stock.

For M3, the money multiplier is derived by utilizing the following equation set:

(5.1) $$M3 = C + D + T + S = (1+c+t+s)D$$

(5.2) $$B = C + RR + ER = (c+r^{RR}+r^{ER})D$$

(5.3) $$RR = r^{RR}(D+T+S+F) = r^{RR}(1+t+s+f)D$$

(5.4) $$ER = r^{ER}(D+T+S+F) = r^{ER}(1+t+s+f)D$$

(5.5) $$B = (c+(r^{RR}+r^{ER})(1+t+s+f))D.$$

C	= currency in circulation	c	= C/D cash deposit ratio
D	= demand deposits	t	= T/D time deposit ratio
T	= time deposits	s	= S/D savings deposit ratio
S	= saving deposits	f	= F/D foreign deposit ratio
RR	= required reserves	r^{RR}	= RR/(D+T+S+F) required reserve ratio
ER	= excess reserves	r^{ER}	= ER/(D+T+S+F) excess reserve ratio

According to equation (4.1) the multiplier is obtained by relating equation (5.1) to equation (5.5):

$$(5.6) \qquad M3 = \frac{1+c+t+s}{[c+(r^{RR}+r^{ER})(1+t+s+f)]KF} B \cdot KF = m \cdot B^{a}.$$

Using the concept of the multiplicatively adjusted monetary base the impact of changes of the required reserve ratio on the multiplier will be neutralized by an opposite move of the adjusted monetary base.
The following formula analyzes the contribution of each component to the growth of the multiplier:

$$(5.7) \qquad \frac{dm}{dt} = \sum_{x} e(m,x) \frac{dx}{dt}$$

with $x = c, t, s, f, r^{ER}$.
The partial elasticity of each component with respect to the multiplier is computed as

$$(5.8) \qquad e(m,x) = \frac{\partial m}{\partial x} \frac{x}{m}.$$

The partial elasticities are derived by application of the quotient rule, where the denominator of the multiplier is written as b:

$$e(m,c) = \frac{c(1-m)}{bm} \qquad < 0$$

$$e(m,t) = \frac{t(1-m(r^{RR}+r^{ER}))}{b} \qquad > 0$$

$$e(m,s) = \frac{s(1-m(r^{RR}+r^{ER}))}{b} \qquad > 0$$

$$e(m,f) = \frac{f(1-m(r^{RR}+r^{ER}))}{b} \qquad < 0$$

$$e(m,r^{ER}) = \frac{r^{ER}(1+t+s+f)D}{B} \qquad < 0$$

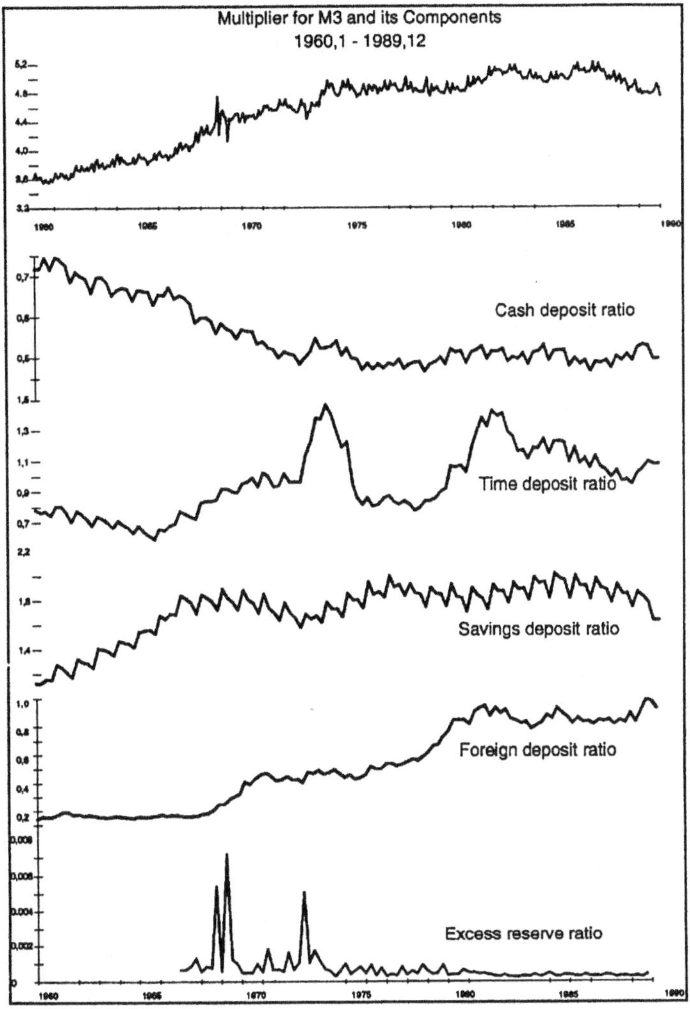
Multiplier for M3 and its Components
1960,1 - 1989,12
Cash deposit ratio
Time deposit ratio
Savings deposit ratio
Foreign deposit ratio
Excess reserve ratio

Figure 5.

Figure 5 provides an overview of the development of the multiplier for M3 and its components. The multiplier has increased almost continuously from a value of about 3.6 in the early 1960s to a value of about 4.8 in the mid-1970s. Then it stayed relatively stable for a while and decreased since the mid-1980s. The cash deposit ratio declined from a value of about 0.75 in the early 1960s to 0.5 in the mid-1970s and is stable since then. Thus, in the first period it contributed to the increase of the multiplier. The time deposit ratio fluctuated considerably between values of 0.6 and 1.4. In periods of an increase, its contribution to the multiplier has been positive and, in periods of a decrease, negative. The savings deposit ratio increased from a value of 1.1 in 1960 to a value of 1.8 in the late 1960s and did not change very much since then. Thus in the first period it generated a positive effect on the multiplier. The foreign deposit ratio stayed relatively constant at a value of 0.15 until the late 1960s, increased almost steadily until the early 1980s, and since then fluctuated around a value of 0.9. A rise of this ratio leads to a decline of the multiplier. Contrary to the previous ratios which are related to demand deposits, the excess reserve ratio is based on total deposits. Until the early 1970s, this ratio fluctuated heavily between values of 0.001 and 0.007. Since then it declined continuously to an extremely small magnitude. The decline of this ratio has a positive impact on the multiplier.

In order to calculate the precise contribution of the various coefficients to the growth of the multiplier the following non-logarithmized formula is applied:

$$\frac{dm}{dt} = \sum_{x} e(m,x)_{t-12} \frac{dx}{dt}. \qquad (5.9)$$

The results are shown in Table 7. It is important to note that in the table the multiplier differs slightly from the values calculated before. This has to do with the limited detail of the available data. For instance, the Bundesbank uses about 24 different required reserve ratios and has changed the definitions of demand and time deposits during the past 30 years. These distinctions can, however, not be completely backed out.

Table 7. Average Annual Growth Rates of the Multiplier for M3 and Growth Contributions of its Components

- per cent -

Period	Multiplier	c	t	s	f	r^{ER}
1960:1 - 1989:12	1.02	0.65	0.10	0.20	-0.24	0.317
1960:1 - 1973:12	2.28	0.75	1.10	0.67	-0.36	0.105
1974:1 - 1989:12	0.01	0.56	-0.71	-0.18	-0.15	0.489

The ratios show substantially different contributions during the subperiods chosen. The strongest positive and least volatile contribution originated from the c-ratio due to its long-run decline. The contributions of the other ratios fluctuated considerably with the t-ratio and the s-ratio even changing their direction. The near stagnation in the growth of the multiplier during the period 1974 to 1989 is due to offsetting influences of the multiplier coefficients.

6 Summary

The investigation of the money supply process in Germany from 1960 to 1989 concludes that:

1. The Bundesbank's monetary policy has always been directed towards the control of monetary aggregates and not interest rates or other intermediate target variables in the monetary sector.
2. Monetary aggregates are indirectly controlled by utilizing the short-term money market rate (call-money rate) as the operational target variable.
3. The announcement of annual targets for the growth rate of a wide monetary aggregate since 1975 implied no principal change in the indirect control procedure but was accompanied by changes in the application of the monetary policy instruments in order to gain closer control of the monetary aggregates.
4. Since the early 1980s the new instrument of security repurchase agreements has been systematically extended so that, in the meantime, refinancing through this mechanism has become the most important source component in the monetary base.
5. During most of the period the Bundesbank has been able to sterilize the impact of foreign reserves on the monetary base. However, periods of excessive growth of the monetary base were almost always periods of a substantial inflow of foreign reserves.
6. A stable cointegration relationship exists between M1 and the multiplicatively adjusted monetary base. Both variables do not deviate from each other in the long-run. Control of the adjusted monetary base implies control of M1 and vice versa.
7. No cointegration relationship between M3 and the multiplicatively adjusted monetary base could be found. Therefore, control of one of these aggregates does not imply control of the other. Since the Bundesbank uses M3 as its target variable, the monetary base is endogenously determined.
8. The multiplier for M3 shows considerable trend movements. The multiplier m3 increased, especially from 1960 to 1975, due to a decline in the cash deposit ratio and increases in the time deposit and savings deposit ratio. Over the total period, growth of the multiplier has most been affected by reductions in the cash deposit ratio and the excess reserve ratio.

References

Bofinger P (1988) Das Europäische Währungssystem und die geldpolitische Koordination in Europa. In: Kredit und Kapital, Vol 21, pp 317-345

Deutsche Bundesbank (1985) Zur langfristigen Entwicklung und Kontrolle des Geldvolumens. In: Monatsberichte, 37 Jahrgang, No 1, January 1985, pp 14-28

Deutsche Bundesbank (1988) Methodische Anmerkungen zur geldpolitischen Zielgröße "M3". In: Monatsberichte, 40. Jahrgang, No 3, March 1988, pp 18-21

Deutsche Bundesbank (1992) Zum Zusammenhang zwischen Geldmengen- und Preisentwicklung in der Bundesrepublik Deutschland, in: Monatsberichte, 44 Jahrgang, No 1, January 1992, pp 20-29

Dudler HJ (1986) Changes in Money-Market Instruments and Procedures in Germany. In: Bank for International Sattlements, Changes in Money-Market Instruments and Procedures: Objectives and Implications, Basle, pp 53-73

Engle R, Granger CW (1987) Co-Integration and Error Correction: Representation, Estimation and Testing. In: Econometrica, Vol 55, pp 251-275

Issing O (1992) Theoretische und empirische Grundlagen der Geldmengenpolitik der Deutschen Bundesbank. In: Wirtschaftsdienst, 72 Jhg, pp 537-548

Jahnke W (1991) Geldpolitik und monetärer Transmissionsprozeß im ökonometrischen Modell der Deutschen Bundesbank, Geld und Währung, Working Paper No 21, Universität Frankfurt am Main

Kremers JJM, Ericsson NR, Dolado JJ (1992) The Power of Cointegration Tests, Board of Govenors of the Federal Reserve Systems. International Finance Discussion Papers No 431

Mastropasqua Chr, Micossi S, Rinaldi R (1988) Interventions, Sterilisation and Monetary Policy in European Monetary System Countries 1979-87. In: Giavazzi F, Micossi S, Miller M (eds) The European Monetary System, Cambridge University Press, Cambridge, pp 252-287

Neumann MJM (1977) A Theoretical and Empirical Analysis if the German Money Supply Process. In: Frowen SF, Courakis AS, Miller M (eds), Monetary Policy and Economic Activity in West-Germany, Fischer Verlag, Stuttgart, pp 73-124

Neumann MJM, von Hagen J (1992) Monetary Policy in Germany. In: Fratianni M, Salvatore D (eds), Handbook on Monetary Policy, forthcoming

Obstfeld M (1983) Exchange Rates, Inflation, and the Sterilisation Problem: Germany, 1975-81. In: European Economic Review, Vol 21, pp 161-189

Sachverständigenrat zur Begutachtung der gesamtwirtschaftlichen Entwicklung (1991): Jahresgutachten 1991/92

Schlesinger H (1985) Zehn Jahre Geldpolitik mit einem Geldmengenziel. In: Gebauer W (Hrsg), Öffentliche Finanzen und monetäre Ökonomie, Fritz Knapp Verlag, Frankfurt am Main, pp 123-147

Siebke J (1972) An Analysis of the German Money Supply Process: The Multiplier Approach. In: Kredit und Kapital, Beiheft No 1, pp 243-272

Siebke J, Willms M (1970) Das Geldangebot in der Bundesrepublik Deutschland. Eine empirische Analyse für die Periode 1958 - 1968. In: Zeitschrift für die gesamte Staatswissenschaft, Bd 126, pp 55-74

von Hagen J (1986) Strategien kurzfristiger Geldmengensteuerung, Verlag Weltarchiv, Hamburg

von Hagen J (1988) Alternative Operating Regimes for Money Stock Control in West Germany: An Empirical Evaluation. In: Weltwirtschaftliches Archiv, Vol 124, pp 89-107

von Hagen J (1989) Monetary Targeting with Exchange Rate Constraints: The Bundesbank in the 1980s. In: Federal Reserve Bank of St. Louis Review, Vol 71, No 5, pp 53-69

Willms M (1971) Controlling Money in an Open Economy: The German Case. In: Federal Reserve Bank of St. Louis Review, Vol 53, No 4, pp 10-27

Endogenous Money and Interest Rates in Germany

Matthias Müller
University of Frankfurt

1 Introduction

The policy of monetary targeting in Germany seems to be in crisis. Being on the horns of the dilemma: the substantial overshooting of the growth rate of M3 on the one hand, and the impossibility of raising short term interest rates in the face of a impending recession and the exchange rate constraints imposed by its leading role in the EMS on the other, the Bundesbank has to shift away from its 'pragmatic monetarism approach'. Besides so called 'special developments', as interventions in the EMS, fiscal policy, wage policy, interest rate subsidies in Eastern Germany and the widespread use of DM-bills in Eastern Europe, the question arises, whether there are more fundamental reasons for the obvious failure of the control of monetary aggregates. Moreover it might be asked, whether some of these 'special developments' are in no way special but constitutional elements of a transmission channel quite different from the one, on which the 'pragmatic monetarism approach' of the Bundesbank is based. Theory of science tells us, that a theory, which explains reality essentially not by its rules, but by its exceptions, should be revised.

Experiencing not only strongly growing monetary aggregates but also rising rates of inflation, the Bundesbank is still commited to anti-inflationary policies. If inflation, as it turns out, is not essentially a monetary phenomenon, there is a need for a theoretical foundation of a new central bank policy for the late 1990s, which might become a better model for a future European Central Bank than monetary targeting.

The concept of 'endogenous money' provides a tool to explain why the policy of monetary targeting must fail, and gives a more realistic view on the process of money creation and the limits of the central bank's control over quantity aggregates. It is argued that the Bundesbank should also theoretically admit to what it actually does, i.e. to control short term interest rates, thus developing a monetary policy which is based on prices, not on quantities. Sticking with monetary targeting on the one hand and frequently failing to meet the targets on the other, will damage the Bundesbank's credibility, which is its main asset in contributing to monetary stability.

The notion to stress the importance of the financial system and its overall liquidity in analyzing the transmission process has been already expressed by the Radcliffe-Committee (1959), Gurley and Shaw (1960) and Tobin (1963), hence questioning the money income causality (Tobin (1970)). However, for more than twenty years economists focused predominantly on the *money view* of the transmission process. But in recent times, economists again shift their interest towards the behaviour of the banking system in the transmission process, as well on the micro economic level (Diamond, Dybvig (1983); Bernanke, Gertler (1987); Gertler, Gilchrist 1992)) as on the macro economic level (Blinder (1987); Bernanke, Blinder (1988)). The specific approach of *endogenous money* and its foundation in the interrelationship between the central bank, commercial banks and the public is elaborated in great detail in Moore (1988) and Wray (1990).

This paper is organized as follows. Section 2 defines the term 'endogenous money supply', and analyzes its behavioural assumptions, its relation to short-term interest rates and the reaction of the central bank. Section 3 analyzes the 'endogenous money supply'-approach in an accounting framework which allows for inside money and gives a view of the causaltity issue using 'multiplier-relations'. Section 4 compares the predictions of the endogenous money approach with the results of the current monetary policy in Germany and presents some preliminary evidence. The paper closes with some conclusions concerning the future monetary policy in Germany and the relevance of monetary targeting for a European Central bank.

2 Endogenous Money Defined

Endogeneity in this context is defined by the *controllability* of a variable by policy. If it turns out that money, whatever monetary aggregate is regarded as 'money', is not controllable by the monetary authority, money is said to be endogenous.[1] Money itself is defined by its functions. These are: medium of exchange, unit of account, store of value and standard of deferred payment. However, these functions are interrelated and 'standard of deferred payment' function arises from the combination of the others.

During the development of the financial system it was experienced that this functions could not only be served by commodity money as gold for example, but also by credit money. As banks established themselves it became known that only a fraction of bank deposits must be held as reserves in order to meet unexpected withdrawals. Thus, the creation of credit money became possible, which did not differ from commoditiy money in its attributes.[2] Hence, the deposit-reserve-ratio determines the expansion of money. However, money creation is only possible, if the public believes in the liquidity of the single bank, as well as the banking system as a whole and its ability to repay the deposits on demand. This is usually guaranteed by the central bank, which commits itself to lending to the banking

---

[1] Desai (1992) p 762, Wray (1992) p 299, for a more detailed treatment see Engle, Hendry, Richard (1983).

[2] It was one of the main issues in the banking-currency controversy, whether bank notes (credit money) was to be regarded as money, see Tooke (1844).

system without any limit in order to maintain this liquidity and to prevent bank runs. This raises the question, whether reserve requirements can limit the expansion of money in terms of quantity restrictions.

There are two reasons for the central bank to require reserve holdings: To provide a primary liquiditiy reserve for sudden withdrawals of deposits and to control commercial bank's credit expansion. In an environment of credit money, where debts are settled with the transfer of deposits, the central bank's commitment to maintain the financial system is conflicting with the attempt to control the monetary base. The functioning of the payment system requires that currency and deposits are traded at par, without any risk premia. The reason is that there may not be a difference between currency and deposits regarding their degree of moneyness. This is guaranteed by the 'lender of last resort'-function of the central bank as well as by deposit insurance.[3] If the central bank refused to lend additional reserves at any price in order to keep the monetary base in line with the monetary targets and if the liquidity of bank's was severely restricted, the confidence in the banking system might be irritated and the stability of the financial system will be endangered.

The volume of credit is by far the largest position on the asset side of the consolidated balance sheet of the banking system. It is by a factor of 1.65 larger than M3 in Germany regarding credit to private households and business enterprises (2.08 regarding total credit).[4] Thus monetary expansion may be a result of the expansion of credit (with the share of monetary capital kept approximately constant over time).

The *endogenous money*-argument is as follows: The central bank cannot restrict the expansion of monetary aggregates, because the expansion is credit demand driven. Commercial banks and other financial intermediaries satisfy the credit demand by supplying additional credit. This credit creates additional deposits. These deposits need to be funded with additional reserves. The banks buy these reserves either from other banks, or from the central bank, or shift their credit expansion towards the euromarkets. The central bank as the 'lender of the last resort' is forced to finance the reserve needs of the commercial banks and thus to create base money. It is the reversion of the usual monetarist approach that a reduction of reserve requirements or an open market purchase creates excess reserves which will be lent to the public, thus creating additional credit supply.

The 'endogenous money supply'-view states that there is first a credit demand, which is always met by commercial banks, as long as the marginal costs of refinancing are lower than the marginal revenues of the loan. It should be thereby kept in mind that banks accepted large credit commitments, which exist off the bank's balance sheets and may be claimed at any time without giving the banks a chance to refuse the credit. In this case there is no way for the central bank but to refinance these credit commitments, if they are claimed. In short: *Loans make deposits; Deposits make reserves; Credit demand makes money supply.*[5] There is no

[3] Goodhart (1988), chapters 6 and 7.
[4] Data for October 1992.
[5] Moore (1988), pp 45-46.

theoretical difference between 'money demand', as determined by public portfolio choices and 'money supply' exogeneously determined by the central bank. Any demand creates its supply, unless interest rates have risen sufficiently to stop additional loan demand. Money demand is simply the willingness of an economic agent to go into debt, money supply is the funding of this debt by a bank. Credit money therefore is a good, to which an inverted 'Say's law' applies, since the 'money supply function' is horizontal in the interest-money space. To be more precise, there is no 'money supply function' independent of the money demand.[6] The ability of commercial banks to create money cannot be limited by the central bank in terms of quantity restrictions, because the liquidity of the banking system must be assured. The central bank's reaction to a credit expansion will not be a tightening of monetary policy in terms of quantity restrictions but a rise in the price of liquidity, hence an increase in the central bank's lending rates.

However, any restrictive monetary policy, which tries to keep base money and thus monetary aggregates close at targets, would cause short term interest rates rise sharply and increase the volatility of financial markets. If central bank's lending rates fluctuate heavily, they will loose their informational content. Of course, the demand for money is reduced when credits are repaid.

In section 3 the argument is derived more formally in an accounting framework, where the role of decentralized decision making and its importance for the monetary transmission process is emphasized.

3 Endogeneity and the Multiplier

The monetarist theory of monetary control consists of two main paradigms:

(i) There is a stable relationship between the monetary base, which is completely under the control of the central bank, since the elements of the monetary base are its liabilities, and some well defined monetary aggregate. The link between the base and money is called the multiplier, which should be empirically stable in time, at least in the long run.

(ii) The money supply is therefore exogeneously determined by the central bank and the 'equation of exchange' can be interpreted as providing a causal link between money and prices, as long as money demand is empirically stable and real income is assumed to be constant.

Taking those assumptions for granted, it is possible to derive the usual policy implications, with monetary targeting being the most important one. This view of the monetary transmission mechanism is termed the *money view*.[7] Since both relations (analogue to (i) and (ii)) are just mathematical identities, they become

---

[6] Moore (1988), p 7.

[7] e.g. Brunner, Meltzer (1990).

theoretical concepts only by making assumptions on the behaviour of the variables and the causal relations between them.[8] This is the reason why it is possible to use them for what is called the *credit view* of the transmission process. Assuming money to be endogenous reverses the causal direction between nominal income and money. It refers to a discussion, as old as the banking-currency debate of the 19th century.

The reversed causality can be established in two ways: First, the money supply is demand driven, as is argued in section 2. Second, the velocity of circulation is not stable. In this paper, the focus is not on 'stable money demand functions'.[9] However, two facts should be kept in mind: First, the banking system in a competitive environment will find financial innovations in order to satisfy a credit demand in the face of a restrictive central bank policy and hence increase the velocity of circulation. Second, an unsatisfied borrower is not restricted with his credit demand to the domestic banking system. He may borrow from abroad, especially the euromarkets or from financial intermediaries outside the commercial banking system, if he is able to overcome informational problems arising with his application for credit.

The further line of argument will concentrate only on the first assumption: given a stable relation between the monetary base and the relevant monetary aggregate, what will happen, if the decision of applying for credit is shifted towards the private sector?[10] The approach contains three elements: It is argued within a financial sector allowing for both, inside and outside money, the demand for inside money is independent of the central bank's behaviour and the interaction between the sectors is analyzed within an accounting framework.[11]

For simplicity of representation, suppose a closed economy with no bonds and consider only M1. Financial intermediation works only through the private banking system. Figure 1 shows the relations in the monetary sector of the economy in the form of balance sheets.

An endogenous money interpretation of these simple model of the financial sector of the economy will argue along the following lines: The central bank supplies central bank credit (CBC) both to the public in form of cash (C) and in form of reserves (R) to the commercial banks. The latter supply credit (K) on the demand of the private sector, which is held as deposits (D) within the banks, thus creating a demand for central bank credit (R) in the amount of a fraction of these deposits. Both the central bank and the commercial banks taken together (i.e. the banking system as a whole) supply credit in the form of central bank credit (outside money) and credit to the private sector (inside money), which in turn is

---

[8] It is worth noting that econometric test of cointegration e.g. between the monetary base and some monetary aggregate simply tests for the long run intertemporal stability of the relationship between these accounting identities.

[9] For a review see Judd, Scadding (1982), for a very early critique Wicksell (1898).

[10] Of course, even the stability of the 'base multiplier' can be severely questioned.

[11] Gurley, Shaw (1960), Harris (1985), Willms (1987).

A	Central bank	L
CBC		C
		R

A	Commercial banks	L
K		D
R		

A	Banking system[a]	L
K		M
CBC		

A	Private sector	L
C		K
D		W

[a] The balance sheet of the banking systems consolidates the balance sheets of the central bank and the commercial banks.

Figure 1. Structure of monetary sector

held by the private sector as money (M).[12] Accordingly, the balance sheet of the private sector contains total credit on the liability side and total money on the asset side. The reason is that by construction of the model the net wealth of the private sector equals the central bank credit and thus the base money. Therefore the monetary base serves as outside money. The division of total credit in inside and outside money components depends at first sight on the supply of central bank credit. If it is supplied on demand, as was argued in section 2, money only depends on inside money, which is the credit demand of the private sector, supplied by the private sector.

While it might be regarded an oversimplification to set total credit $K+B=M$ in the model shown above, it does not disregard factors relevant to the endogenous money argument. $K+B=M$ simply states that the relation between bonds and loans is approximately constant over time.[13] Moreover, this is essentially the same assumption, which guarantees a stable money demand function in monetarist models. This model can easily account for broader monetary aggregates by adding savings and time deposits both on asset side of the private sector account and on the liability side of the account of the banking system. Adding government bonds to the asset side of the banks and the public and on the liability side of the central bank, thus transforming the central bank's account into the account of the public sector, allows for fiscal policy. Expanding to an open economy means adding international reserves to the central bank's account.

[12] It is clear, that this argument is independent of the definition of the monetary aggregate.

[13] An explanation of the role of loans and bonds in determining the total equilibrium amount of credit give Bernanke, Blinder (1988).

It is also possible to split the total holding of cash between the public and the banking sector. But the simple representation shown above is sufficient for proposing the main argument in favor of the 'endogenous money' view and keeps the algebraic treatment quite simple. However, it reflects the notion that aggregate demand and thus price-level-stability is the result of an interaction of independent economic agents, stemming from private sector decision taking, not discretionary actions of the central bank.

From the budget constraints in figure 1 a multiplier relation between inside money, which is private credit, and the money supply can be derived. It is important to mention that this kind of analysis works with the same behavioural assumptions, as the usual textbook base-money-multiplier approach does.

Combining the budget constraint of the central bank and the definition of M1 gives the well-known multiplier relation:

(3.1) $$M = \frac{1+c}{c+r} B$$

Multiplying the right-hand side by (1-r)/(1-r), denoting c = C/D and r = R/D and r < 1 gives:

(3.2) $$M = \frac{(1+c)}{(1-r)} \frac{(1-r)}{(c+r)} B$$

Noting that

(3.3) $$B = C + R = cD + rD$$

and

(3.4) $$K = D - rD = (1 - r)D$$

thus

(3.5) $$D = \frac{1}{1-r} K$$

Substituting in 3.3 and rearranging gives:

(3.6) $$B = \frac{c}{1-r} K + \frac{r}{1-r} K = \frac{c+r}{1-r} K$$

(3.7) $$K = \frac{1-r}{c+r} B$$

Substituting 3.7 into 3.2 gives a 'multiplier-equation' depending on credit instead of the monetary base:

(3.8)
$$M = \frac{c+1}{1-r} K$$

It is worth mentioning that nothing has changed concerning the elements of the multiplier itself, the currency deposit ratio and the required reserve ratio. Equation 3.8 expresses just another aspect of the causality issue from a different point of view, using the same analytical framework.

Equations 3.6 and 3.8 summarize the argument and allow the reversion of the causality betwen money and credit. While 3.6 determines the demand for central bank credit by the commercial banks resulting from private credit demand, 3.8 does so for any choosen monetary aggregate.

If it is accepted that the decision to go into debt is a decentralized decision, taken in the private sector of the economy and that the central bank cannot exert a rigorous control of the monetary base in terms of quantity restrictions, it is the creation of inside money, which determines the quantity of money. This rises the question for an adequate central bank policy within this theoretical framework, because from an endogenous money perspective, inflation is no monetary phenomenon, because money supply is not independent of money demand, thus there cannot be an excess supply that would 'drive up' the price level. Obviously this argument leaves no room for a 'real balance effect'.

4 Endogenous Money and the Bundesbank

The Bundesbank's record in achieving its targets is somewhat mixed, to say the least. On the one hand, the Bundesbank was successful in maintaining low rates of inflation until 1992, on the other hand it frequently failed to meet the respective monetary targets. Summarizing the well-known relative success regarding that issue: From 1975 to 1992 the Bundesbank failed to meet its targets in 10 cases, it was successful in 6 cases, for 1975 and 1976 evidence is debatable. It is reasonable to expect the Bundesbank to fail to meet its 4.5 to 6.5 target in 1993 again. So, what are the reasons?

It is commonly accepted that the contemporary monetary expansion in Germany is primarily a reflex of the domestic credit expansion. If money is endogenous, the Bundesbank cannot restrict the expansion of monetary aggregates, because this expansion is credit demand driven. On the other hand this says nothing about the causes of inflation, which may be determined by higher wages or taxes, fiscal policy or just by rising inflationary or business expectations.

The new Bundesbank's price-gap theory partly reflects the endogenous nature of money at least in the short run.[14] Also the fact that the Bundesbank has changed its monetary target to broad money M3 in 1986 and just recently started to pay attention to the development of money creation at the euromarkets by watching M3E(xpanded) demonstrates that it is not unaware of the arguments put forward in the preceeding section. Raising the Lombard rate up to 9.75 percent in December 1991, did not slow down the expansion of monetary aggregates, but the further growth of M3 is the kind of reaction one should expect according to the 'endogeneous money' argument. High and rising interest rates indicate optimistic business expectations thus rising credit, and result in rising money demand. Figure 2 shows the relation between money market rates and the yearly rate of change in credit to the private sector, including private sector bonds:[15]

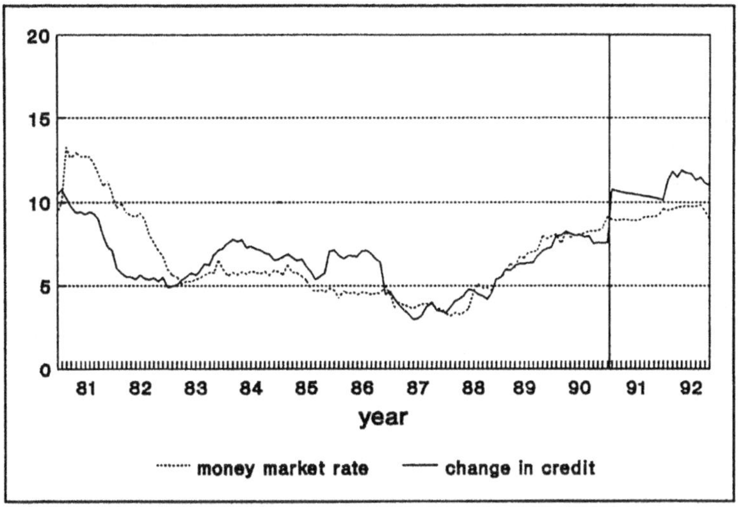

Figure 2. Private sector credit expansion and the money market rate 1981-1992
The data for 1991 has been adjusted for the base effect, resulting from German reunification
Source: Deutsche Bundesbank

As can be easily seen both series move closely together, indicating rising credit demand in face of a restrictive monetary policy.

Perhaps the most obvious evidence for endogeneous money is the so called base-drift. Next year's monetary target is calculated from the existing stock of money, independent of whether it was on target or not. There is a simple

---

[14] Hallman, Porter, Small (1991), Deutsche Bundesbank 1992, Issing (1992).

[15] Goodhart (1984) chapter 4 finds similar evidence for the UK.

explanation for the base-drift: Since the central bank can easily expand its base money by open market purchases, it cannot reduce base money by open market sales: Commercial banks usually do not hold marketable securities as assets, except for the trading needs of their customers and as secondary liquidity reserves. The majority of assets are loans with a low degree of liquidity, since the informational structure of credit relations make them non-marketable. They cannot be easily sold in secondary markets. Hence it is difficult for the central bank to remove central bank money from the banking sector. Moreover, it is the role of banks as financial intermediaries in the economy to transform highly liquid liabilities into less liquid assets in their balance sheet. This asymmetry means regarding the price-gap approach that there are no economic factors yielding the surplus amount of money to vanish in the long run.

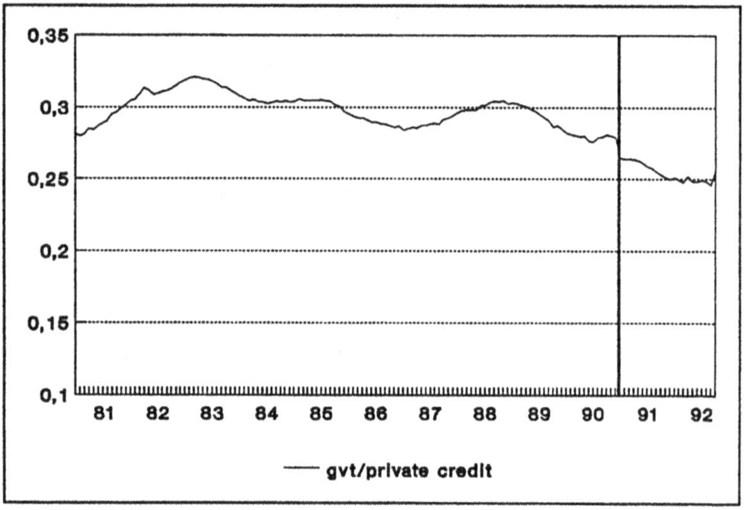

Figure 3. Ratio of public to private sector credit
Source: Deutsche Bundesbank

The argument that the recent domestic credit expansion mainly results from non-interest-elastic government debt is not covered by the facts. As figure 3 demonstrates, the ratio of public-sector credit to private-sector credit is remarkably stable over time from 1/1975 to 10/1992 and has been *sinking* since 1991. This is further evidence in favor of the argument that private credit is not very sensitive to interest rate changes as long as there are positive business expectation, thus confirming interest rate spread theories of the transmission mechanism.[16] However, it should be noted that the figures for private and business credit contain interest-rate-subsidized credits as well.

It is not necessary to discuss all instruments of the Bundesbank's monetary policy in the light of the 'endogeneous money approach'. The kind of instrument is of no importance to the endogeneous money argument, but of cause, the reduction of minimum reserve requirements in February 1993 e.g. will reduce the role of off-shore markets.

The successful sterilization of the huge expansion in the liquidity of the banking system that followed the interventions in the foreign exchange markets last quarter of 1992 shows again that credit expansion is demand determined. If thepublic is expected to demand whatever amount is supplied, the additional liquidity should have been converted fully into credit and hence, money. Since no one could be forced to take a credit, the credit expansion did not take place, according to the latest pessimistic business expectations and the surplus in liquidity could be sterilized by cutting down repurchase agreements.

To sum up: If the banking system as a whole still has potential liquidity, which may consist of

(i) unused credit lines either with commercial banks home or abroad or the central bank
(ii) stocks of marketable securities or bills of exchange
(iii) possibilities to economize the existing stock of deposits in order to increase the velocity of circulation

the central bank cannot limit the domestic credit expansion, neither in the short nor in the long run. Under the institutional conditions of Germany, first of all the lagged-reserve-accounting system, the banking system has all these opportunities easily available so that the Bundesbank may hit its monetary targets only in a stable macroeconic environment, thus earning the benefits from a transmission process quite different from the propagated 'pragmatic monetarism'-approach.

The biggest crisis ever within the EMS was caused when the Bundesbank lowered its lending rates insufficiently in September 1992. There emerged a clear divergence between the existing role of the DM as the anchor currency in the EMS and the Bundesbank's struggle to keep monetary expansion at target. The resulting interventions in the foreign exchange markets increased the growth rate of the monetary aggregates even more. One might ask, whether it is worth, bringing the EMS nearly to an end just for pursuing a monetary policy based on an inadequate view of the domestic transmission process.

[16] e.g. Tobin 1978.

5 Conclusions

The assertion that the Bundesbank controls M3 and thus inflation, obviously no longer holds. Sticking with monetary targeting will damage the Bundesbank's credibility, and hence its ability to influence inflationary expectations. As these spread more, inflation will increase as a consequence.

If the endogeneous money approach holds, we must have a fresh look upon the monetary transmission process. Aggregate demand is no longer determined by the central bank's money supply, but by the credit demand of the public. Since credit demand seems not to depend too much on nominal interest rates - especially not on short term rates - but rather on the economic expectations of the borrowers and their banks, how should the central bank influence the economy? The central bank's main asset is its credibility, which can be used to stabilize business and inflationary expectations, thus stabilizing the economy. Credibility must be achieved by pursuing a policy, which is likely to achieve its targets. Hence monetary targeting does no longer meet this condition it should be terminated.

The role of business expectations in the transmission process became obvious during the U.S. 'credit crunch'. Lowering interest rates did not cause a monetary expansion until banks and borrowers started to expect the overcoming of the current recession. This also demonstrates that credit rationing may be an important factor to undermine the central bank's intentions, although first evidence from survey data shows that there seems to be no credit rationing in quantity terms in Germany.[17]

A new monetary policy, which relies on credit demand rather than money supply has still to be developed. Since its transmission channels will not be well defined, but loose and indirect, it will be more difficult to explain central bank's actions to the public, even to the well informed part of it. But it might perform better than a monetary policy, which starts intervention somwhere in the middle of the monetary transmission process. The robustness of the quantity theory of money as a guideline for monetary policy has been so successful, because it is quite easy to explain and widely understood. However, to ensure the credibility and the success of a future European Central Bank a monetary policy has to be suggested, which is aware of the credit demand in the economy instead of the money supply.

---

[17] v.Köppen (1993).

References

Bernanke BS, Gertler M (1987) Banking and Macroeconomic Equilibrium. In: Singleton K, Barnett WA (eds) New Approaches to Monetary Economics, New York pp 89-111

Bernanke BS, Blinder AS (1988) Credit, Money, and Aggregate Demand. In: American Economic Review, Vol 78, No 2, May, pp 435-439

Blinder AS (1987) Credit Rationing and Effective Supply Failures. In: Economic Journal, Vol 97, June, pp 327-352

Brunner K, Meltzer AH (1990) Money Supply. In: Friedman BM, Hahn FH (eds) Handbook of Monetary Economics, Vol 1, Amsterdam, pp357-398

Committee on the Working of the Monetray System (1959) Report. London

Desai M (1992) Endogenous and Exogenous Money. In: Newman P, Milgate M, Eatwell J (eds) The New Palgrave Dictionary of Money and Finance, pp 762-764

Deutsche Bundesbank (1992) Zum Zusammenhang zwischen Geldmengen- und Preisentwicklung in der Bundesrepublik Deutschland. In: Monthly Report, Vol 44, No 1, January, pp 20-29

Diamond DW, Dybvig PH (1983) Bank Runs, Deposit Insurance, and Liquidity. In: Journal of Political Economy, Vol 91, No 3, pp 401-419

Engle RF, Hendry DF, Richard JF (1983) Exogeneity. Econometrica, Vol 51, No 2, pp 277-304

Gertler M, Gilchrist S (1992) The Cyclical Behavior of Short Term Business Lending: Implications for Financial Propagation Mechanism. Paper Presented at the 7th Annual Congress of the European Economic Association, August

Gurley JG, Shaw ES (1960) Money in a Theory of Finance. Washington

Goodhart CAE (1984) Monetray Theory and Practice: The UK Experience. London

Goodhart CAE (1988) The Evolution of Central Banks. Cambridge

Hallman JJ, Porter RD, Small DH (1991) Is the Price Level Tied to the M2 Monetary Aggregate in the Long Run? In: American Economic Review, Vol 81, No 4, September, pp 841-858

Harris L (1985) Monetary Theory. New York

Issing O (1992) Theoretische und empirische Grundlagen der Geldmengenpolitik der Deutschen Bundesbank. In: Wirtschaftsdienst, Vol 10, pp 537.548

Judd JP, Scadding JL (1982) The Search for a Stable Money Demand Function: A Survey of the Post-1973 Literature. Journal of Economic Literature, Vol 20, September, pp 993-1023

Moore BJ (1988) Horizontalists and Verticalists: The Macroeconomics of Credit Money. Cambridge

Tobin J (1963) Commercial Banks as Creators of 'Money'. In: Tobin J (1971) Essays in Economics, Vol 1: Macroeconomics, New York pp 272-282

Tobin J (1970) Money and Income: Post Hoc Ergo Propter Hoc? In: Tobin J (1971) Essays in Economics, Vol 1: Macroeconomics, New York pp 497-514

Tobin J (1978) Monetary Policies and the Economy: The Transmission Mechanism. In: Tobin J (1982) Essays in Economics, Vol 3: Theory and Policy, Cambridge pp 497-514

Tooke T (1844) An Inquiry into the Currency Principle. London

v Köppen I (1993) Bankenverhalten und Wirksamkeit der Geldpolitk - Theorie und qualitative Evidenz. Geld - Währung - Kapitalmarkt Working Paper No 30, February

Wicksell K (1898) Geldzins und Güterpreise. Jena

Willms M (1987) Geldangebotstheorie. In: Thieme J (ed) Geldtheorie. Entwicklung, Stand und systemvergleichende Anwendung, Baden Baden

Wray LR (1990) Money and Credit in Capitalist Economies: The Endogenous Money Approach. Aldershot

Wray LR (1992) Commercial Banks, the Central Bank, and Endogenous Money. In: Journal of Post Keynesian Economics, Vol 14, No 3, Spring, pp 297-310

The Endogeneity of Money: Concepts, Methods and Doctrinal Influence of Monetary Theory

Andreas Beyer
University of Frankfurt

1 Introduction

One of the most discussed topics in monetary theory is whether money is endogenous or exogenous. Since there are no generally accepted definitions of exogeneity and causality such discussions must, as Hoover (1988) states, "proceed gingerly through a terminological minefield." The purpose of this paper is to show that the usage of different notions of exogeneity and causality yields very different conclusions about the influence of money in relation to other economic variables. In Section 2 the distinction between economic and statistical exogeneity is briefly discussed. Section 3 describes Granger's definition of causality and its application to money supply. That inadequate assumptions of exogeneity have serious impacts on estimated parameters and on forecast behaviour of econometric (structural) models is shown in Section 4. In Section 5 the definition of exogeneity by Engle/Hendry/Richard (1983), which provides a framework for statistical tests of exogeneity is explained. Based on this definition, Hoover recently has shown that the monetarist view concerning money and causality can, at least, be posed into question. Section 6 describes the main steps of Hoover's (1991) analysis and in Section 7 a conclusion is presented.

2 Economic and Statistical Exogeneity

2.1 The Necessity of a Conceptual Distinction

Koopmans (1950) describes two main principles to distinguish between endogenous and exogenous variables.
1. Departmental principle: variables are exogenous if they are determined outside the scope of economics, such as natural events.
2. Causal principle: variables are exogenous, if they influence other (endogenous) variables without being influenced thereby.
Concerning the question whether money is determined exogenously or not, a

departmental distinction obviously is not possible. Relevant, instead, is the criterion of causality. Modelling causal relationships is possible within both, economic and econometric models. Koopmans (1950) stresses the difference between economic and statistical exogeneity: For reason of simplification, in the economic model the influence of endogenous on exogenous variables can be neglected whilst the econometrician must be convinced (e.g. by statistical tests) that such an influence on variables treated as exogenous can be ruled out. Statistical exogeneity therefore implies that the disturbances in the equations of the exogenous variables[1] are distributed independently from the disturbances in the equations explaining the endogenous variables.

2.2 Exogeneity Econometric Models

Since in general economic data are not the result of laboratory experiments, it is not possible to draw conclusions about cause and effect from the data alone. If causal relationships are modeled in econometric models, the causal direction must be postulated a priori and very often this is provided by economic theory. Then, from a structural model the reduced form can be derived. Johnston (1984) notes:

> "The reduced form indicates that there is one-way causation in the model in the sense that the exogenous variables influence the current endogenous variables, but there is no feedback in the opposite direction: current endogenous variables do not influence the exogenous variables."(p.8)

However, contradictions may arise if there are different competing theories about how to treat a variable such as the money-stock, where keynesian and monetarist models yield different causal directions. The monetarist view favours the causal chain from money via prices to income as Cagan (1965):

> "The conclusion that long-run price movements are primarily due to changes in the money stock suggests that any causal connection must run from prices to the output variables."(p.260)

whereas real business cycle models as quoted by Hoover (1988) say:

> "It is planned movements in output that induce movements in deposits rather than autonomous movements in deposits causing movements in output as Friedman and Schwartz would have it."(p.56)

One way to find a "solution" of this dispute would be if causality assumptions could be tested on statistical grounds. Granger (1969) therefore developed a notion that is explained in the next section.

---

[1] Equations that explain exogenous variables must not contain endogenous variables.

3 Causality and the Flow of Time

3.1 Granger's (1969) Definition

Granger's definition of causality is based upon the time sequence of the realisations. Assuming *stochastic* variables, the dependence of the flow of time is implied by the central assumption that the future cannot cause the past. He defines:

> "Y_t is causing X_t, if we are better able to predict X_t using all available information than if the information apart from Y_t had been used"(p.428).

where the series $\mathbf{X_t}$ and $\mathbf{Y_t}$ contain all realisations from $-\infty$ to t. The criterion for the goodness of prediction is the error variance of the linear predictor of $\mathbf{X_{t+1}}$. Y is causing **X**, if $\sigma^2(X_{t+1} | X_t, Y_t) < \sigma^2(X_{t+1} | X_t)$.

This definition provides a framework to test three hypotheses of causality in the sense of Granger: "**Y** causes **X**, but **X** does not cause **Y**" and vice versa and "**Y** causes **X** *and* **X** causes **Y**". If the last hypothesis is not rejected then a feedback is occuring from **X** to **Y**.

Granger applies the test for causality according to the following model:

$$X_t = \sum_{j=1}^{m} a_j X_{t-j} + \sum_{j=1}^{m} b_j Y_{t-j} + e_t \tag{3.1}$$

$$Y_t = \sum_{j=1}^{m} c_j X_{t-j} + \sum_{j=1}^{m} d_j Y_{t-j} + u_t \tag{3.2}$$

where $\mathbf{e_t}$ and $\mathbf{u_t}$ are uncorrelated white-noise error terms. Both equations are estimated seperately. The null hypothesis "**Y** causes **X**" is *not* rejected, if the coefficients $\mathbf{b_j}$ in (3.1) are significantly different from zero. Analogous to this, the null hypothesis "**X** causes **Y**" is *not* rejected, if the coefficients $\mathbf{c_j}$ in (3.2) are significant different from zero. If both hypotheses together are not rejected, a feedback relationship exists between **X** and **Y**.

3.2 Money and Causality (I): The Analysis of Sims (1972)

Granger's definition of causality seemed to provide an appropriate framework to apply statistical tests on the question whether money causes income or vice versa.

Sims (1972) developed a test for Granger-causality that is based on Granger's central argument that future events cannot cause the past. The application of that test "identifies the causal direction" and is described by Sims as resting on a "sophisticated version of the *post hoc ergo propter hoc* principle". Sims claims that for a unique causal direction running from X to Y it is necessary and sufficient that in a regression

$$(3.3) \qquad Y_t = \sum_{j=1}^{m} a_j X_{t-j} + \sum_{j=1}^{m} b_j X_{t+j} + cX_t + e_t$$

all the coefficients b_j of the future values of X are *not* significantly different from zero. A nonexisting feedback from Y to X together with unidirectional causality from X to Y has two important implications: first, a theortical causal relationship, which is formulated as a regression of Y on past and present X can be interpreted as an economic causal relation as well. Second, Granger-noncausality from Y to X is necessary and sufficient to avoid any correlation of X with the residuals. Hence, the condition of "strict" exogeneity is fulfilled such that inconsistent estimates in a regression of Y on X can be avoided.[2]

Sims applies this test procedure asking if there is "statistical evidence that money is 'exogenous' in some sense in the money-income relationship?" He uses US-data for 1949-1968 regressing M1 and, with the same result, the monetary base on GNP. Granger-causality tests reject the hypothesis of a causal direction from income to money but they do not reject the opposite direction:

> "The evidence agrees quite well with a null hypothesis that causality runs entirely from money to GNP, without feedback."(p.541)

Hence, this is necessary and sufficient for his theorem to get consistent estimates and Sims concludes:

> "No evidence appears to contradict the common assumption that money can be treated as exogenous in a regression of GNP on current and past money."(p.550)

4 The Ambivalence of Exogeneity: Contradiction and Critique

4.1 The Contradiction in Sims' (1972) Theorem

In this paragraph the distinction into economic and statistical exogeneity (Section 2) is now discussed with relation to Sims'theorem (see footnote 2). Apart from the decision *which* variable to treat as exogenous, additional aspects have to be taken into account in any structural econometric model, such as identification restrictions and the question whether the model is complete. Concerning the es-

---

[2] "When [X Y]' has an autoregressive representation, Y can be expressed as a distributed lag function of current and past X with a residual which is not correlated with any values of X, past or future, if and only if, Y does not cause X in Granger's sense." Sims (1972), p.545.

timation properties, the relationship between consistent estimates and exogenous regressors can be demonstrated with the following model:

(4.1) $$Y_t = \gamma X_t + \beta_{11} Y_{t-1} + \beta_{12} X_{t-1} + \zeta_t$$

(4.2) $$X_t = \delta Y_t + \beta_{21} Y_{t-1} + \beta_{22} X_{t-1} + \eta_t$$

where ζ_t und η_t are uncorrelated white-noise errors.
From Sims' theorem it follows, that γ in (4.1) can be estimated consistently if and only if there is no Granger-causality from Y to X. This implies that in equation (4.3)

(4.3) $$X_t = \Pi_{21} Y_{t-1} + \Pi_{22} X_{t-1} + \nu_t$$

Π_{21} must be equal to zero. Since (4.3) is the reduced form of X_t, (4.1) and (4.2) imply the restriction

(4.4) $$\Pi_{21} = \frac{\delta \beta_{11} + \beta_{21}}{1 - \gamma\delta}$$

However, it can be shown[3] that γ in (4.1) can be estimated consistently if and only if δ equals zero in (4.2) because only then X_t und ζ_t in (4.1) are uncorrelated, i.e. only then X_t is strictly exogenous. But the condition that $\Pi_{21} = 0$ is neither necessary nor sufficient for consistency, since from $\delta = 0$ and $\beta_{21} \neq 0 \rightarrow \Pi_{21} \neq 0$ and from $\delta \neq 0$ and $\beta_{11} = -\beta_{21}/\delta \rightarrow \Pi_{21} = 0$.

Hence, the invalidity of Sims' theorem is shown and even if Granger-causality is considered equivalent to economic causality, it does not imply statistical exogeneity.[4]

The definitorical gap between economic and statistical exogeneity was shown even more lasting by the critique of Lucas (1976). The basic idea behind his critique is explained in the following paragraph.

4.2 The Critique of Lucas (1976)

Due to the predictive-failure of many econometric models in the early 70's (structural macro-models as well as single equation models for money demand), Lucas criticised the application of such models for political purposes, i.e. predictions and policy simulations. Lucas assumes that agents have rational expectations. This implies that agents know the control variables and the decision rules of the policy-makers, i.e. "the true model" with its parameters. In his critique Lucas refers to the consequences of a change in the parameters due to policy

---

[3] e.g. Johnston (1984), p.272.

[4] In a footnote Hoover (1988) remarks: "It has been suggested that the logical error is so egregious that Sims must have his tongue in his cheek."

decisions. Such changes in control variables are recognised immediately by the agents and hence they adapt their economic behaviour to the new parameters. Since conventional econometric models do not sufficiently take into account these structural changes they produce wrong forecasts. Furthermore, a model can only produce forecasts due to parameters that were estimated under a particular regime. Since a regime shift due to a policy-change yields a shift in the parameters, the consequences of that policy change cannot be simulated by an econometric model that does not take into account these parameter changes. Instead, a new model has to be estimated. Lucas' argumentation implies a fundamental critique against traditional econometric models: They should not be employed for neither long-run forecasts nor policy-simulations, respectively. An answer, however, to this critique is the definition by Engle Hendry and Richard (1983) which is explained in the next section.

5 Statistical Exogeneity - Part of a Methodological Concept

5.1 The Definition by Engle, Hendry and Richard (1983)

The motivation for the Engle/Hendry/Richard approach goes back to Koopmans' claim for a distinction between economic and statistical exogeneity. Their statistical concept provides definitions for weak, strong and super exogeneity. Employing simple models, these three definitions are exposed in the next paragraphs.

5.1.1 Weak Exogeneity

Assume the following bivariate linear regression model:

$$y_t = \beta x_t + e_t \tag{5.1}$$

where e_t is the non-systematic component of the model and y and x are stochastic variables. They are underlying the joint density function $D(y_t,x_t;\Psi)$, which is entirely characterised through the parameter vector Ψ.
$Z_t = [y_t\ x_t]'$ represents the vector of the jointly distributed stochastic variables at every time t. Z_t is assumed to be a normal, independent and identically distributed (niid) stochastic process. The joint density can be factorised into a conditional and a marginal distribution, such that

$$D(Z_t;\psi) = D(y_t,x_t;\psi) = D(y_t|x_t;\psi_1)\cdot D(x_t;\psi_2) \tag{5.2}$$

The first two moments of the conditional distribution $D(y_t|x_t;\psi_1)$ are $E(y_t|x_t) = \beta x_t$ and $Var(y_t|x_t) = \sigma^2$. Hence, the conditional distribution in (5.2) is a representation of the parameters that are the unknown "parameters of interest" in the regression model (5.1), i.e. $(\beta,\sigma^2) \equiv \theta$.

The marginal distribution $D(x_t;\psi_2)$ represents the exogenous process. If it is to be neglected for the estimation of the parameters of interest its parameters must be "nuisance parameters", i.e. they do not contain any relevant information for the estimation of θ. The values of ψ_2 must not restrict those of ψ_1 which means that they are variation free. They define:

> "X_t ist weakly exogenous for the parameters of interest, if there exists a reparameterisation such that (i) θ is a function of ψ_1 ($\theta = h(\psi_1)$) and (ii) ψ_1 und ψ_2 are variation free ($(\psi_1,\psi_2) \in \Psi_1 X \Psi_2$)."(p.282)

Weak exogeneity is sufficient for efficient estimates in linear non-dynamic models such as (5.1). In (4.1) X_t is weakly exogenous for γ, if $\delta = 0$ in (4.2). In this case strict exogeneity is implied by weak exogeneity.

5.1.2 Strong Exogeneity

If an estimated model is used for forecast purposes, it is convenient to use all the relevant information of the past, i.e. the history of the variables of the joint distribution. In dynamic models as well, the history of the variables is relevant. Assume the following dynamic linear regression model

$$y_t = \beta_0 x_t + \beta_1 x_{t-1} + \alpha y_{t-1} + e_t \tag{5.3}$$

with e_t as in (5.1). Now $Z_t = [y_t,x_t]'$ is no longer assumed to be an independent process but, instead, a normally distributed, stationary stochastic process. Compared with (5.2) the factorisation changes in so far as the history of the process has to be taken into account. Formally this is done by writing the past of Z_t as $Z^\circ_{t-1} \equiv (Z_1,Z_2,...,Z_{t-1})$. This yields the factorisation

$$D(Z_t|Z^\circ_{t-1};\psi) = D(y_t|Z^\circ_{t-1},x_t;\psi_1)\cdot D(x_t|Z^\circ_{t-1};\psi_2) \tag{5.4}$$

For (5.3) to be estimated the parameters of interest, $\theta = (\beta_i,\alpha,\sigma^2)$ are functions of ψ_1. Hence, x_t is still weakly exogenous for θ, and also in this model θ can be estimated by the conditional distribution alone, ignoring the marginal. Nevertheless, if y_t has to be forcast, it must be taken into account that the exogenous process $D(x_t|Z^\circ_{t-1};\psi_2)$ contains the history of $y_t \equiv Y^\circ_{t-1}$, such that a feedback relation between x and y - if it exists - influences the marginal distribution. To avoid this, it is necessary to assume that Y°_{t-1} is not contained in Z°_{t-1}, i.e. there is no feedback from y to x. Their definition for strong exogeneity says:

> "If X is weakly exogenous with respect to θ and there is no Granger-causality from Y to X, then X is strongly exogenous with respect to θ." (p.282)

Hence, strong exogeneity of the right hand side variables allows to make forecasts for the endogenous variables without knowing the exact marginal distribution of the exogenous variables.

5.1.3 Super Exogeneity

The definition of super exogeneity can be seen as an econometric answer to the Lucas-critique. Weak and strong exogeneity are related to constant regimes. A change in the parameters of control variables might also change the structural parameters of the model. Therefore it is of particular interest to show under which conditions a regime shift leaves the structural parameters of the model unchanged. Weak exogeneity of the marginalised variables per se does not exclude a behavioural change of the agents due to an intervention in control variables. Having

$$(5.5) \qquad D(Z_t \mid Z^o_{t-1};\psi) = D(y_t \mid Z^o_{t-1},x_t;\psi_1)\cdot D(x_t \mid Z^o_{t-1};\psi_2)$$

it is therefore necessary that the parameters of $D(y_t \mid Z^o_{t-1},x_t;\psi_1)$ are structural invariant with respect to changes in the parameters of the exogenous process. Structural invariance means that the parameters of ψ_1 remain constant if ψ_2 changes due to interventions. Hence, they formally define:

> "A variable ist super exogenous with respect to the parameters of interest θ, if it is weakly exogenous for θ and if the conditional distribution $D(y_t|Z^o_{t-1},x_t;\psi_1)$ is structurally invariant." (p.284)

Applied for structural models this means that super exogenous variables allow for policy simulations. Forecasts are valid, even if control variables are shifted by interventions, i.e. if they are not stationary.

Hence, if in a model the assumption of super exogeneity is justified, the Lucas-critique can be refuted.

5.2 Testing for Exogeneity Assumptions

The exogeneity definition of Engle/Hendry/Richard provides a framework for testing exogeneity assumptions on statistical grounds. Although it is possible to run statistical tests for exogeneity based on definitons of predeterminedness and strict exogeneity, these tests underly overidentification restrictions which have to be tested, too. Under certain conditions tests for strict exogenity, e.g. Wu (1973), that are testing for correlation between right hand side variables and disturbances are sufficient for weak exogeneity. In such a case it is necessary firstly to specify the exogenous process $D(x_t \mid Z^o_{t-1};\psi_2)$ as in equation (4.2). Richard (1982) puts forward that it is paradoxical if a marginal model must be estimated to test whether it is relevant for the estimation of the parameters of interest. In general strict exogeneity is neither necessary nor sufficient for consistent estimations of the parameters of interest and it does not guarantee the invariance of the parameters either.

Alternatively to such parametric tests, indirect tests for the underlying (statistical) assumptions of a model and its implications for the residuals can be employed, such as:

- Tests for ex-post forecast accuracy
- Tests for parameter constancy
- Tests for structural breaks
- Tests for normality
- Encompassing tests.

Applying these tests reveals the role of the residuals in the LSE-Approach as the "non-systematic part" of the model rather than "disturbances", underlying certain a priori assumptions.

The application of this approach and the link between causality and exogeneity concerning money and prices are described in the next section.

6 Causality and Controllability

6.1 The Notion of Simon

Alternatively to Granger's (1969) time and forecast related causality definition, the notion of Simon (1953) is based on asymmetric relationships between the variables of a system. Asymmetry in this sense depends on the controllability of one variable by another variable: **Y** is controllable, if the value of **Y** can be forecast by a change of **X**, i.e. if the model is invariant with respect to interventions in **X**. Simon (1953) states that

> "Any such intervention would alter the structure but leave the model (and hence the causal ordering) invariant. Hence, causal ordering is a property of models that is invariant with respect to interventions within the model, and structural equations are equations that correspond to specified possibilities of intervention."(p 27).

6.2 Money and Causality (II): The Analysis of Hoover (1991)

6.2.1 Statistical Foundations

Based on Simon's (1953) notion of causality, Hoover (1991) examines the causal relationship between money and prices:

> "Supposing the Federal Reserve can control the stock of money, can it thereby also control the level of prices (or the rate of inflation)?" (p.382).

An important role in Hoover's analysis play events in economic policy such as price controls and expansion of the money stock by the central bank. These events are determinants of the hypotheses formulations for statistical tests which are based on the Engle/Hendry/Richard (1983) definition of super exogeneity. Assuming that money (M) and prices (P) can be represented by a joint density, different factorisations represent different causality directions. A priori they are (statistically) equivalent if none of the distributions underlies any restrictions. A regression of M on P then cannot be distinguished statistically from a regression of P on M and both conditional models are said to be observational equivalent. Hence

$$(6.1) \qquad D(M,P) = D(M|P)\bullet D(P) = D(P|M)\bullet D(M)$$

The second equals sign in (6.1) is no more valid, if the stability of the conditional and marginal distribution is influenced due to interventions on control variables. If a particular intervention in M or P can be related to changes in the pattern of stability of the conditional models, this yields conclusions about the super exogenous character of the corresponding control variables. If P is super exogenous and the causal direction runs from P to M, then the conditional distribution **D(M|P)** must remain stable although there might be interventions in P, and hence a shift in the exogenous process **D(P)** is irrelevant for the parameters of interest. In contrast, if an intervention in M changes the parameters of **D(P|M)**, then the intervention is not parameter invariant and hence M is not super exogenous.

6.2.2 Hoover's Empirical Results

The corresponding distributions of (6.1) are represented by models that are estimated with US data for 1950-1985 according to the criteria of the "LSE-Methodology". Potential parameter shifts due to interventions in variables were confirmed by statistical tests. The tests for the stability performance of the corresponding models show that **D(M|P)** is more stable than **D(P)** but that **D(P|M)** is less stable than **D(M)**. For Hoover this evidence gives support for the view that prices influence money but that money does not influence prices as proclaimed by monetarists. However, a consensus between this and the monetarist position is seen by Hoover in so far as in the long run a strong correlation exists between money and prices though, from correlation alone a causal direction cannot be derived as it is applied by Friedman and Schwartz (1963).

7 Conclusions

Based on Koopmans' (1950) claim for a distinction into economic and statistical exogeneity, the definitions of weak, strong and super exogeneity by Engle/Hendry/Richard (1983) provide a framework for testing exogeneity assumptions on statistical grounds. Statistical exogeneity of a variable in an econometric model depends crucially on the parameterisation of the corresponding model. *If* a variable can be treated as exogenous with respect to the parameters of interest, it is the underlying formulation of that particular model, i.e. the underlying distribution which determines the exogeneity of the variable.

Concerning the question whether money is exogenous or endogenous with respect to prices, Hoover (1991) shows for the US that the conditional distribution of prices is more stable when money is marginalised out rather than money is included. Hence, prices are exogenous with respect to money. In Simon's sense a causal direction from exogenous to endogenous variables (here from prices to money) can be interpreted as an asymmetric relationship between control and controllable variables. From Hoover's results it follows that it is money which is "controlled" by prices and not vice versa as the monetarist's view would suggest. However, these results do not allow for a general statement like "money is exogenous in the economy".

A different approach in determining the causal direction between money and prices was employed by Sims (1972). However, it was shown that relying on the results of Granger-causality tests can be dangerous: They imply the opposite direction of argumentation in the sense that economic and statistical exogeneity is derived from *statistical* causality. It can yield very misleading results since Granger-causality must not be understood as logical causality.

References

Cagan P (1965) Determinants and Effects of Changes in the Stock of Money, 1875-1960. New York: Columbia University Press

Deutsche Bundesbank (1992) Zum Zusammenhang zwischen Geldmengen- und Preisentwicklung in der Bundesrepublik Deutschland. Monatsberichte der Deutschen Bundesbank, January

Engle RF, Hendry DF, Richard JF (1983) Exogeneity. Econometrica, Vol 51, No 2, pp 277-304

Engle RF, Hendry D (1990) Testing Super Exogeneity and Invariance in Regression Models. Institute of Economics and Statistics. Discussion Paper No 100, Oxford

Florens JP, Mouchart M, Richard JF (1976) Likelihood Analysis of Linear Models. CORE-Discussion Paper No 7619, Louvain-La-Neuve

Friedman M, Schwartz A (1963) A Monetary History of the United States. Princeton, NJ: Princeton University Press

Granger CWJ (1969) Investigating Causal Relations by Econometric Models and cross-spectral Methods. Econometrica, Vol 37, No 3, pp 424-438

Haavelmo T (1944) The Probability Approach in Econometrics. Econometrica, Vol 12 (Supplement)

Hausman JA (1978) Specification Tests in Econometrics. Econometrica, Vol 46, No 5, pp 1251-1271

Hendry DF, Richard JF (1982) On the Formulation of Empirical Models in Dynamic Econometrics. Journal of Econometrics, Vol 20, p 3-33

Hoover KD (1988) The New Classical Macroeconomics. A Sceptical Inquiry. Oxford: Basil Blackwell

Hoover KD (1991) The Causal Direction between Money and Prices. An Alternative Approach. Journal of Monetary Economics, Vol 27, pp 381-423

Johnston J (1984) Econometric Methods. 3rd ed, New York: McGraw Hill

Judge G, Griffiths W, Carter Hill R, Lütkepohl H, Lee TC (1985) The Theory and Practice of Econometrics. Second Edition, New York: John Wiley

Koopmans TC (1950) When is an Equation System Complete for Statistical Purposes? Chapter 17 in: Statistical Inference in Dynamic Economic Models. New York: John Wiley, 1950

Lucas RE Jr (1976) Econometric Policy Evaluation: A Critique. In: Brunner K, Meltzer A (Hrsg) (1976) The Phillips Curve and Labor Markets. Carnegie Rochester Conference Series on Public Policy, Vol 1, pp 19-44. Amsterdam: North-Holland. Printed in: Lucas (1981) Studies in Business-Cycle Theory. Oxford, Basil Blackwell, pp 104-130

Mann HB, Wald A (1943) On the Statistical Treatment of Linear Stochastic Difference Equations. Econometrica, Vol 11, No 3,4, pp 173-220

Mizon G, Richard JF (1986) The Encompassing Principle and its Application to Testing non-nested Hypotheses. Econometrica, Vol 54, pp 657-678

Mood M, Graybill F, Boes D (1974) Introduction to the Theory of Statistics, 3rd ed Singapore: Mc-Graw-Hill

Nakamura A and M (1981) On the Relationships among several Spezification Error Tests presented by Durbin, Wu and Hausman. Econometrica, Vol 49, No 6, pp 1583-1588

Richard JF (1980) Models with Several Regimes and Changes in Exogeneity. Review of Economic Studies, Vol 47, pp 1-20

Richard JF (1982) Exogeneity, Causality, and Structural Invariance in Econometric Modelling. Chapter 7 in: Chow GC and Corsi P (ed) (1982) Evaluating the Reliability of Macro-economic Models. New York: John Wiley

Simon HA (1953) Causal Ordering and Identifiability. Chapter 1 in: Models of Man. New York: John Wiley, 1957

Sims CA (1972) Money, Income and Causality. American Economic Review, Vol 62, No 4, pp 540-552

Sims CA (1980): Macroeconomics and Reality. Econometrica, Vol 48, No 1, pp 1-48

Spanos A (1986) Statistical Foundations of Econometric Modelling. Cambridge: Cambridge University Press

Wold H (1954) Causality and Econometrics. Econometrica, Vol 22, No 2, pp 162-177

Wu DM (1973) Alternative Tests of Independence between Stochastic Regressors and Disturbances. Econometrica, Vol 41, pp 212-235

Currency Competition and Endogenous Money: Experiences from the Suffolk System, 1819-1858

Stephan L. Kalb
European University Institute, Firenze

1 Introduction

This article studies competing currencies in Massachusetts under the so-called Suffolk Clearing System, 1819-1858. It provides information on the operation of a monetary system in which banks competitively issued bank notes, serving as the media of exchange and convertible into a monetary commodity (gold or silver). The article contributes to the general reconsideration of the need for outside bodies to intervene and regulate market forces in the financial system by exploring the consequences of laissez-faire in the supply of bank money.

Currency competition is a controversial issue. Even strong supporters of laissez-faire in other sectors of the economy are opposed to competing currencies and accept the state monopoly of note issue as an indispensable condition for monetary stability. The best example of this view is Milton Friedman (1959) who objects to a system with competitively supplied convertible currency on a fractional reserve basis for the following reason:

> "In fraud as in other activities, opportunities for profit are not likely to go unexploited. A fiduciary currency ostensibly convertible into the monetary commodity is therefore likely to be overissued from time to time and convertibility is likely to become impossible."(p.6)

Hence, in Friedman's view competition does not provide an effective limit to the volume of a fiduciary currency. For the currency to remain fiduciary, the cost of producing additional units must be kept lower than the value of the notes. In holding this position Friedman stands in line with the *Currency School*, which proposed strict regulation of the issue of paper money because of the dangers of overissue, on the grounds that convertibility alone would not prevent banks from overissuing. Loyd (1858) argued

> "The desire to extend his own issue is the motive of each issuer; this motive will lead each party to ... look upon contraction as a favorable opportunity, not for contracting, but for expanding his own issues, with the view and in hope of possessing himself of the ground which his rival has receded."(pp.98-99)

This was undoubtedly the predominant view on the topic until Friedrich von Hayek

(1976, 1978) and others[1] suggested that the path to monetary stability was simply to open up banking to the same competitive forces that operate effectively in other sectors of the economy. This was by no means a new idea. Advocates of *Free Banking* argued that the banking system could be trusted to operate effectively with few external constraints or regulations, and adherents of the *Banking School* believed that competitive banks are incapable of creating any excess issue. For both the belief that bank money is endogenous is central. In Tooke's (1844) words:

> "It is not in the power of Banks of Issue, including the Bank of England, to make any direct addition to the amount of notes circulating ... the prices of commodities do not depend upon the quantity of money indicated by the amount of bank notes; but on the contrary, the amount of the circulation medium is the consequence of prices."(pp.122-123)

Most advocates of competing currencies regard, in addition to appropriate liability regulation, the convertibility of bank notes into a commodity money as essential for preventing overissue within the banking system. If a bank were to increase its circulation in excess of demand, redemptions would reduce the bank's specie reserves and hence, contract its note issue. While writers like White (1984) consider direct redemptions by consumers as sufficient, Parnell and Fullarton[2] argued for an organized note exchange system.

Such a mechanism was used under the Suffolk System. Convertibility, required by law, was enforced by a clearing system that evolved in the market. However, the immense growth of the supply of bank money under this system raises doubt with regard to the claim that money is endogenous and currency competition non-inflationary. This is the question considered here.

The organization of this article is as follows. Section 2 provides an overview of the monetary system in Massachusetts as a background for the analysis. In section 3 the question of the endogeneity of money and the relationship between money and prices will be examined. Furthermore the safety of bank money will be appraised and explanations for the strong increase in the volume of bank money will be discussed. Section 4 offers some concluding remarks.

[1] E.g. Klein (1974), Tullock (1975), Vaubel (1977), Girton and Roper (1979).

[2] See Smith (1936, p 62) and Fullarton (1845, p 67).

2 Money and Banking in Massachusetts, 1819-1858

2.1 The Money Stock

The monetary system of Massachusetts was, like in the rest of the United States, on a bimetallic standard from 1786 to 1873. The Dollar of the United States was defined as a particular weight of gold or of silver and served as the unit of account.[3] Gold and silver coins as well as paper money, redeemable into gold or silver, served as media of exchange.

The Constitution of the US gave to Congress the power "to coin money and regulate the value thereof" (Article I, Section 8). However, this did not imply that the quantity of gold and silver coins was under the control of the monetary authority, because in 1793 a number of foreign gold and silver coins were also made legal tender.[4] Official exchange rates between these foreign coins were fixed according to their gold and silver weight. Although only gold and silver coins (specie) were legal tender the largest part of the circulation consisted of paper money redeemable in specie. For 1816 the Secretary of the of Treasury (1856, p. 51) estimated the ratio of circulating coins to circulating paper money at 1:10 on average for the entire US.

In Massachusetts redeemable paper money was for the most part issued by so-called *State Banks*, i.e., banks chartered by the State. Section 10 of the federal Constitution excluded the States themselves from issuing paper money but left them entirely the right to regulate banking in their territories. In Massachusetts a law was passed limiting the business of banking, including the issue of bank notes, to authorized banks and *State Banks* were chartered by special acts of the legislatures of the State of Massachusetts.[5]

In addition to the State Banks, bank notes were issued by the Boston branch of the Second Bank of the U.S. (1816-1836). These notes suffered from a comparative disadvantage in serving as media of exchange because only notes of denominations of ten dollars or more were issued while State bank notes were denominated even in fractional parts of the dollar (Secretary 1856, p. 56). Hence, the share of the notes issued by the Second Bank was in 1819 only about 10 % of all bank notes issued in Massachusetts.[6] As Table 1 shows, in most years the average holding of State Bank

---

[3] The Gold Dollar and Silver Dollar weight was slightly adjusted at times. In 1786 the Gold Dollar was 24.6268 in grains Fine, the Silver Dollar was 375.64 Fine (International Monetary Conference 1879, p. 437-453). Whenever the resulting mint ratio of about 1:15 was below the world ratio the U.S. was in fact on a silver standard.

[4] Act of February 9, 1793, Section 1.

[5] Acts of Massachusetts 1799, Ch. 32.

[6] In 1819 the Boston branch of the Second Bank had a circulation of $ 254,400 (Elliot 1845, p. 767) while circulation of the State Banks was $ 2,464,057.

money per head of the population was below the smallest denomination of notes issued by the Second Bank (10 $). Because of their high denomination we consider notes of the Second Bank as bearer bonds, usually not serving as media of exchange and exclude them from the analysis.[7]

The total volume of bank notes issued by State Banks in Massachusetts is presented in Table 1. One can easily see that both the number of banks and the volume of circulation increased tremendously over this period. Both figures doubled between 1820 and 1830 as well as between 1830 and 1836. Furthermore the average holding of bank notes per head of the population trebled within fifteen years from about $ 5 to about $ 15.

Table 1. Number of State Banks in Massachusetts and their Note Circulation

Year	Number of Banks	Circulation of Bank Notes	
		in US $	per Head
1820	28	2,614,734	4.99
1822	33	3,132,552	5.79
1824	37	3,842,641	6.88
1826	55	4,549,814	7.91
1828	61	4,884,538	8.24
1830	63	5,124,090	8.39
1832	83	7,122,850	11.19
1834	103	7,650,147	11.54
1836	117	10,892,249	15.82
1838	120	9,400,512	13.16

Sources: Comptroller of the Currency (1878, p. 98 - 99) and Hunt's Merchants' Magazine

2.2 Banking

Entry into banking was essentially free regardless of the fact that a law opened the business of banking only to incorporated banking companies. The system is not considered as *free banking*, which would have required that opening a bank and issuing bank notes were open to anyone meeting some standard requirements, but recent research by Sylla (1985) and Ng (1988) claims that obtaining a charter was only a

[7] There is also a data problem. For most years data on the circulation of the Boston branch of the Second Bank is not available, there are only data for New England as a whole.

formality.[8] While for the first charter in 1784 for the Massachusetts bank much attention was paid to the "public interest" of the charter, as the number of banks grew concern about the public interest also diminished (Lamoreaux 1986, p. 549-650). This *de facto* free entry may also have been the reason why there was little use made of the free banking law, passed in 1851.

Banks located in Boston were, on average, larger than country banks with respect to their capital stocks. In 1824 the smallest bank had a capital of $ 68,000 (Oxford Bank) and the largest bank had a capital stock of $ 1,800,000 (State Bank).[9] Legal limits upon the volume of bank note circulation of individual banks were fixed according to the bank's capital. The limit was 150 % until 1825, 100 % between 1825 and 1829, and 125 % thereafter of a bank's capital.[10] There was no provision relative to keep a particular liquidity reserve in specie. Notwithstanding, if a bank failed or refused to redeem their notes on presentation, a penalty of 2 % a month, payable by the bank to the bill holder was imposed by law (Knox 1903, p. 361). Thus, bank note holders themselves served as lender of last resort.

The liability rules that applied to the stockholders are well summarized by Root (1895):

> "In case of any loss or deficiency arising from mismanagement, the stockholders were to be individually liable in their private capacities, to an amount not exceeding the stock held by them; and upon the expiration of the charter the stockholders were to be liable in their private and individual capacities for the payment of all bills outstanding, in proportion to the stock held."(p.256)

In addition, directors were individually liable if the bank note circulation in relation to the banks' capital exceeded the legal limit (Dewey 1910, p. 115).

2.3 The Suffolk Clearing System

The initiative to create a clearing system in Massachusetts originated from the Suffolk Bank after which the System was named.[11] In 1819 the Bank decided to engage in the "foreign money business", i.e., dealing with bank notes issued by banks outside Boston. These bank notes, so-called *foreign notes*, circulated in Boston at varying discounts whereas bank notes issued in Boston were accepted at par. Discounts varied

---

[8] This view is also shared by Dowrie (1936), p 182 and Lamoreaux (1986). Ng (1988) found that the provision of free banking laws was not followed by the entry of new banks. However, he does not conclude that entry had already been relatively free under chartered banking but that both chartered banking and free banking had effective provisions restricting entry.

[9] Commonwealth of Massachusetts (1824).

[10] See Root (1895), p 256 and Bank Commissioner (1850), p 120.

[11] The ultimate source on the Suffolk Bank and the Suffolk System is Whitney (1878). Other references are Lake (1947), Trivoli (1979), Fenstermaker and Filer (1986), and Mullineaux (1987).

according to the distance the holder of a bank note had to travel to collect specie in exchange for the note, and the financial standing of the issuing bank. Whitney (1878, p. 2) reports "How great the discount was he (the merchant) could learn only by consulting his "Bank note Reporter," or by enquiring at the nearest exchange office..." Several bank note brokers, the Boston Exchange Office, and some Boston banks were engaged in exchanging country banknotes against Boston notes at varying discounts and thereby fixed the market prices for these notes. Price quotations of bank notes revealed information to buyers and sellers of bank notes as the secondary market had a strong incentive to monitor the quality of the received bank notes and to buy only at adequate prices.

The Suffolk Bank basically internalized part of the secondary market for bank notes. It bought bank notes at the market discount and the respective issuing banks were offered the opportunity to open accounts with the Suffolk for the purpose of clearing incoming bank notes, or be faced with frequent redemptions. A committee of the Suffolk bank formulated the conditions as follows (Whitney 1878):

> "That if any bank will deposit with the Suffolk Bank five thousand dollars as a permanent deposit, with such further sums as shall be sufficient from time to time to redeem its bills taken by this bank, such bank shall have the privilege of receiving its own bills at the same discount at which they are purchased... "(p.7)

> "... should any bank refuse to make the deposit required, the bills of such banks shall be sent home for payment at such times and in such manner as the directors may hereafter order and direct."(p.8)

This scheme meant increased deposits for the Suffolk Bank. For the country banks it meant either keeping a deposit with Suffolk, or facing the threat of frequent demands for redemption. In consequence, one way or the other, discounts on country banknotes fell to less than one-half per cent (Hammond 1957, p. 552). However, with decreased discounts profits were shrinking and soon the Suffolk Bank became dissatisfied with its scheme. The pressure one single bank could apply was limited and the formation of a more general system, including all the Boston banks, was considered.

In 1824 the Suffolk Bank suggested to each of the six Boston banks the raising of a fund for the purpose of sending home the bills of the country banks and creating a clearing system similar to the one existing but with the participation of all the Boston banks. The six Boston banks, dissatisfied with their limited banknote circulation, agreed to raising this fund, expecting that this measure would materially increase their circulation (see Appleton 1831, p. 18).

According to the agreement, the Suffolk Bank should, as the agent of the associated banks, receive from them all their foreign money to send it home for redemption. As an alternative to being faced with immediate redemptions, the country banks were offered the opportunity to keep an account with the Suffolk Bank for the redemption of their bills. The required permanent deposit was a minimum of $ 2000 for banks with a capital of $ 100,000 and under, free of interest. In consideration of such a deposit the Suffolk Bank than redeemed bills to the issuing bank, provided the bank kept a sufficient amount of funds in its account in addition to the permanent deposit. Rather than have their notes sent home for payment, in which case specie was received, soon almost all banks in New England had joined the system and kept deposits at the Suffolk Bank. Under this system all bank notes of associated banks could be exchanged or redeemed in Boston in specie at par.

The Suffolk Bank discontinued receiving country money in 1858, when a rival institution (The Bank of Mutual Redemption) was organized by a number of country banks and a single Boston bank (see Lake 1946). The large profits that the Suffolk Bank had been able to realize through the non-interest bearing permanent deposits of the country banks had motivated the establishment of an alternative clearing institution. Several of the banks which held stock in the Bank of Mutual Redemption withdrew their deposits from the Suffolk Bank and announced that their notes could be redeemed at the new Bank.

3 Banks, Bank Money and Prices

3.1 The Endogeneity of Bank Money

An important question for the success of a system with competing currencies is whether the volume of competitive supplied monies is endogenous. If money is endogenous the financial system is only capable of expanding the volume of money in line with demand, not exceeding it.[12] Then the issuing banks cannot autonomously increase their issue, but only indirectly via stimulating demand, e.g. by offering better services. In contrast, if the inside money issued by competing issuing banks were exogenous, banks would have an unlimited ability to expand the money supply and influence the price level as well as real economic variables. Then, as predicted by Friedman and others, currency competition would lead to an infinite price level.

If the volume of circulation are to be treated as the decision variable for a bank, the relation between resources required for and revenues obtained from issuing bank notes determine an individual bank's circulation. Banks serve as financial intermediaries by bringing borrowers and lenders together - granting loans is the usual means by which banks issue "promises to pay gold or silver", i.e. bank notes.

[12] See e.g. Desai (1990).

In a simple model the balance sheet of an issuing bank contains specie reserves (*R*) and loans (*L*) on the asset side and capital (*K*) and bank notes (*M*) on the liability side. This results the following balance sheet constraint:

$$R + L = K + M$$

Assumed the bank's capital is fixed an enlargement of interest-bearing loans would add to the bank's gross income but would usually require an increase in its issuing activity as well as in its reserve holding. Since bank money entails a legal claim against the issuer to pay specie on demand an increase in the volume of bank notes involves, *ceteris paribus*, an increase in reserve holding to meet possible redemptions of bank notes via the clearing system. If a bank over-issued, it would quickly face the prospect of paying out specie or having to pay the legal penalty to the note holder for not redeeming its notes. No bank can supply money unless demanders are willing to hold it.

Endogenity of the quantity of bank money implies elasticity of the quantity of bank money, that is to say, the note circulation expands and contracts in accordance with the needs of the economy. Variations in the demand for bank money, due to variations in the volume of trade or to variations in aggregate output, have an direct effect on the volume of bank money.

3.2 New Entries of Banks and the Expansion of Bank Money

In the literature it is sometimes claimed that the increasing number of banks, due to unrestricted entry, led to an increase in the volume of circulation.[13] This would contradict the claim convertible inside money is endogenous. Since in the period under investigation Massachusetts experienced a substantial increase in the number of banks as well as in the volume of circulation, the direction of causality between the two variables can be tested.

In the following regressions the growth rates in the volume of circulation and, alternatively, the growth rates of the number of banks is estimated using past growth rates of both circulation and the number of banks. The first regression tests whether past growth rates of the number of banks had a positive impact on the current growth in the volume of circulation. The results, presented in Table 2, reveal that growth rates of the number of banks in the past are insignificant in explaining the present growth rate in circulation.

The alternative hypothesis that past growth rates of the volume of circulation had a positive influence on the current growth in the number of banks, is tested with the

---

[13] See e.g. Gouge (1935), p 48, Marcuse (1907), p 17, or Nussbaum (1957), p 65.

second regression. The causality is supported by the data. Both the growth in the volume of circulation between t=1 and t=2 and between t=2 and t=3 had a significant impact on the increase in the number of banks in the present period. Thus, the growth in the number of banks was demand driven.

Table 2. Regression Results (1819 - 1858)

	$Ln(Circ_{t=0} / Circ_{t-1})$		$Ln(Banks_{t=0} / Banks_{t-1})$	
Regressor	Coefficient	t-value	Coefficient	t-value
CONSTANT	.0771536	2.29461	.0163406	1.13065
Ln(C1/C2)	-.1988734	-1.14160	.1767749	2.36083
Ln(C2/C3)	-.0727461	-0.36248	.1845150	2.13899
Ln(B1/B2)	-.1793933	-0.46846	.1603316	0.97408
Ln(B2/B3)	-.0610925	-0.16841	.0468406	0.30042
R^2	.056		.278	
F(4,35)	.520		3.370	
DW	1.980		1.908	

Notation: $ln(C1/C2) = Ln(Circulation_{t-1} / Circulation_{t-2})$

3.3 Bank Money and Prices

Unfortunately we are not really able to test whether money had an impact on prices. The data needed to test this relationship are not available. First of all, movements in the stock of bank money issued by State banks do not give an overly accurate picture of movements in the overall stock of money. Since Massachusetts' bank money circulated in other parts of the country and money issued in other States circulated in Massachusetts, the volume of bank notes issued by the State Banks of Massachusetts is only an approximation of the total supply of paper money. Furthermore, we have no estimate of the amount of gold and silver circulating in Massachusetts.

Second, there is also no information about the general price development in Massachusetts for the respective period. The only price index found is a price index on farm products in Massachusetts (see figure).[14] This farm price index provides some information about the behavior of the general price level, since in the first 20

[14] The index is taken from Rothenberg (1979). Warren and Pearson (1933), p 10-13 provide a wholesale price index for the U.S. The index of bank money is calculated from the data presented in Comptroller (1878), p 98-99.

years of the 19th century agricultural products contributed in a large part to GNP. However, supply fluctuations which are typical of agricultural products may have made the prices of farm products fluctuate more than the prices for other products.

Although these problems mean that an accurate test of the causality between money and prices is not possible, the available data, presented in Figure 1, provide some insight in the relationship between money and prices.

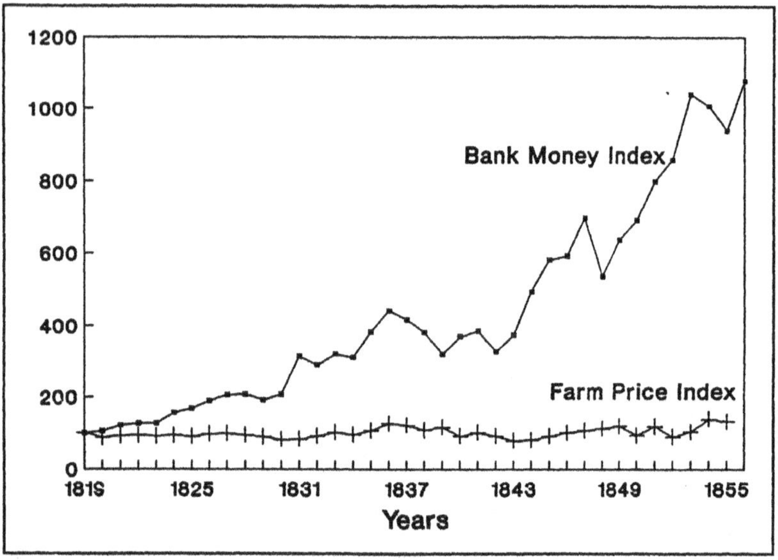

Figure 1. Indices for Farm Prices and Bank Money, 1819 - 1855
Sources: See text

The figure shows the supply of bank money and the index of the main farm products. There was a large increase in Massachusetts bank money supply, especially after 1830, while the price index remained fairly stable. Taken the definition of inflation given by Laidler and Parkin (1975, p. 741): "Inflation is a process of continuously falling value of money" we can conclude that there was no inflation in Massachusetts in the first third of the 19th century. Even with the limited data available we can also conclude that since there was no inflation, the competitive provision of bank notes was not inflationary. The quantity of money varied without affecting the value of the currency in terms of gold. The evidence suggests that the quantity theory of money, in the sense of causality running from changes in money to changes in prices, may not be applicable to the economy under a convertible currency.

3.4 The Safety of Bank Money

Bank notes issued by State Banks were promises to pay gold or silver on demand. There is no risk involved with holding bank notes as long as the banks can always pay the coins they promise. But in cases of temporary or permanent inability of an issuing bank to pay specie on demand, the value of its bank notes depends heavily on the liability regulation.

As mentioned before, the liability of stockholders was limited. If the capital stock of a failing bank was insufficient to redeem the bills issued, the stockholders were liable for the deficiency in an amount equal to their stock. In addition, bank directors were liable if the bank note circulation exceeded the respective legal limit. The latter provision was associated with a circulation to capital ratio between 1 and 1.5 and therefore provided additional protection to the note holders. It is conceivable that the combination of liabilities prevented possible problems arising from the inability of stockholders to adequately monitor the behavior of the directors of the banks.

The actual ratio of circulation to capital in relation to the liability limit of the stockholders, aggregated for the entire banking system in Massachusetts, is presented in Figure 2. The figure shows that on the aggregate only about 50 % of the average bank's capital was reached, which was well below the liability limit of the stockholders.

One might object, that there may have been differences between different banks, but also individual banks did for the most part not reach the liability limit of the stockholders. For two years there is exact data available, 1830 and 1835.[15] In 1830 the bank with the highest circulation to capital ratio kept approximately a circulation equal to its capital. In 1835 one bank had a circulation equal to 110 % of its capital and two other banks kept a circulation almost equal with their capital stocks. Consequently, even when banks failed, the note holders were generally unaffected.[16] Thus, currencies issued by banks in Massachusetts have been save media of exchange.

The low circulation to capital ratios should, however, not entirely be attributed to the liablity regulations, but also to competitive pressures. Whenever money demand allowed banks, in principle, to expand their circulation, new entries set limits on the possible expansion of existing banks. This argument is supported by the findings of section 3.2: increasing demand for bank money was accomodated by new entries of banks.

---

[15] See Commonwealth of Massachusetts (1830) and (1835).

[16] For the period before 1840 Hunt's Merchants' Magazine (1840), p 144 estimates the losses to bank note holders have been less than 0.4 % of total bank money issued. There is no data for the years after 1840.

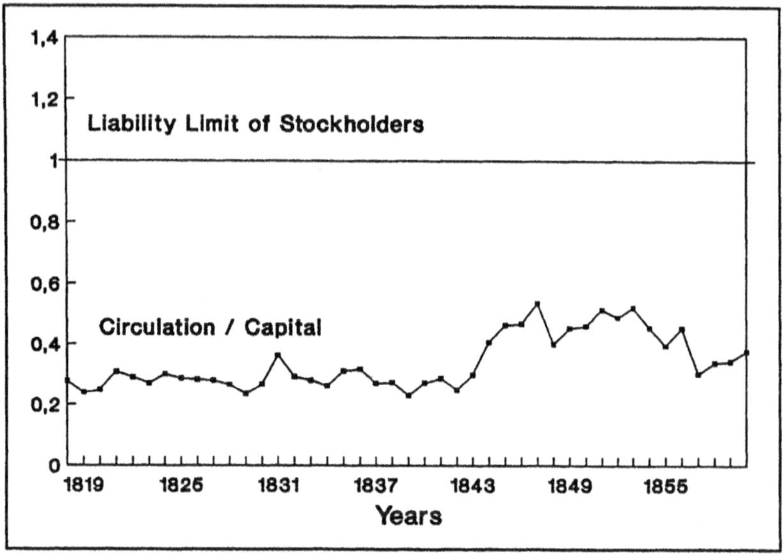

Figure 2. Average Ratio of Circulation to Capital of Banks in Massachusetts.
Sources: See text

3.5 Increased Demand for Bank Notes

As the enormous increase in bank money was not followed by an increase in the price level, there must have been a substantial increase in the demand for bank notes. One explanation is the increase in real income or the fall of interest rates during the respective period, which, according to the standard theory of money demand, increases the demand for real balances for transaction purposes.

Another explanation is the increase in the "quality" of bank notes. After the introduction of the Suffolk System all bank notes issued in Massachusetts were accepted at par to gold and silver. The fixed exchange rate system led to a reduction in information costs for the general public and therefore increased welfare. More important, the uncertainty regarding future purchasing power of a bank note was substantially lessened. To a certain extent centralized note clearing in Boston created confidence that each bank note issued by one of the member banks of the clearing system could be redeemed at par at any time. Since a particular value of real balances involved a smaller expected risk than before, agents were willing to hold more balances than before.

4 Concluding Remarks

The banking experience of Massachusetts, 1819-1858, strongly suggests that liberal financial regimes can be very successful. Paper money, convertible into gold or silver, was issued competitively by private banks, but contrary to the hypothesis by Friedman, neither inflation nor signs of instability have been observed. Although there has been a large increase in the quantity of bank money during the respective period it was not accompanied by rising prices. The evidence supports the claim that convertible inside money is endogenous.

The success of the Suffolk System rested on several factors: (1) convertibility of bank notes in specie at par, (2) organized bank note clearing, (3) de facto free entry of banks, and (4) mixed stockholder-manager liability. Consequently, banks had strong incentives to follow sound banking practices and to provide save currencies.

References

Appleton N (1831) An Examination of the Banking System of Massachusetts. In: Reference to the Renewal of the Bank Charters, Stimpson & Clapp, Boston

Bank Commissioner of the Commonwealth of Massachusetts (different years) Annual Report, Senate Documents, Boston

Comptroller of the Currency (1878) Annual Report to the Second Session of the Forty-Forth Congress of the United States, Government Printing Office, Washington

Commonwealth of Massachusetts (different years) A True Abstract from the Statement of the President and Directors of the different Banks, Boston

Desai M (1990) Endogenous and Exogenous Money. In: Eatwell J, Milgate M and Newman P (Ed) The New Palgrave: Money, Macmillan, London and Basingstoke

Dewey DR (1910) State Banking Before the Civil War, National Monetary Commission, 61st Con Senate 2nd Sess, Doc No 581, Washington

Dowrie GW (1936) Money and Banking, John Wiley & Sons, New York

Elliot J (1845) The Funding System of the United States and of Great Britain, Blair and Rives, Washington

Friedman M (1959) A Program for Monetary Stability, Fordham University Press, New York

Fullarton J (1845) On the Regulation of Currencies, John Murray, 2nd Ed, London

Girton L, Roper D (1979) Substitutable Monies and the Monetary Standard. In: Dooley M, Kaufman H and Lombra R (Eds) The Political Economy of Policy Making, Beverly Hills and London

Goodhart CAE (1988) The Evolution of Central Banks, MIT Press, Cambridge, Mass

Gouge WM (1835) A Short History of Paper-Money and Banking in the United States, B&S Collins, New York

Hammond B (1957) Banks and Politics in America from the Revolution to the Civil War, Princeton

Hayek FA von (1976) Choice in Currency. A way to Stop Inflation, The Institute of Economic Affairs, London

_____ (1978) Denationalization of Money - The Argument Refined, Hobart Special Paper No 70. The Institute of Economic Affairs, 2nd Ed, London

Hunt's Merchant's Magazine and Commercial Review (1840) Ed by Freeman Hunt, New York

International Monetary Conference (1879) Senate Executive Document No 58, 45th Congress, 3rd Session, Washington D.C.

Knox JJ (1903) History of Banking in the United States, New York

Klein B (1974) The Competitive Supply of Money. Journal of Money Credit and Banking, Vol 8

Laidler D and Parkin M (1975) Inflation: A Survey. Economic Journal, Vol 85

Lake WS (1947) The End of the Suffolk System. Journal of Economic History, (November)

Lamoreaux NR (1986) Banks, Kinship, and Economic Development: The New England Case. Journal of Economic History, Vol XLVI, No 3 (September)

Loyd SJ (Lord Overstone) (1858) Tracts and Other Publications on Metallic and Paper Currency, Longman, Brown & Co, London

Marcuse P (1907) Betrachtungen über das Notenbankwesen in den Vereinigten Staaten von Amerika, Heymanns Verlag, Berlin

Mullineaux DJ (1987) Competitive Monies and the Suffolk Bank System: A Contractual Perspective. Southern Economic Journal, Vol 53, No 4, April

Ng K (1988) Free Banking Laws and Barriers to Entry in Banking, 1838-1860, Journal of Economic History, Vol XLVIII, No 4 (December)

Nussbaum A (1957) A History of the Dollar. Columbia University Press, New York

Redlich F (1951) The Molding of American Banking - Men and Ideas, Hafner, New York

Root LC (1895) New England Bank Currency: Current Redemption Developments. Sound Currency, Vol II, No 13, June 1

Rothenberg WB (1979) A Price Index for Rural Massachusetts. Journal of Economic History, Vol XXXIX, No 4 (December)

Secretary of the Treasury (1856) Report on the State of the Finances for the Year ending 6-30-1855, 34th Congress 1st Session, ExDoc No 2, Washington

Smith VC (1936) The Rationale of Central Banking, King & Son London

Sylla R (1985) Early American Banking: The Significance of the Corporate Form. Business and Economic History 14 (March), pp 105-123

Tooke T (1844) An Inquiry into the Currency Principle. The Connection on the Currency with Prices and the Expediency of a Separation of Issue from Banking, London

Trivoli G (1979) The Suffolk Bank, A Study of a Free-enterprise Clearing System. The Adam Smith Institute, London and Leesburg, Va

Tullock G (1975) Competing Monies. Journal of Money, Credit, and Banking, Vol 7

Van Fenstermaker J, Filer J (1986) Impact of the First and Second Banks of the United States and the Suffolk System on New England Bank Money. Journal of Money, Credit, and Banking, Vol 18, No 1 (February)

Vaubel R (1977) Free Currency Competition. Weltwirtschaftliches Archiv Vol 113

Walker A (1857) The Nature and Uses of Money and Mixed Currency, Craslus, Nicholas & Co, Boston

Warren GF and Pearson FA (1933) Prices. John Wiley & Sons N.Y.

White LH (1984) Free Banking in Britain: Theory, Experience, and Debate, 1800-1845, Cambridge University Press

Whitney DR (1878) The Suffolk Bank, The Riverside Press, Cambridge

Part II

Towards an European Central Bank Policy Design

Economic Convergence and Monetary Union*

Francesco Papadia and Ciro Schioppa
Banca d'Italia, Roma

1 Introduction and Summary

The Maastricht Treaty has acknowledged, and translated into precise criteria and indicators, the need for increased economic convergence to enter the final phase of Economic and Monetary Union (EMU). In this paper, we examine the improvement in the process of economic convergence since the creation of the EMS in 1979 and until mid-1992, as well as the expectations of market participants on the evolution of the process over the period 1992-96. We also try to assess the extent of the adjustment still to be made by comparing it to the adjustment already implemented during the 80s. We reach four main conclusions:

(i) Economic convergence, expressed in terms of inflation, interest, and exchange rates, has improved considerably during the life of the EMS, but remains incomplete and differentiated amongst countries
(ii) Market participants do not expect a significant improvement in the convergence process over the next five years
(iii) The adjustment still to be made, which should basically affect the budget deficit and the rate of inflation, seems to be beyond the reach of Greece, extremely demanding, but not impossible, in the case of Italy, Spain and Portugal
(iv) Successful adjustment policies and confidence of market participants on the results of such policies are thoroughly interlinked and cannot survive in isolation.

---

* The opinions expressed are the authors' and do not necessarily reflect those of Banca d'Italia. The help of G. Boccuzzi, G. Cellai, S. Leoni, F. Panfili and D. Porciani in preparing the statistical material is gratefully acknowledged. The paper has been written and presented before the crisis of August-September 1992 in the EMS which led to the devaluation, and then to the suspension of compulsory interventions for the lira, the abandonment of the ERM by the pound, the devaluation of the peseta, as well as to severe tensions for other currencies in the system. These events will have important consequences for the achievement of economic convergence and monetary union which are not taken into account in this paper. By accident, or because of policy mistakes, the smooth transition towards EMU illustrated in this paper will not be achieved. The analysis of the options available after the crisis to achieve convergence and EMU is for another paper.

2 The Starting Point

From an economic point of view, the present stage of the EMU process can be described by referring to the concept of "price of money". As is well-known, the price, or value, of money can be defined, first of all, as an external value, namely as units of national currency necessary to buy one unit of foreign currency. Secondly, it can be expressed, on an inter-temporal basis, as a rate of interest. Thirdly, it can be defined in terms of goods and services: the aggregate price level measures the average price of the goods and services produced in a certain country and its reciprocal expresses the purchasing power of money, i.e. the price of money in terms of goods and services.

Basically, EMU implies a continuous equalization of the price of money across participating countries, i.e. a constant exchange rate and the same nominal rate of interest and of inflation. Of course, in case of full monetary union, i.e. when only one currency circulates, this condition would be automatically fulfilled. To evaluate how far we have progressed towards EMU, we have to ascertain what are the remaining divergences in the price of money in the various EEC countries.

2.1 Exchange Rate Stability

Figure 1 shows that a clear trend towards stability of exchange rates has been recorded in Europe in the period 1979-1991, i.e. during the life of the EMS. Currency re-alignments of the French franc, Belgian franc, Dutch guilder, Italian lira, Danish krona, and Pound sterling vis-à-vis the Deutsche mark have become less and less frequent over time and no re-alignment has actually taken place since January 1987. Furthermore, the one-year forward exchange rate[1] which can be taken as an indicator, albeit imperfect, of exchange rate expectations shows that the ERM parities have become more credible: as from mid-1989, it generally lies within the fluctuation margins, whereas previously it used to lie outside, with the exception of the Dutch guilder.

In the chart we have also plotted the value of an indicator of foreign exchange market expectations over longer time horizons: the forward exchange rates for maturities from one to five years calculated on the basis of the interest rate differentials prevailing at mid-1992, assuming that they fully reflect the forward exchange premium or discount. The chart shows, that the forward rate for maturities beyond one year lies beyond fluctuation margins in the case of the Italian lira, the French franc and the Danish krona, a proof that exchange rates expectations have not yet fully stabilized.

The trend towards more stable exchange rates has occurred in spite of the declining role played by market interventions by European monetary authorities.

---

[1] For a similar analysis see Committee of Governors (1992) and Frankel (1991).

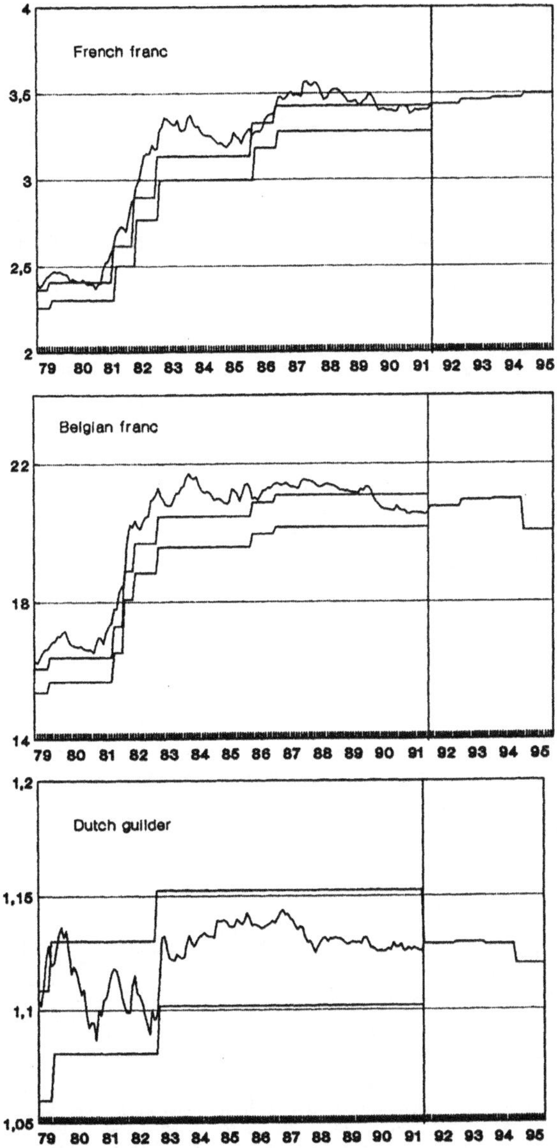

Figure 1. Forward exchange rates and ERM margins (vs. Deutsche Mark)
Source: B.I.S.

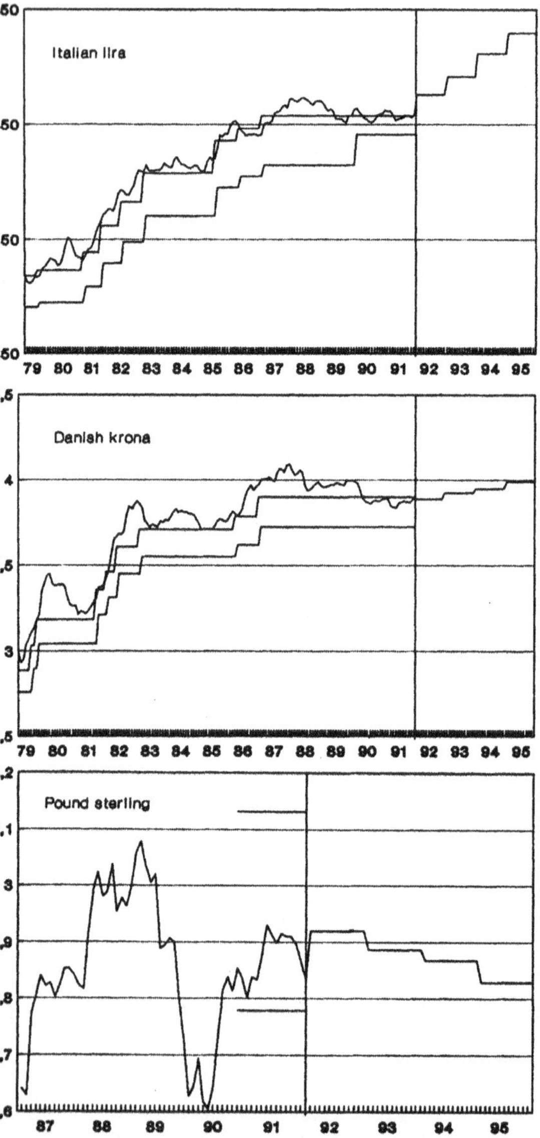

Figure 1. Forward exchange rates and ERM margins (vs. Deutsche Mark) (continued)
Source: B.I.S.

The actual number of days in which monetary authorities have intervened in the foreign exchange markets has been on a clear, even if not continuous, downward trend which has reinforced itself since the mid-eighties. This notwithstanding, the overall size of yearly interventions was larger in the most recent years than in the initial years of the EMS in the case of Italy and France due to the larger average size of daily interventions. However, the increase in interventions was smaller than that of other nominal magnitudes, such as international trade and national incomes, which have swelled, in dollar terms, by a factor of 2.3, confirming the diminishing role of interventions in keeping exchange rates stable.

2.2 Interest Rate Convergence

The process of convergence has extended itself to the inter-temporal price of money, i.e. to interest rates. This is shown by the gradual reduction of long-term interest rate differentials vis-à-vis the average rate of interest on the three currencies with the lowest rate of inflation (figures 2a and 2b). However, substantial differences still prevail on certain currencies (in particular the Greek drachma, the Portuguese escudo, the Spanish peseta and the Italian lira) and, according to market expectations, these will not be reduced noticeably by 1997, the deadline for EMU. In fact, calculating from the term structure prevailing at mid-1992 the five-year forward interest rates expected over the next five years, there is no evidence of a significant reduction of differentials[2] with respect to the three countries with lower inflation (figures 2a and 2b; for Portugal and Greece there are no comparable data).

In the case of Italy, a further indication about interest rates expectations is given by the evolution of the pricing of the options contained in the "Certificati del Tesoro con opzione" (CTOs).[3] A comparison between the secondary-market yield of a CTO over a *three-year* horizon and the secondary market yield of a fixed-rate *three-year* Treasury bond gives the value attributed by the market to the *call*-option contained in the CTO. Instead, a comparison between the secondary-market yield of a CTO over a *six-year* horizon and the secondary market yield of a *six-year* fixed-rate bond gives the value attributed by the market to the *put*-option. The value of the two options depends, inter alia, upon the market expectations about the yield which will prevail on a three-year maturity asset in three year time. Namely, if the market expects, *ceteris paribus*, an increase (decline) in yields, the value of the call-option will decline (increase), whereas the price of the put-option will increase (decline).

---

[2] The above calculations have been performed on the basis of market yield curves, not on the basis of zero-coupon yield curves. Therefore, our calculations are an approximation of forward interest rates.

[3] CTOs are fixed-rate Treasury bonds, with a maximum maturity of six years, containing an option to be exercised three years after issue. Depending on the relevant time horizon, CTOs can be alternatively regarded as a portfolio containing: a) a short-term (three-year) fixed-rate asset plus a call-option; b) a long-term (six-year) fixed-rate asset plus a put-option. The following analysis draws heavily upon Martina and Rossetti (1992).

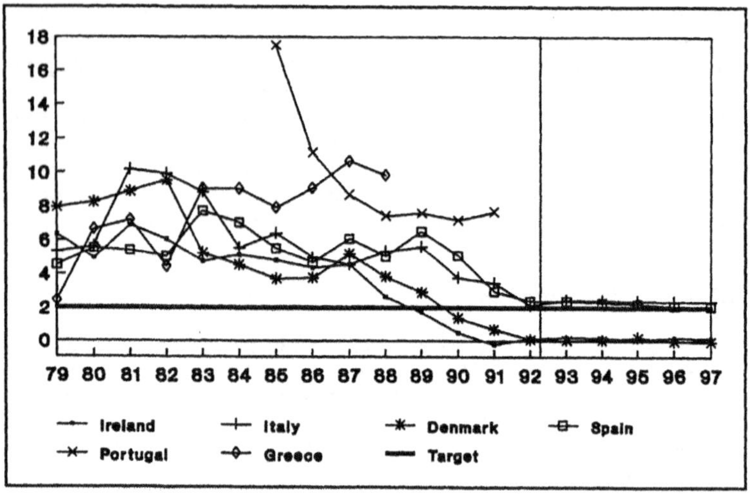

Figure 2a. Nominal long-term interest rates (differentials vis-a-vis the three EEC countries with the lowest inflation rates)

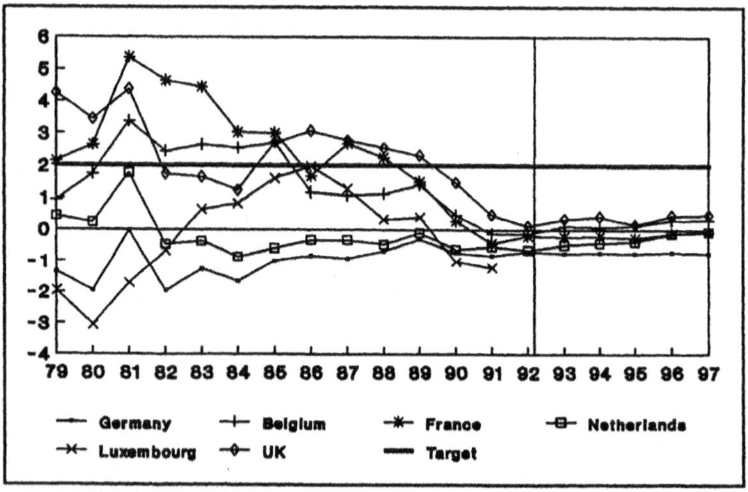

Figure 2b. Nominal long-term interest rates (differentials vis-a-vis the three EEC countries with the lowest inflation rates)
Source: Commission of the European Communities, Annual Economic Report 1991-92, No. 50, December 1991

Over the period February 21, 1991 - June 12, 1992 (figure 3), the value of the put-option has been positive, but declining, whereas the value of the call-option has normally oscillated around zero. The evolution and the level of the price of the two options proves that investors in Italian Treasury bonds have attributed a gradually declining probability to the event of an increase in three-year yields and little, if any, probability to a decrease in yield. This confirms the idea of an improving, but incomplete, convergence.

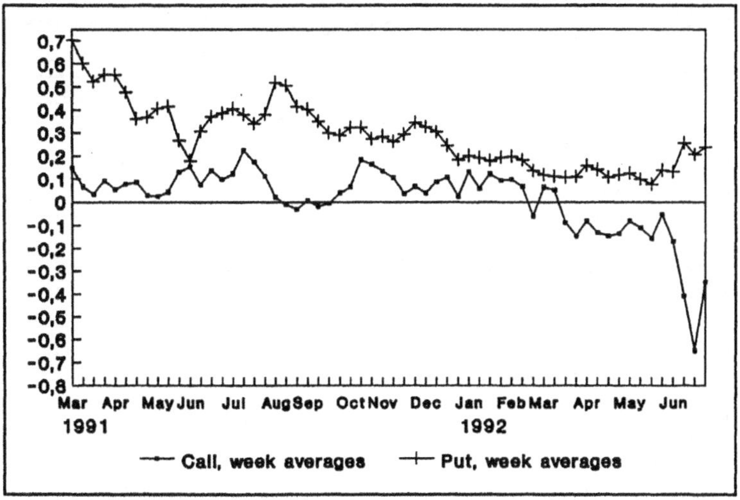

Figure 3. CTO: Put and Call Options
Based on week averages
Source: Bloomberg

2.3 Inflation Convergence

The third definition of the price of money, i.e. that in terms of goods and services (measured as inflation rate differentials for the twelve EEC countries vis-a-vis the three countries with the lowest rate of inflation): figures 4a and 4b, also show a clear trend towards convergence. Nevertheless, this is far from being achieved and, on the basis of the EEC Commission forecasts, it will not be achieved in the near future.

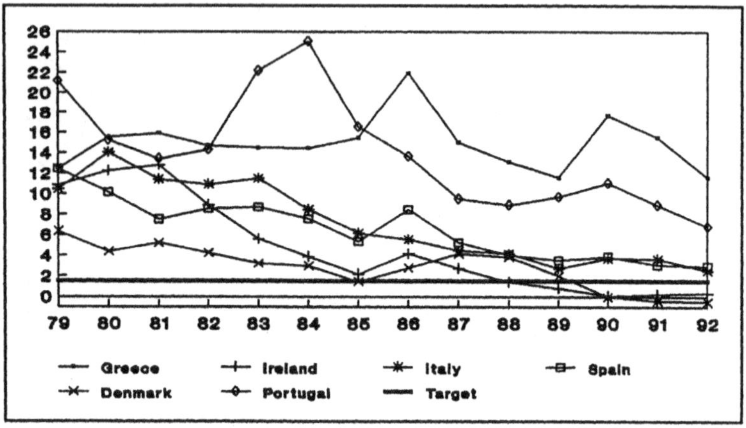

Figure 4a. Inflation rate differentials 1979 - 92 (vis-a-vis the three countries with the lowest inflation rates)

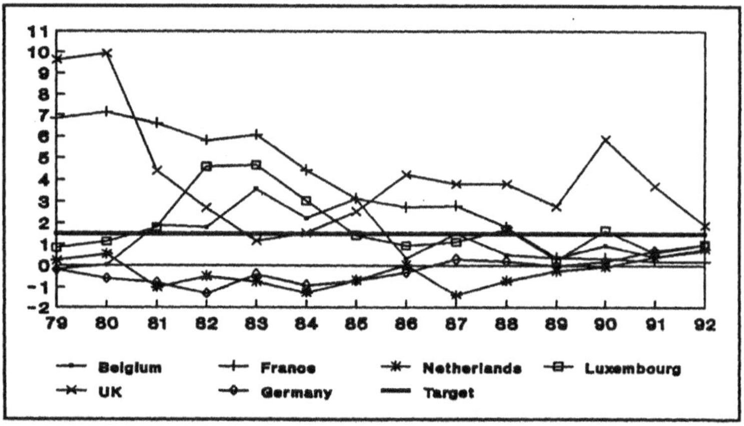

Based on annual % changes in the price deflator private consumption.

Figure 4b. Inflation rate differentials 1979 - 92 (vis-a-vis the three countries with the lowest inflation rates

Source: Commission of the European Communities, Annual Economic Report 1991-92, No. 50, December 1991

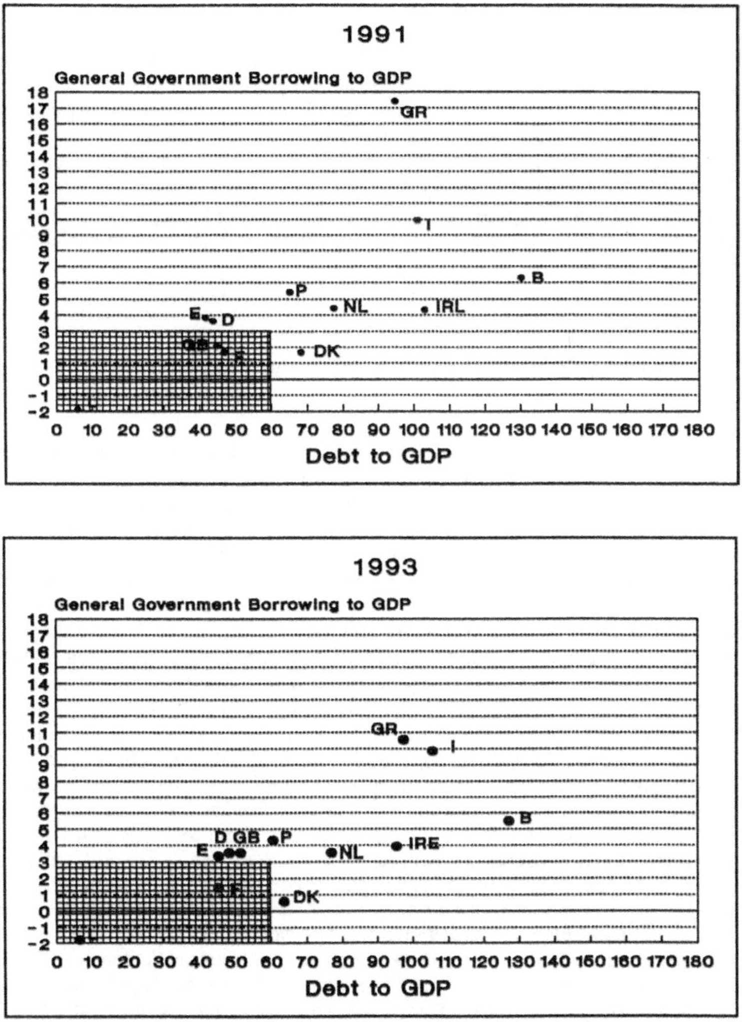

Figure 5: Debt to GDP and General Government Borrowing to GDP Ratios (1991 and 1993)
Source: Commission of the European Communities, Annual Economic Report 1991-92

2.4 Convergence of Public Finances

One of the factors which might explain the incompleteness of economic convergence is the different course of fiscal policy in the various EEC countries. Apart from extreme cases, such as Italy and Greece, many other countries show high deficit- and debt-to-GDP ratios (figure 5). The forecast of the EEC Commission predict an improvement in the overall situation in the course of 1992-1993, but no major turnaround.

Overall, the evidence presented illustrates that, while a strong convergence has taken place in the last decade, its degree varies across countries and has not yet been fully achieved.

3 The Outline of the Course Traced in the Treaty

According to Treaty provisions, 1996 will mark the launching of the complex procedure which shall lead to the third stage of Economic and Monetary Union: in 1997, if a majority of the Member States enter it, in 1999 otherwise. One basic element of this procedure is the assessment of the degree of economic convergence which will have been achieved in the period of about three years between now and mid-1995, a date by which the Treaty provides for the respect of criteria relating to four variables - the same which were considered above to evaluate the situation from which the Community may move to the final stage of the Union: exchange rates, interest rates, inflation rates, public finance conditions.

As for exchange rates, the Treaty envisages that, a country must maintain its currency in the narrow band of the EMS for at least two years, without devaluing on its own initiative. As for interest rates, in the year before the start of the procedure to enter stage three, their level is required not to exceed by more than 2 percentage points that of the three Community countries closest to price stability. As for the rate of inflation, the margin is fixed at 1.5 percentage points. Finally, as far as public finances are concerned, only those countries which, in the judgement of the Council of Ministers of the Community, do not have an excessive budget deficit will be able to participate in EMU from the start. This judgement is, in turn, formulated on the basis of a complex procedure in which the Commission plays an important role. The procedure will be started if two quantitative criteria are systematically violated: a ratio of public deficit to GDP equal to 3 per cent; a ratio of public debt to GDP equal to 60 per cent. More precisely, paraphrasing the Treaty, the first criterion is violated if the deficit-to-GDP ratio is higher than 3 per cent, unless it has declined substantially and continuously and reached a level that comes close to 3 per cent or, alternatively, the excess over 3 per cent is only exceptional and temporary and the ratio remains close to the reference value. The second criterion is instead violated if the ratio of public debt to GDP exceeds 60 per cent, unless the ratio is sufficiently diminishing and approaching the reference value at a satisfactory pace.

4 An Economic Path

The figures of section 2 have pointed out the marked convergence of monetary conditions achieved in the eighties by the Member States of the Community. However, they also show that, in the eyes of the market, convergence is not seen to improve enough to meet the strict requirements established in Maastricht to enter the third stage of the Union in the three years or so now available. It is therefore natural to try to ascertain how the adjustment effort which is still necessary compares to the one made in the eighties.

The deficit or, more precisely, the public sector net borrowing, which can be reasonably considered an exogenous variable, is the most useful starting point for our analysis. Of course, this variable is not perfectly exogenous, being influenced, in turn, by changes in inflation and in the level of activity; however, it is undoubtedly "more exogenous" - if such concept is legitimate - than other variables on the basis of which economic convergence will be assessed.

Table 1 obviously confirms what had been shown in figure 5: in 1991 only four countries - Denmark, France, Luxembourg and the United Kingdom - complied with the 3 per cent parameter (below which a country is assumed not to have an excessive deficit). To evaluate the effort yet to be made, one can examine whether the matching by each country of its best performance over a three-year period in the past decade could be enough to fulfil the target established in the Treaty.

As it is shown in the last column of the table, a correction of that kind would more than suffice for all Community countries, with the exception of Italy and Greece, the two Member States recording the highest deficit and, at the same time, those which have carried out less effective remedial measures in the eighties. In a sense, the result is trivial: it is obvious that the countries which have implemented insufficient correction measures record a high deficit. However, the calculation illustrates in a vivid manner that for these countries the adjustment must be much deeper than the one implemented in the eighties. The qualitative conclusion does not change if the reference period is lengthened to the seventies: Italy, for instance, succeeded in achieving an adjustment equal to 3.6 percentage points of GDP between 1975 and 1977, twice as much as that carried out between 1985 and 1988, but still insufficient in comparison with the target set in Maastricht.

However, one can wonder whether, by adopting remedial measures like those taken by Denmark (10.6 per cent), Ireland (7.7 per cent), Luxembourg (6.9 per cent) and Portugal (5.2 per cent), Greece and Italy would succeed in reaching their targets. The comparison indicates that an even larger correction than the one carried out by Denmark between 1983 and 1986 would be necessary in order to bring Greece close to the target; a much smaller correction - close to that implemented by Luxembourg - would instead suffice for Italy to get to the target.

Table 1. Convergence criteria established by the Maastricht Treaty: net borrowing-to-GDP ratio

Country	Net borrowing-to GDP ratio 1991 (1)	Best performance over 3 years (reduction) (2)	Value of the ratio if the best performance is repeated (1)-(2)
Belgium	6.3	3.8 (81/84)	2.5*
Denmark	1.7*	10.6 (83/86)	°
West Germany	3.6	2.3 (82/85)	1.3*
Greece	17.3	3.3 (81/82)	14.0
Spain	3.9	3.6 (85/88)	0.3*
France	1.5*	1.5 (86/89)	0.0*
Ireland	4.1	7.7 (86/89)	°
Italy	9.9	1.6 (85/88)	8.3
Luxembourg	-1.9°	6.9 (81/84)	°
Netherlands	4.4	2.3 (82/85)	2.1*
Portugal	5.4	5.2 (84/87)	0.2*
United Kingdom	1.9*	3.9 (85/88)	°

Source: EC Commission, Annual Economic Report, European Economy, n. 50, December 1991

* Value lower than or close to 3 per cent

° Negative value

As indicated above, the other parameter on which the judgement about the existence of an excessive deficit is to be based is the level, and the behaviour, of the public debt-to-GDP ratio. In table 2, as in figure 5 above, it can be noticed that, in 1991, seven countries recorded a ratio exceeding the critical threshold of 60 per cent (Belgium, Denmark, Greece, Ireland, Italy, the Netherlands, and Portugal) but for four of them the ratio was already significantly declining, while three countries could not fulfill the requirement: Greece, Italy, and the Netherlands. Analogously to what has been said on net borrowing, these are countries which have not implemented sufficient adjustment measures in the eighties: as a matter of fact, in these countries the ratio of debt to GDP has constantly increased during the eighties and in the early nineties. However, it is evident from the second column of the table that, if these countries implemented corrections of the same magnitude as those carried out by Denmark, Ireland, and Portugal, they could easily comply with the criterion established by the Treaty.

Table 2. Convergence criteria established by the Maastricht Treaty: public debt-to-GDP ratio

Country	Public debt/GDP 1991	Best performance over 3 years (reduction)
Belgium	129.5*	5.1 (88/90)
Denmark	67.5*	14.0 (84/87)
West Germany	46.4*	0.5 (88/90)
Greece	95.6	increase
Spain	45.6*	2.1 (87/90)
France	47.0*	0.8 (89/90)
Ireland	102.8*	17.8 (87/90)
Italy	100.8	increase
Luxembourg	6.9*	5.1 (86/89)
Netherlands	78.2	increase
Portugal	65.0*	6.8 (88/90)
United Kingdom	44.6*	12.4 (86/89)

Source: EC Commission, Annual Economic Report, European Economy, n. 50, December 1991

* Indicates the countries respecting the parameter established in Maastricht: lower than 60 per cent or decreasing value

The statistics above indicate that the rule established for the debt-to-GDP ratio does not represent an additional constraint with respect to that set for borrowing. This is not surprising: the ratio decreases whenever the numerator (the debt) increases at a lower rate than the denominator's (the GDP). But, if the ratio of debt to GDP exceeds 60 per cent, the 3 per cent constraint relating to the deficit implies a lower debt growth rate than the 5-6 per cent which can be considered normal, even in low-inflation conditions, for GDP and thus the debt to GDP ratio would be decreasing.[4]

---

[4] In fact

(1) $$H = dB/dS = G - T + iB$$

where H indicates the government deficit, B the debt, G public expenditure, T total revenues, Y income (small letters will indicate the ratios of these variables to income), i the nominal rate of interest and S time. If we divide through by Y, we obtain:

(2) $$(dB/dS)\ (1/Y) = h = g - t + ib.$$

The Treaty imposes an upper limit on h equal to 3%. By calculating the derivative of the debt/income ratio with respect to time, we obtain:

(3) $$db/dS = (dB/dS)\ (1/Y) - (dY/dS)\ (B/Y^2).$$

Substituting equation (2) into equation (3), we obtain:

(4) $$db/dS = g - t + b\ [i - (dY/dS)\ (1/Y)].$$

Since $(dY/dS)\ (1/Y) = y$ where y indicates nominal growth, equation (4), which describes the motion of the debt to GDP ratio, can be rewritten as:

(4a) $$db/dS = g - t + b\ (i - y).$$

Substituting from equation (2), we obtain:

(5) $$db/dS = h - y\ b.$$

For instance, if the debt to GDP ratio (b) equals 60%, the rate of growth (y) equals 5%, and the

The situation concerning the inflation targets is illustrated in Table 3. From the first column it appears that, by using 1991 data, five countries would have exceeded the limit of 4.3 per cent derived from the Treaty, as illustrated above. Nevertheless, with the exception of Greece and Portugal, the excess over the reference value would have been relatively limited, close to or lower than 2 per cent in the case of Spain, Italy, and the United Kingdom. Furthermore, again with the exception of Greece, the required correction is much smaller than the one already carried out in the best three-year period of the eighties. This clearly indicates that most of the path has already been covered, even if it must be taken into account that the progress in the eighties was favoured by the exceptional fall in oil prices.

Table 3. Convergence criteria established by the Maastricht Treaty: inflation

Country	Inflation 1991	Excess over the Maastricht margin	Best performance over 3 years (81/90)
Belgium	3.2°	-	6.5 (83/86)
Denmark	2.4*	-	3.9 (83/86)
West Germany	3.5	-	3.4 (83/86)
Greece	18.3	14.0	7.4 (86/89)
Spain	5.8	1.5	6.3 (84/87)
France	3.0*	-	6.8 (83/86)
Ireland	3.0*	-	9.9 (82/85)
Italy	6.4	2.1	9.4 (83/86)
Luxembourg	3.4°	-	7.2 (83/86)
Netherlands	3.2°	-	3.6 (81/84)
Portugal	11.7	7.4	18.5 (84/87)
United Kingdom	6.5	2.2	6.2 (81/84)

Source: EC Commision, Annual Economic Report, European Economy, no. 50, December 1991

* Indicates the three countries with the lowest inflation rate

° Indicates the countries within the margins established by the Maastricht Treaty (average of the three best-performing countries in terms of inflation plus 1.5 per cent = 2.8 + 1.5 = 4.3 in 1991, and = 2.6 + 1.5 = 4.1 in 1993)

Two considerations qualify, but do not contradict, this result. Firstly, the inflation performance of the countries closest to price stability should improve further,

constraint on the deficit ($h <= 3\%$) is respected, the debt to GDP ratio would remain constant over time; instead, for any value of b higher than 60% the ratio would decrease, thus respecting the criterion of the Treaty of a declining debt to GDP ratio. Incidentally, this also implies that the steady state value of the debt to GDP is 60% when the deficit is 3% and the growth rate is 5%. This is one of the arguments which led to the establishment of this quantitative value as a convergence criterion.

thus making the task of the pursuers more difficult: if, for instance, the "front squad" achieved an inflation rate of 1.5 per cent instead of the current 2.5 per cent, all the other countries should improve their performance by as much. Secondly, the level of inflation does not depend only on the macroeconomic policy, but also on a host of specific, at times contingent factors, which make comparisons more difficult. This is clearly demonstrated by the fact that even inside a single country the inflation rate varies from one city to the other. For instance, P. Giucca and M.A. Antonicelli have found that inflation differentials equal to or higher than 1 per cent are not unusual among the cities of Italy or those of the United States. From this viewpoint, the 1.5 per cent margin to be applied to the inflation rate of the countries closest to price stability is more an adjustment to take account of these specific effects than a factor allowing a significantly different inflation rate.

Taking these elements into account, the improvement in price performance to be achieved by Spain, Italy and the United Kingdom with respect to the inflation recorded in 1991 is more around 4.0 per cent than around 2.0 per cent. This remains much smaller than the one achieved in the best three-year period of the eighties.

As indicated above, the fourth variable on which convergence is assessed is the interest rate. Table 4 shows that in 1991 three countries (besides, presumably, Greece, for which no comparable data is available) had interest rates which would have exceeded the level required by the Treaty: Portugal, Italy, and Spain. However, with the exception of Portugal, the excess is modest, lower than 2 per cent, and, in any case, much smaller than the reduction recorded in the best three-year period of the eighties. Also in this case, the bulk of adjustment has already been accomplished.

Of course, all the variables examined above are, in the economic reality, linked to one another and actions aimed at influencing one of them necessarily affect the others. To grasp the richness of such connections, it would be necessary to consider them jointly, in a comprehensive econometric model.

This has been done recently for the Italian case by Banca d'Italia (1991). The results are encouraging: a reduction of non-interest expenses by 4 percentage points of GDP in 1996 with respect to 1991 and an increase in revenue by 2 percentage points in the same period would cause a reduction of interest expenses by 1.5 percentage points of GDP and bring the public deficit to 3 per cent in 1996, causing a reduction of the debt-to-GDP ratio beginning in 1994. The tight fiscal policy, a behaviour of wages more consistent with price stability and the continuation of the monetary policy lines pursued so far, ensuring the stability of the lira in the narrow band of the EMS, would take the rate of inflation down to about 2 per cent in 1996. The tight policies necessary to achieve the Maastricht objectives would not cause a reduction of real income - indeed, this would continue to grow, albeit at a reduced rate over the next two years; unemployment, however, would have a certain tendency to rise, also because of the increase in the labour force over the next few years.

Table 4. Convergence criteria established by the Maastricht Treaty: interest rates

Country	Long-term interest rates 1991	Excess over the Maast-richt margin	Best performance over 3 years (reduction)	Nomi-nal inte-rest rates	One-year real inter-est rates Dec. 1991	One-year infla-tionary expect-ations Dec. 1991
Belgium	9.3°	-	3.9 (83/86)	9.5	7.0	2.2
Denmark	10.1*	-	8.9 (82/85)	9.7	8.8	1.0*
West Germany	8.6	-	2.6 (81/84)	9.5	5.1	4.1
Greece	...	...	...	22.3	4.2	17.9
Spain	12.4	1.0	5.5 (83/86)	12.3	7.7	4.4
France	9.0*	-	5.2 (83/86)	9.7	6.9	2.0*
Ireland	9.2*	-	4.3 (82/85)	10.3	7.3	2.7*
Italy	12.9	1.5	6.3 (83/86)	12.0	5.1	6.4
Luxembourg	8.2°	-	2.4 (85/88)	-	-	-
Netherlands	8.9°	-	3.6 (81/84)	9.5	4.5	4.4
Portugal	17.1	5.7	11.2 (85/88)	14.2	6.4	7.9
United Kingdom	9.9°	-	4.1 (81/84)	10.6	6.9	3.4

Source: EC Commission, Annual Economic Report, European Economy, n. 50, December 1991; based on A. Levy, Research Department, Banca d'Italia, document for internal use
(1) Based on EEC surveys
* Indicates the three countries with the lowest inflation rate
° Indicates the countries within the margins established by the Maastricht Treaty (average of the three best-performing countries in terms of inflation plus 2 percent = 9.4 + 2 = 11.4)

Similar exercises are not available for other Community countries and, in any event, it is useful, following a portfolio approach, to see what conclusion can be derived from an entirely different methodology consisting of concentrating on a few fundamental relationships rather than a full econometric model.

The first relationship links the rate of inflation to the public deficit through the interest rate. The nominal interest rate can be decomposed into two parts, the real interest rate and the expected rate of inflation.[5] Table 4 shows that the average nominal rate reaches the level of 10 per cent in the countries with the lowest inflation rate (France, Denmark and Ireland) and that inflation expectations are responsible for 2 full percentage points of this overall level. However, in Greece, Portugal, Italy and Spain, the countries with the highest level of interest rates, the inflationary component of interest rates is much higher (18 per cent in Greece, 8 per cent in Portugal, 6 per cent in Italy and 4 per cent in

[5] In this exercise, we have used one-year interest rates; inflation expectations have been estimated on the basis of the surveys carried out by the EEC Commission, according to the methodology elaborated by F. Papadia and V. Basano, used by A. Levy.

Spain). This means that if these countries were able to stabilize the inflationary component of interest rates around the average level of France, Denmark and Ireland, nominal interest rates could be reduced to the levels required by the Treaty. Therefore, the goal of inflation convergence coincides, to a large extent, with the goal of nominal interest rate convergence.

A note of caution is necessary: the relationship between the nominal interest rate and the inflation rate is neither direct nor immediate. As a rule, the real interest rate has a tendency to increase when the inflation rate falls. The data contained in Table 4 seem to confirm this empirically observed regularity, since the average real interest rate of the three low-inflation countries is around 8 per cent, whereas the real rate for the three high-inflation countries is around 5 per cent. However, even if an increase in real interest rates would be recorded, it is unlikely that it would fully offset the reduction in nominal interest rates caused by the decrease in the rate of inflation. In the case of Italy, even if the real interest rate rose to the average level of the low-inflation countries, the decrease in the inflationary component should still determine a fall in the nominal rate of around 2 per cent, enough to achieve the Treaty target.

The reduction in the nominal interest rates would have, in turn, positive feed-backs on the public deficit, made up of the primary deficit and interest expenses. The beneficial effects on the deficit are proportional to the level of the debt-to-GDP ratio.[6] For instance, if the debt equals the GDP, as in Italy's and Greece's case, a reduction in the interest rate of a full percentage point would be translated, in the long term, into an equal change of the deficit-to-GDP ratio. The fall in the inflation rate would therefore help in containing the deficit through the decline of interest rates. However, only in the case of Portugal the magnitude of this effect is similar to the fiscal correction which is necessary to achieve a 3 per cent deficit-to-GDP ratio. In the case of Greece and Italy, the required adjustment is much larger, whereas for the other countries which are beyond the 3 per cent target, such as Belgium, Ireland, Spain and the Netherlands, no significant contribution to the reduction in the public deficit can be expected from the fall in the rate of inflation and in the rate of interest.[7] A decisive reduction in the primary deficit, and indeed the achievement of a sizable primary surplus, appears to be necessary.

Improvements in the primary balance are also necessary to reduce the debt-to-GDP ratio in all the countries which have a ratio above 60 per cent and in which no trend towards reduction has appeared so far. In fact, the decline in inflation cannot have, by itself, any positive effect on this indicator; on the contrary, since an increase in the real interest rate can be expected, the

---

[6] See note 4, equation (2).

[7] Equation (2) in note 4 can be used to show the effects of inflation on the deficit to GDP ratio. In fact, splitting the nominal rate of interest (i) in its real (r) and inflationary (p) components, we can write: $h = g - t + ib = g - t + (r + p)b$

If r remains constant in spite of changes in p, the changes of h will be proportional to b: if $b = 0$, a lower inflation rate will not affect h; if $b = 1$, h will decline by as much as the rate of inflation. If r varies with p (i.e. $dr/dp = a < 0$), the change in h will be reduced correspondingly.

debt-to-GDP ratio will tend to increase.[8]

Another positive, albeit difficult to measure, element to be considered is given by the effects of the fiscal restraint on the real interest rate and on the inflation rate. The lower absorption of resources due to the reduced primary deficit should lower the real rate of interest, as well as favouring a decline in the inflation rate.

On the whole, the effects we have considered so far should facilitate the achievement of the targets indicated in the Treaty. However, not all the effects are mutually beneficial. Apart from a possible increase in the real interest rate due to the decline in inflation, the recessive effects of a policy of fiscal restraint should not be overlooked. Even a mild recession would have unwanted consequences on the budget deficit, given its well-known cyclical behaviour. This, in turn, would feed-back on the debt-to-GDP ratio, which would also be affected by the lower rate of growth of the economy.

However, one should not ignore either the positive effects that a strong fiscal action would have on market expectations. In this regard, the experience suggests that the favourable effects on expectations are far from negligible. Moreover, one should not forget that in certain countries the policy-mix remains highly unbalanced, with rather loose fiscal policies and very tight monetary conditions. In these countries, successful fiscal adjustment could therefore lift part of the burden on monetary policy.

The idea that a strong correction of large fiscal imbalances does not necessarily cause losses in economic activity and employment is not contradicted by the evidence relating to the European countries which have carried out this kind of correction. Figures 6 and 7 report the government deficit and the level of GDP and unemployment (as index numbers) of the countries that in the eighties have achieved a significant reduction in their fiscal imbalances: Denmark, Portugal, Belgium, and Ireland.

There are of course some differences among the various countries but also some significant similarities, in particular between Denmark, Ireland[9] and Portugal which have enacted the most determined adjustment plans: real income kept growing during and after the adjustment, while unemployment was initially unchanged but subsequently decreased substantially. In Belgium instead, a much weaker adjustment effort corresponded to an increase in unemployment for two years, reabsorbed only over the following five years. Of course, one cannot take these examples as a proof that the correction of serious fiscal imbalances does not have deflationary effects, inter alia because the deficit, employment and income are simultaneously determined and one cannot take the deficit as the exogenous variable moving around the endogenous income and employment. The suggestion

---

[8] Splitting nominal income growth (y) in its real (q) and inflationary (p) components, we can rewrite equation (4a) of note 4 as: $db/ds = g - t + b\,(r-q)$,
which shows that the debt-to-GDP ratio varies with the real interest rate and real growth, while the rate of inflation does not affect the ratio directly, though the effects of inflation could come through its influence on the real rate of interest.

[9] For a detailed analysis of the cases of Denmark and Ireland reaching similarly optimistic conclusions, see Giavazzi and Pagano (1990), as well as "Maastricht Watch" (1992).

one derives from these experiences is, nonetheless, strong.

The conclusion we can draw from the analysis above is that, from an economic point of view, the targets indicated by the Treaty do not constitute an impossible task for most EEC countries. This, of course, cannot ensure that the targets will be achieved. A very strong political will is necessary, especially in pursuing the goal of reducing the fiscal deficit, the achievement of which would greatly facilitate the achievement of all other objectives.

A strong determination in pursuing convergence would have immediate consequences on financial markets, through the lowering of inflation expectations. In fact, financial markets base their equilibrium upon expectations and adjust to changes in expectations rapidly and fully, thus anticipating the trend towards convergence and favouring such convergence. On foreign exchange markets, the trend towards stability will be reinforced decisively, given that there will be no reason for realignments. The maintenance, for two years before the beginning of Phase three, of exchange rates within the narrow band and the absence of realignments will mark the achievement of the fourth criteria of convergence set by the Treaty. It is possible, however, that the market will ask for even more stability, similar to the one recorded on the Dutch guilder-Deutsche mark exchange rate since many years. In that case, the present margin of 2.25 per cent would be too wide and its reduction, either *de jure* or *de facto*, would appear both possible and necessary. As a matter of fact, the Danish authorities proposed such measure last year, but it was rejected by the Council of Ministers on the ground that it was unwise to restrict the margins without having implemented a coherent plan for EMU. Of course, the proposal could be reconsidered when the Treaty will be ratified. The higher expected stability in exchange rates would, in turn, feed-back on long-term interest rates, thus favouring convergence and the achievement of the target indicated by the Treaty.

On the basis of the analysis developed so far, it is apparent that the adjustment measures necessary to achieve the Treaty targets and the market reactions to such measures would activate a "virtuous circle". Symmetrically, if the adjustment measures encountered unexpected obstacles, the whole convergence process could be arrested and even reversed: in a certain sense, once adjustment is started it cannot be stopped. For instance, doubts on the authorities' determination in pursuing convergence targets could give new strength to inflationary expectations and jeopardize the overall adjustment action. The trust of market participants is an indispensable ingredient of the whole operation and only credibility can ensure such trust; in turn, credibility depends upon the authorites' readiness and determination in pursuing adjustment.

Denmark

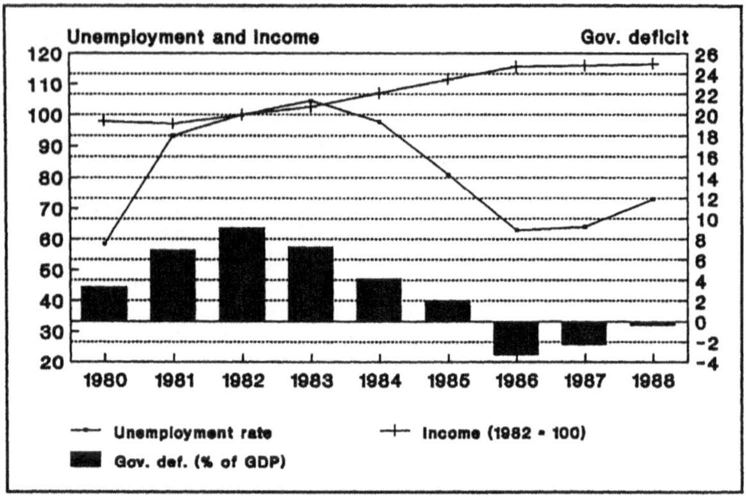

Adjustment begins in 1982; ends in 1986

Portugal

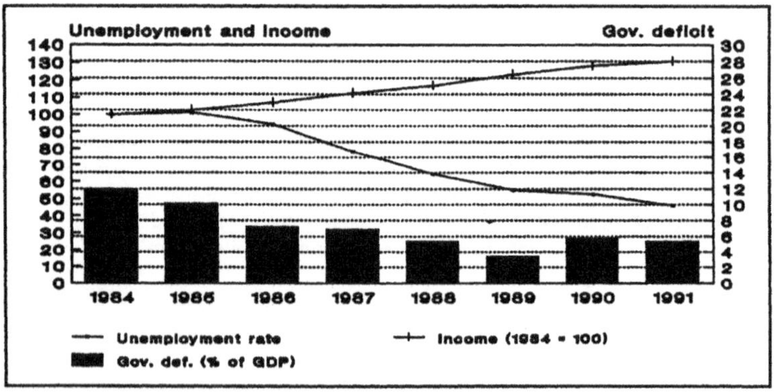

Adjustment begins in 1984; ends in 1989

Figure 6.

Source: see table 1

Belgium

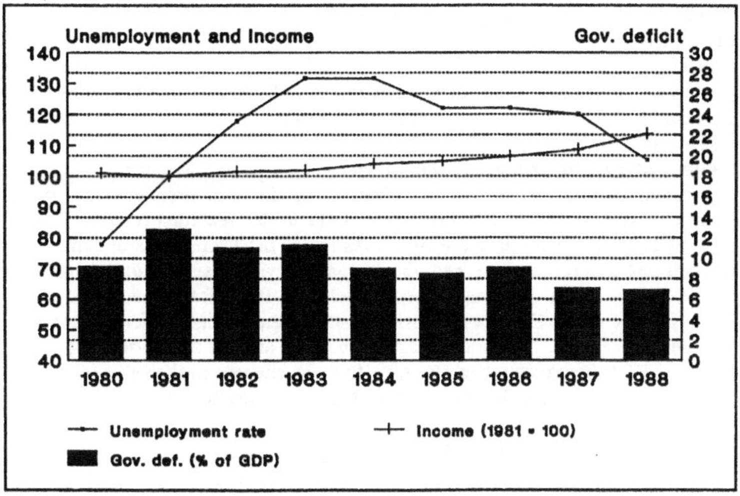

Adjustment begins in 1981; ends in 1985

Ireland

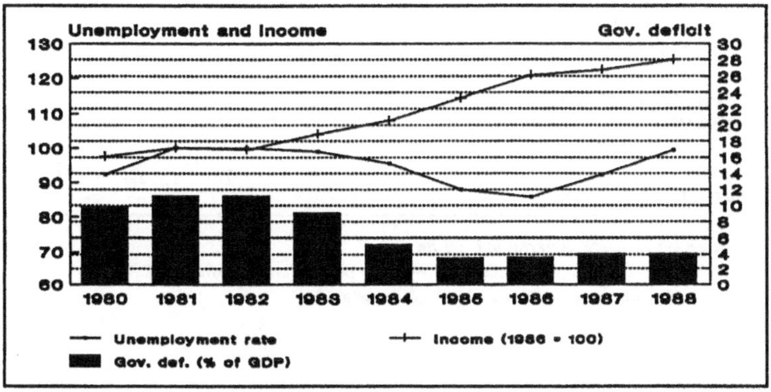

Adjustment begins in 1986; ends in 1989

Figure 7.

Source: See table 1

The proof of a fundamental, mutual relationship between market expectations and the success of the whole EMU endeavour has been given, painfully but very clearly, by the market reactions to the negative result of the Danish referendum on the Maastricht Treaty.

In a very short-term analysis, based on daily data, we can assume the *ceteris paribus* condition and think of the rejection of the Treaty by the Danes as the equivalent of a laboratory experiment: what happens if the market expectation of a successful EMU is shaken?

Table 5 shows the changes in the yields of European and American ten-year government bonds, as well as the changes in the spot exchange rate of the Deutsche Mark and Dutch guilder against the dollar recorded on June 3, 1992, the day after the announcement of the results of the Danish referendum. As far as the bond market is concerned, the increase in yields is statistically significant in the case of Spain, Sweden, Denmark, Belgium, Italy, France and U.K., as well as in the case of the ECU bond market. Instead, the change in yields recorded in the German, Dutch, Irish and American markets are not statistically significant. As for the foreign exchange markets, neither the changes in the value of the DM, nor the changes in the Guilder are statistically significant.

Table 5. Market reactions to the Danish referendum

	Bond markets[(a)]						
	E	S	USA	NL	DK	B	IRL
Average daily change[(c)]	0.003	0.004	0.005	0.002	0.000	0.000	0.002
Upper Limit[(d)]	0.063	0.095	0.115	0.048	0.064	0.055	0.086
Lower Limit[(d)]	0.057	0.086	0.125	0.044	0.064	0.054	0.083
Change in yields on 3/6/92	0.312	0.203	0.009	0.029	0.170	0.072	0.035
Significant change?	yes	yes	no	no	yes	yes	no

(a) yields on ten-year government bonds
(c) on the basis of the yields recorded over the period january-june 1992
(d) average change minus/plus 2 standard deviation

Table 5. Market reactions to the Danish referendum (continued)

	Bond markets(a)					Forex Market(b)	
	I	GER	ECU	F	UK	DEM	NLG
Average daily change(c)	0.002	0.000	0.001	0.000	0.006	0.001	0.001
Upper Limit(d)	0.065	0.059	0.071	0.061	0.138	0.024	0.497
Lower Limit(d)	0.062	0.059	0.073	0.060	0.127	0.026	0.499
Change in yields on 3/6/92	0.214	0.012	0.270	0.127	0.137	0.013	0.003
Significant change?	yes	no	yes	yes	yes	no	no

(a) yields on ten-year government bonds
(b) spot rate against the US dollar
(c) on the basis of the yields recorded over the period january-june 1992
(d) average change minus/plus 2 standard deviation

Source: Bloomberg
Note: E=Spain; S=Sweden; USA=USA; NL=Netherlands; DK=Denmark; B=Belgium; IRL=Ireland; I=Italy; GER=Germany; F=France, UK=United Kingdom.
DEM=D-Mark; NLG=Dutch Guilder.

Some results of the "experiment" are quite in line with our expectations. For instance, the increase in yields recorded in Italy and Spain shows that certain bond markets have been adversely affected by the fading of convergence expectations. Other results are unexpected: how to explain the increase in yields in France and Denmark, the only countries which already comply, together with Ireland, with the Treaty targets? However, the result which is really extraordinary and interesting is the *absence* of any reduction in long-term yields in Germany and the Netherlands and of any noteworthy appreciation of their currencies against the dollar.

An interpretation of these results is that EMU, and its anticipation by the market, accomplishes a Pareto improvement: what is gained in terms of lower inflationary expectations by countries which still have to complete their adjustment, such as Italy and Spain, is not lost by those countries which have already completed it, such as France, and not even by the "anchor country", Germany. Another, but mutually consistent, way to interpret these results is that markets see EMU as a device to obtain the *lowest*, not the *average* inflation, as feared by many critics.

The idea underlying this conclusion is that the level of the exchange rate and of long-term yields depends, inter alia, on inflationary expectations. The absence of any effect of the Danish "no" on German and Dutch long-term yields, as well as on exchange rates towards currencies outside the EMS, means that inflationary expectations have not been reduced in "virtuous countries" due to the lower probability of EMU. Instead, the increase in yields in other countries, as well as the depreciation vis-a-vis the DM, should indicate a deterioration in inflationary expectations in the "not-yet-convergent" countries.

References

Banca d'Italia (1991) Annual Report, Rome

Committee of Governors of the EEC (1992) Annual Report. Basle, Bank for International Settlements

Frankel J (1991) The European Monetary System: Credible at Last? NBER Working Paper no 3819

Giavazzi F, Pagano M (1990) Can Fiscal Contractions be Expansionary? The Tale of Two Small Countries. NBER Working Paper no 3372

Martina L, Rossetti A (1992) Emissioni di CTO nel 1992. Rome, Banca d'Italia, mimeo

Maastricht Watch, Rapporto semestrale sullo stato della convergenza all'Europa dell'economia italiana, CER, IAI, IRS and Prometeia; September 1992, n 0

Five Years to Prepare the Final Stage of EMU: A German View

Hans-Jürgen Treutler
Landeszentralbank in Hessen, Frankfurt

1 The EMU Debate in Germany

Whether the final stage of EMU will start at the earliest possible date, i.e. 1997, or at the latest date, i.e. January 1, 1999, or at any time in between, in any case there is not much time left to prepare the 3rd stage, considering the ambitious objective of EMU and the huge work to do. However, due to the outcome of the referendum in Denmark the time schedule agreed in the Maastricht Treaty on European Union (EC treaty) may have become uncertain.

In Germany the public debate on EMU began rather late. Before the Maastricht decisions there was not really a discussion of this issue, neither in the general public nor in the political area, although at an early stage the Bundesbank had pointed out to the far-reaching significance and the implications of a monetary union. Obviously the Maastricht decisions came unexpected, especially because the public was not prepared for. This is somewhat surprising as the Maastricht decisions in fact constitute a logical step within a long-lasting development. This process began with the Werner plan in the sixties, currency "snake" and EMS in the seventies and continued with the summit in Hannover (1988) that charged the Delors committee with preparing an EMU concept; the EC summit in Rome (October 1990) then set the starting date of the second stage of EMU.

The response to the Maastricht decisions in Germany has tended to be rather sceptical. Worries and anxieties concentrate on

- the surrender of the D-Mark
- insufficient harmonization of financial policy
- additional financial burden.

Especially getting aware of loosing the D-Mark caused a kind of shock due to the strong ties of the German population to its currency which have their roots in special historical experience:

- the experience of the two hyperinflations in Germany in this century has led to a high degree of sensitivity attached to currency issues
- the stability success of the Bundesbank has set high standards
- the symbolic significance of the Deutsche Mark for the economic recovery after World War II.

In addition increasing fears have emerged that the Maastricht decisions could entail further financial burdens primarily for the big member countries like Germany which already pays higher amounts into the budget of the EC commission than other countries. Such a suspicion is being reinforced by the establishment of a "Cohesion Fund" by the Maastricht agreement with which the aim of promoting economic and social cohesion and solidarity among the member states has been fixed. What is considered to be another critical issue is the imbalance of the Economic and Monetary Union on the one hand and the Political Union on the other hand. The argument that mainly the insufficient harmonization of the financial policies entails the risk of financial and economic instability, is often mentioned in this context. Summarizing the discussion it has to be noted that the effective resp. expected weaknesses and risks of EMU dominate the debate. Only a few comments deal with advantages and chances of an extended currency area which e.g. were emphasized in the paper of the EC Commission "One market, one currency", i.e. elimination of exchange rate risks and transaction costs and the chance of extending the stability oriented policy of the Bundesbank to the other member states.

2 Some Critical Aspects of EMU

2.1 Stability Consensus

Even the Bundesbank has appreciated that the EC treaty and in particular "...the Statute of the future European System of Central Banks is likely to create the legal basis enabling monetary policy in the monetary union to be geared to stability."[1] However, this is certainly not a guarantee that a successful stabilization policy will be implemented in reality. As experience in Germany shows, a successful monetary policy requires certain institutional patterns, in particular legally guaranteed independence of the central bank, commitment to the primary objective of price stability, the ban on the monetary financing of government deficits. However, the succes of a monetary policy is also a "result of a social consensus".[2] A monetary union, therefore, does not concern monetary policy alone, but is - as the Bundesbank has often stressed - "... an irrevocable joint and several community which in the light of past experience, requires a more far-reaching association, in the form of a comprehensive political union, if it is to prove durable.[3]

In Germany there has traditionally been a widespread consensus on the necessity and priority of a monetary policy geared to price stability. Stabilization policy therefore receives full support from the great majority of the public, the

[1] Deutsche Bundesbank, February 1992, p 51.
[2] Richter (1992).
[3] Deutsche Bundesbank, October 1990, p 41.

economists, the media and even the politicians as it is unpopular being in opposition to the policy of the Bundesbank. There is not any comparable or similar tradition in other EC countries. It is true, in Maastricht all participants have declared their readiness and their willingness to pursue a stability oriented monetary policy, but what matters is that already in the transition period this idea will be translated into appropriate concrete action.

2.2 Convergence Criteria and Firm Time Schedule

As the Maastricht Treaty amendment provides on the one hand for clear convergence criteria to be met by every country that desires access to the 3rd stage and on the other hand sets a firm latest date for the commencement of the final stage, this involves the risk that the criteria for the entry in stage 3 will not be taken as serious as necessary. The Bundesbank therefore has emphasized that "... the fulfillment of the entry criteria or the convergence conditions must not be impaired by any dates set".[4] To meet the entry criteria some countries will have to make vigorous efforts. It is true the EC Commission has to submit reports on the convergence progress in the member states to the ECOFIN council, but in evaluating the financial position it has to be examined whether exceedings of the reference values have "substantially" resp. "sufficiently" declined. Under "due account of the reports" and "on the basis of the recommendation of the Council" (ECOFIN) the Council in the composition of the Heads of States or of Governments, by a qualified majority, decides whether and at which date the 3rd stage will start and which countries are granted to participate. That means considerable room of manoeuvre has been granted to the Council to decide on the eligibility of member states to participate in the final stage. In particular at the latest starting date the propensity could increase to evaluate any exceedings of the reference values rather generously, in order to avoid having to commence the final stage only with a small number of member states. If member states can achieve to be granted eligible without having to fulfil the entry conditions their convergence efforts in the transition period could be impaired.

2.3 Financial Burden

The EMU is likely to entail additional financial demands on the countries with strong economies. Member states which face structural deficits will no longer have the possibility of safeguarding their competitiveness by exchange rate adjustments. Increasing demands for additional measures of regional and structural promotion are likely to expect. As all wage and salary payments will be made in the same single European currency, wage disparities within the community will, at least optically, emerge more clearly than before. A tendency to aggressive wage claims,

[4] Deutsche Bundesbank, February 1992, p 52.

especially in countries with a lower income level, cannot be ruled out. Countries which have to cope with difficulties in meeting the public debt criteria for entry in the final stage probably might claim for support from the community. As a consequence of the Maastricht decisions the EC Commission has presented only a few months later the so-called "Delors-II-package" demanding for additional payments of the member states into the Community budget of 21 billion ECU which mainly are designated to financing measures of economic structure policy.

In Germany fears about such additional financial burden for the EMU must be seen against the background of the current high public sector deficits due to the massive financial transfers to eastern Germany. The Bundesbank has urged several times that deficits on the present scale can only be tolerated for a short time and that growth in public expenditure must be reduced. Therefore, in the years ahead there will be no room of manoeuvre for substantially increasing transfers to the EC budget. Besides, from a more fundamental point of view as well, it seems to be reasonable not to expect too much success and benefits of a policy geared to promoting economic structures. Experience in this field has generally been rather disappointing. For instance, disparities in income and on the labour markets between the EC countries have hardly been reduced despite the Community raised considerable amounts for this purpose in the past. Also the Italian experience with the financial aid for the southern part of the country to promote economic structure, does not give much reason for optimism with regard to sustainable success of a policy aiming at promoting economic structures.

3 Tasks of Preparing the Final Stage

In the transition phase the main tasks of preparing the final stage are from my point of view the following ones:

- safeguarding the credibility of the European monetary policy
- improving the convergence with the aim of fulfilling the conditions set in the EC treaty
- elaboration of a monetary policy concept for the European Central Bank (ECB).

3.1 The Credibility of the European Monetary Policy

Credibility under the present conditions is one of the primarily important prerequisites for a successful stability-oriented monetary policy. Gebauer (1988) expressed the view that the credibility of the monetary policy of the Bundesbank is even the main reason for its success. However, the reputation of the central banks of the member states cannot automatically be transfered to the ECB, but the European Central Bank will have to earn its credibility anew by succeeding in stability. To be sure the EC treaty, in particular the statute of ESCB, creates a satisfactory legal basis for future European monetary policy: independence of the ECB, commitment to price stability as the priority aim, the ban of government financing. In addition in Maastricht all parties have declared their willingness to pursue a policy aiming at stability, but there is still a certain scepticism, especially in Germany, whether this readiness will turn out to stand in reality. In this context it would be an important positive sign, if other member states granted full independence to their national central banks very early in the transitional period. This would demonstrate clearly that these countries take seriously a strictly anti-inflationary monetary policy course.

Outside Germany it is referred to that other countries have made large progress in implementing stability-oriented policies and that the inflation rate in some other countries is meanwhile lower than in Germany. However, it has to be reminded to the fact that this success has partly been reached by pegging the exchange rate of the currencies of those countries to the D-Mark, giving the D-Mark the so-called "anchor role". The monetary policy in that countries necessarily had to adopt the policy stance of the Bundesbank in order to avoid having to devaluate their currencies. The question is whether the readiness towards a consequent stabilization policy will stand when in the final stage of the EMU the D-Mark will no longer play the "anchor role". But it has to admit that there are also positive signs of an increasing European stability consciousness, at least among the central banks of the member states. The recently published first Annual Report of the Committee of the Governors of the EC central banks declares full support to a stability-oriented monetary policy what justifies a certain confidence with regard to the future European monetary policy.

Incidentally it is not unimportant where the ECB will have its seat. From the German point of view it should be a location with a convincing stability tradition, as the "genius loci" is in fact of great importance. In addition the ECB should not be located at a place where any government has its seat.

3.2 Convergence Progress

At present the convergence record shows that large efforts will be necessary to reach the convergence level set by the Maastricht decision for entry into the final stage. Currently only three countries meet all four criteria, these are Denmark, France and Luxemburg. Some countries exceed only slightly one or more criteria, for instance Germany, Great Britain and the Netherlands, so that they have good chances to eventually reach the goal by time. For the other countries especially the debt criteria means a high hurdle, which in some cases may hardly be overcome.

Prof. Issing, Member of the Directorate of the Bundesbank, recently illustrated the size of the efforts necessary to cut down a high public debt ratio to the level of the entry criteria within the few years left until the commencement of the final stage by the following example: Taken a debt ratio for 1991 of 100 % and assuming a GDP growth rate of 6 % p.a. a budget surplus of 1 % of the GDP would have to be achieved every year to bring down the debt ratio to 60 % until 1998 (resp. a budget surplus of 3,5 % would be necessary to reach the 60 % level already by 1996).[5] Therefore, it has to be expected with a certain probability that some countries will claim on the exception clause of art. 104c paragraph 2 of the EC treaty which under certain circumstances allows to grant participation in the final stage without fulfilling the entry criteria.

Without any doubt improving the convergence is primarily up to the individual countries. This is being stressed in art. 109e paragraph 2 EC treaty, which states that already before the beginning of the 2nd stage every member country shall "...adopt, where necessary, ... multiannual programmes intended to ensure the lasting convergence necessary for the achievement of economic and monetary union, in particular with regard to price stability and sound public finances ..." However, the Commission will also have to play an important role in the convergence process, as it has been charged by the EC treaty with the so-called "monitoring":

- Already before the beginning of stage 2 the Commission has to submit reports to the Council on the "... progress made with regard to economic and monetary convergence ..." (art. 109e paragraph 2 (b)).
- From the beginning of the second stage "...the Commission shall monitor the development of the budgetary situation and of the stock of government debt in the Member States with a view to identifying gross errors ..." (art. 104c paragraph 2).

If a member state does not fulfill the requirements of the convergence criteria, i.e. if it exceeds the reference values, the Commission shall prepare a report for the Council. Where the existence of an excessive deficit is decided, the Council shall make recommendations to the member state concerned (art. 104c paragraph 7). If there will not been taken effective action in response to the recommendation the Commission may make its recommendation public (paragraph 8). Further sanctions set in art. 104c paragraph 11 may be applied not until the beginning of stage 3. The possibility of the community institutions to exert influence on the efforts of the member states to improve the convergence may be considered to be rather weak and insufficient. Nevertheless, moral suasion, public pressure and published criticisms by the EC Commission may have the proper effect, provided the criteria for the entry in the final stage will be strictly applied. Within the "monitoring" the Commission will also have to pay attention to any attempt of member states to manipulate the situation of the public finance, e.g. by shifting public expenditures into so-called "shadow budgets".

Certain constraint on reducing excessive budget deficits will also be exerted by the ban on monetary financing of government deficits that comes into effect from the beginning of the 2nd stage. In some countries central bank lendings play an important role in the financing of public budgets like in Greece, Italy and Portugal. If instead of monetary financing, often granted free of interest or at

[5] Issing (1992).

preferential interest rates, governments have to borrow from the market, this will certainly have its disciplining effect.

4 Elaboration of a Monetary Policy Concept

The EC treaty and the statute of the ESCB contain clearly institutional conditions for the monetary policy of the European Central Bank (ECB), but what remains to be clarified is the way the common European monetary policy shall have to be implemented. It is true that the European Monetary Institute (EMI) to be established at the beginning of the 2nd stage, shall "... prepare the instruments and the procedures necessary for carrying out a single monetary policy in the 3rd stage ..." (art. 109f paragraph 3). Hitherto the discussion about this issue has not gained momentum yet. Here, an interesting field for research may open up for the academic scene over the years ahead. The hitherto heard remarks from central banks on this issue were limited to pointing out to the principle of subsidiarity (art. 3b EC treaty). The vice-governor of the Banque de France, Mr. Lagayette, for instance, has emphasized that the national central banks remain integral components of the ESCB; members of the Central Bank Council of the Bundesbank have claimed for a high degree of decentralization of the European monetary policy.

The elaboration of a concept for the European monetary policy concerns the following levels:

- formulation of the monetary target
- instruments to be applied
- organisational structure.

4.1 Formulation of Monetary Goals

The ultimate goal of the European monetary policy has been unequivocally determined in art. 105 paragraph 1 EC treaty:
"The primary objective of the ESCB shall be to maintain price stability." The ESCB may support the general economic policy of the community, but only "...without prejudice to the objective of price stability." As the instrument of price control, fortunately, is not provided for and as the monetary policy cannot exert direct influence on the price level, the ECB will have to choose a monetary intermediate target. Theoretically, the following monetary targets would be possible: exchange rate, interest rate resp. term structure of interest rates and money stock.

In the past some EC countries had geared its monetary policy to the exchange rate of its currency, in particular towards the D-Mark as the "anchor" currency within the EMS. A comparable exchange rate orientation, say towards the

US-dollar or the yen, would certainly not be a suitable monetary policy goal of the ECB. The US-dollar as well as the yen could not really be regarded as anchor currencies for the future single European currency, neither with respect to their stability performance nor to the relative weights of the concerning economic areas.

The interest rate level has also been used as a monetary policy target by some countries. Those countries who had pegged the exchange rate of their currencies to another currency had necessarily to pursue an interest rate oriented monetary policy, for they had to keep the interest rate difference to the "anchor" currency on a certain level. But apart from that, interest rates have played an independent role as a monetary target in some countries, what often had led to a low interest rate-oriented monetary policy serving to enhance economic activity. However, from a theoretical as well as a practical point of view interest rates are not only an inappropriate but even more a doubtful monetary policy indicator or intermediate target. On the one hand it is not clearly established by tested hypotheses to which extent medium and long-term market interest rates are influenced by monetary policy or by market forces. On the other hand interest rates are not a suitable leading indicator for the development of the price level. In pursuing a certain interest rate goal, monetary policy therefore tends to an "oversteering" and may lead to instability of the whole system. In addition, due to the great importance of interest rates for the overall economic activity and for the interest expenditures of the government budget in case of a high public debt stock, an interest rate-oriented monetary policy is permanently in danger to be urged to contribute to supporting economic activity and to reduce the interest burden of public budgets. The conclusion, therefore, should be: The priority of safe-guarding price stability provided for in the EC treaty rules out a monetary policy aiming at a certain interest rate goal.

For some years the term structure of interest rates has been receiving support as monetary policy indicator. In particular for monetary theorists the term structure of interest rates in this context has become something like a "pet subject", certainly in response to the increasing difficulties occurred in some countries with the correct definition of the money stock indicators. Gebauer[6] has suggested, the Bundesbank should apply a term structure of interest rates approach instead of a money target. In fact, several theoretical and statistic-mathematical surveys have found the term structure of interest rates quite suitable as monetary policy indicator, but there are serious doubts on this qualification from a practical and political point of view.[7] It remains unclear, for instance, how a term structure of interest rates target should have to be quantified at a certain time: has the monetary policy stance to be tightened up or is it strict enough? In addition, here again it has to be pointed out that neither the level of interest rates on the markets nor their term structure can be fully controlled by the central bank, among other things, because of the external influences which in an open system sometimes dominate the domestic financial markets. Besides,

---

[6] Gebauer (1988).

[7] Hesse, Roth (1992) p 18.

applying the term structure of interest rates as a monetary target or indicator the central bank, like in the case of an orientation towards the interest rate level, is in danger to be drawn into the discussion of supporting short term economic activity.

Therefore, in my view, the ECB should decide in favour of the money stock as its monetary intermediate target. The money stock has by and large proved to be the best suitable indicator for monetary policy. It is true, that the Bundesbank has failed sometimes to meet its quantified money stock target. What is decisive, however, is that the Bundesbank obviously has been able to present convincing reasons for it. Money stock targets show in particular advantages from a practical and political point of view. If it is correct that the success of the monetary policy depends largely on its credibility, also the monetary intermediate target will have to be credible and understandable for the general public. This demand is excellently met by the money stock. Such a general acceptance of the money stock target is, among other things, necessary, as otherwise it could not fulfil its information function aiming at encouraging adjustment behaviour of the various social groups towards the stability-oriented monetary policy. A money stock target is the best way of protecting monetary policy against its instrumentalization in favour of the economic policy. A money stock target published at the beginning of the year and accepted by the general public makes it more difficult to politicians, governments or other interest groups to put pressure on the central bank to support economic policy. A money stock target makes it easier to pursue a monetary policy oriented at the productive potential and strengthens to a certain extent the de facto independence of a central bank.

The choice of a money stock target for the European monetary policy would of course raise some questions with reference to practical issues. How can an European money stock be identified? Does an aggregation of the national money stocks lead to a suitable definition of the European money stock? Does such a money stock show a sufficient correlation to the European GNP or the price level? Is the money demand function in the European countries sufficiently similar? A sub-committee of the Committee of the Governors of the EC central banks has been dealing for some years with the harmonization of the monetary aggregates of the EC countries. In its annual report published in April 1992 the Committee has pointed out that the money stock aggregates in the broader sense are already defined quite similarly. The Committee suggests to apply, where appropriate, the harmonized money stock aggregates, which some countries have already decided to adopt. Therefore, some progress has been made in this field, but as the Committee of the Governors emphasizes, there is some work left to do.

4.2 Monetary Instruments

With reference to the monetary instruments the question is on the one hand whether the ECB will set official interest rates like lombard and discount rate and on the other hand in which way liquidity will be provided to the individual banks resp. the banking system as a whole. The ESCB will certainly have to provide a central bank facility which banks can use to bridge temporary liquidity needs, i.e. a facility like the lombard loans granted by the Bundesbank in the way of current account lending. The interest rate of such lendings is something like a "penalty rate", i.e. the highest rate charged by the central bank, and forms a kind of upper limit to the call money rate on the money market. A discount rate could of course be set only if the instrument of discount lending was used at all (what will be discussed below). So-called repo rates would be another interest rate instrument of the ECB; the Bundesbank sometimes has been using this instrument by offering fixed rate repos. Regarding the liquidity policy there are on the one hand instruments which are likely to be adopted by the ECB without difficulties as they are already being used by most national central banks like, for instance, open market transactions in the form of repurchase agreements. They can serve as an instrument for both longer-run liquidity provision and "fine-tuning" of the money market as they can be offered at different periods to maturity.

Other liquidity policy instruments are employed by some but not all national central banks so that it will have to be decided whether it is necessary to harmonize them and which one should be adopted by the ECB. From the German point of view this refers in particular to the minimum reserve instrument that the Bundesbank regards to be an essential part of its stabilization policy, for it forms the "string" which ties the banks to the central bank as a rise in bank lendings and money creation leads to increasing minimum reserve requirements. Minimum reserves are by some people seen to be the "ultimate" reason of the stability success of the Bundesbank.

Should the ECB not adopt the minimum reserves as monetary policy instrument this, therefore, could be regarded as a lack of willingness pursuing a strictly stability-oriented European monetary policy. Admittedly, the minimum reserve instrument is not uncontested in Germany, especially of course by the banks but also by some academic economists. However minimum reserves, in any case, facilitate the practical liquidity policy as they make it easier to the central bank to determine the liquidity needs of the banking system as a whole. By reason of this practical aspect the ECB, in my opinion, will hardly be able to refrain from using the minimum reserve instrument. In providing the EMU-banking system as a whole with central bank liquidity the ECB requires a reliable forecast of the liquidity needs of all banks. National central banks, as experience shows, may manage to steer the liquidity of their banking systems without requiring minimum reserves due to their long forecast experience or, if necessary, by intervening in the money market several times a day. However, the ECB, at least in the initial period, will need a firm base for its practical liquidity management. Without minimum reserve requirements it would hardly be possible to make a forecast of the union-wide liquidity needs with sufficient exactness, since there is almost no experience or indication to what magnitudes banks want to hold voluntarily ECB balances. Probably the European banking system would permanently be provided with too much or too less liquidity with the consequence of large fluctuations of the money market interest rates.

In the liquidity policy of the Bundesbank the discount lendings continue in playing an important role. Although repurchase agreements have become the dominating refinancing instrument, about one third of the total refinancing volume is still done by discount lending (e.g. 70 billion D-Mark in April 1992). To carry on using the discount window after the entry in the final stage of EMU would certainly be possible only if the monetary policy instruments were not completely harmonized within the ESCB, because other national central banks which do not use the discount instrument anymore would presumably not be prepared to introduce this instrument, since the discount business is rather complicated and requires a certain technique and special organisational prerequisites which cannot be easily created (e.g. assessment of the solvency of the parties who have signed the bills, handling of the bills, use of bills in lending between non-banks etc.). It has been often argued in favour of the discount instrument that central bank money should not be provided only through buying government securities but also on the basis of private debt instruments like bills. In addition it is pointed out that discount lendings of the central bank create direct contact to the enterprises and increase the effectiveness of the interest rate policy as the interest rate of discount lendings of the banks are closely linked to the discount rate of the central bank. However, there are on the other hand objections to the discount instruments, especially if discount lendings are granted at preferential rates within certain rediscount quotas. Such refinancing quotas, as experience shows, can easily produce attempts of the government to demand for special rediscount facilities in favour of certain purposes of structural policy. Nevertheless, the basic idea of the rediscount policy, i.e. not to base central bank lendings on public debt alone but also on private enterprises debt, should be taken into account by the ECB when it will decide on the monetary policy instruments to be used for implementing European monetary policy.

4.3 Centralized versus Decentralized Monetary Policy

Concerning the organisation and distribution of responsibilities with regard to the implementation of the monetary policy of the ECB a distinct preference in favour of a high degree of decentralization seems to emerge on the part of national central banks. This view can be substantiated by referring to art. 106 paragraph 1 of EC treaty: "The ESCB shall be composed of the ECB and of the national central banks." In addition art. 12 of the statute of the ESCB says: "To the extent deemed possible and appropriate... the ECB shall have recourse to the national central banks to carry out operations which form part of the tasks of the ESCB." Considering moreover the principle of subsidiarity, thus the EC treaty regulations have to be interpreted in the sense that all the tasks have to be transferred to the national central banks which they can properly perform, whereas the ECB shall have to confine itself to the tasks which have necessarily to be carried out in a centralized way.

It is uncontested that the ECB determines the principles of the monetary policy. This is explicitly provided by art. 12 of the statute: "The Governing Council shall adopt the guidelines and take the decisions necessary to ensure the performance of the tasks ... The Governing Council shall formulate the monetary policy of the

Community including, as appropriate, decisions relating to intermediate monetary objectives, key interest rates and the supply of reserves in the ESCB, and shall establish the necessary guidelines for their implementation." Thus the choice of the monetary intermediate goal as well as the setting of a quantified target lie within the authority of the ECB. This applies to the key interest rates as well, for a common currency area requires, of course, a uniform interest rate level.

With reference to the implementation of the European monetary policy the statute speaks only of the "necessary guidelines" to be set by the ECB. Obviously, it is not intended to have refinancing and open market operations implemented primarily or to a considerable extent by an own and centralized "operational arm" of the ECB. Such a model of a completely centralized implementation of the monetary policy within the ESCB seems to be envisaged, for instance, in Great Britain, for there it is often argued that a broad and efficient financial market is needed to carry out the European monetary policy so that London had to be regarded as the "natural choice" for the location of the ECB, at least for its "operational arm". However, such a model of the implementation of European monetary policy does, of course, not meet the interests of the other national central banks. In addition, the spirit and the wording of the EC treaty suggests the ECB should carry out own refinancing and open market operation, if any, only to a limited extent, for instance to meet temporary liquidity needs of the banks, whereas otherwise the ECB should confine itself to the setting of guidelines.

Within these guidelines various models are conceivable concerning the degree of self-responsibility of the national central banks in implementing the European monetary policy. A model formed similar to the distribution of tasks within the Federal reserve system in the USA between the board and the "desk" would, for instance, provide for the highest room of manoeuvre to the national central banks (considering all of them as "desk"). In this case the ECB would pre-set a certain target for the money market interest rates, e.g. a range of 9-9,25 % p.a., and the national central banks would have to secure that the rates on their local money markets shall not exceed or fall below that target range. In which way this aim was achieved and which monetary instruments were used, would benefit up to the national central banks. Such room of manoeuvre of the national central banks would allow to take consideration of the national specialities in the use of monetary policy instruments. This, for instance, would open up the opportunity to the Bundesbank to maintain the rediscount instrument, although, of course, not at preferential interest rates. However, it seems to be doubtful whether large differences in the use of monetary policy instruments would be acceptable in the longer run. If, for instance, the German banks had to borrow central bank balances from the Bundesbank in the way of resdiscounting bills, causing comparatively high costs, whereas the banks in other countries could use the less complicated open market operations, the German banks would certainly complain of their disadvantages in competitiveness. In any case, the "federal reserve" model would presumably tend to a centralization of the liquidity provision within the ESCB. Differences in the interest rates on the various local money markets, which could hardly be avoided, would lead to permanent disturbing arbitrage transactions. Therefore the internationally acting banks would certainly be inclined to centralize their liquidity management operations at the big financial places. In the end only one "operational center" or a few one would be likely to arise.

Therefore it seems to be necessary to harmonize at least to a certain extent the monetary instruments within the ESCB. Here it could be helpful to make a distinction between the supply of central bank funds for covering basic and current liquidity needs of the banks as it is being exercised by the Bundesbank. For the covering of the basic needs the ECB, for instance, could set refinancing quotas, either directly for all individual banks or for the national central banks which had to distribute the quotas to the banks in their area according to calculation methods which they can set independently. It would not be necessary that the refinancing quotas had to be used only in the way of rediscounting bills, but it could left up to the national central banks to decide how the quotas could be used, e.g. by lombard loans, repurchase agreement or in another appropriate way. This model of the implementation of European monetary policy would secure that at least to the extent of the quotas every national central bank was involved in providing the banking system with liquidity. The supply of central bank money in excess of the quotas would have to be arranged through open market operations, namely on a scale necessary to maintain money market interest rates within the target.

Basically quite another approach would be pursued by employing instead of the national central banks the ECB with the task to steer the money market interest rate within the pre-set target. In this case, too, the ECB could set quotas for the liquidity supply of each national central bank, however not the national central banks but the ECB had to provide for the liquidity balance on the money market as a whole carrying out own open market operations with the aim to maintain the target interest rate level. At least in the initial phase such a centralized liquidity steering would certainly face some difficulties. Supplying the liquidity through only a few financial centers would require a market proceeding of liquidity distribution among the various local money markets which might not be as efficient as necessary to avoid unduly interest rate fluctuations. Therefore, operations geared to the liquidity balance on the market should better be carried out at the "local" level by the national central banks in permanent coordination with the ECB.

An even more centralized implementation of the European monetary policy would make national central banks to something like ECB-branches with purely technical tasks. Refinancing quotas, e.g. would be set by the ECB on the basis of a uniform calculation method for all individual banks within the monetary union, the liquidity needs of the banking system as a whole would be estimated by central forecasts and all open market operations would be carried out by the central ECB office itself. Carrying out repurchase agreements, for instance, the national central banks would merely collect the bids of the banks and transmit them to the central ECB office which had to decide on the allocation. Apart from that to the national central banks were left only the book-keeping tasks. At this stage it is hard to believe that the national central banks would accept such a role. Therefore this model must be considered highly inadequate at least in the initial period of the ESCB.

5 The Ecu Issue

While the preparation of the final stage has to focus on convergence progress and the design of a feasible monetary policy concept, the Ecu issue is rather unimportant from my point of view. Indeed the EMI is, due to art. 109 f EC treaty, supposed to "...facilitate the use of the Ecu and oversees its development ...". In some EC countries promoting Ecu is considered to be of great importance but for the functioning of the EMU, to my mind, it does not play any significant role, whether the Ecu will be more or less used in the transition period. Even if the current "basket" ECU should smoothly turn to a uniform currency Ecu in the final stage, what is meanwhile generally considered to be rather probable, there is no reason to be seen why the use of the Ecu should yet be promoted. At a certain day in the final stage all currency amounts will be changed from the hitherto existing national currencies to the final single currency whatever its name will be according to the market exchange rates at that date. Any preceding exercise of handling the present basket ECU or accustoming to the name "Ecu" does not seem necessary. In addition, it is not likely to expect, that the general public will practically become accustomed to the Ecu, as the present "basket" ECU is not supposed to be used for normal daily payments; until now the Ecu plays a greater role only in securities transactions and interbank business. The German experience with the currency union between western and eastern Germany in 1990 shows, that a change of currency does not entail great technical difficulties; the people in eastern Germany have become easily and fast accustomed to the new currency.

6 Summary

For a stability-oriented monetary policy within the EMU it is essential to achieve a convergence in price stability as well as in public budget deficits and public debt in Europe before the commencement of the final stage. Participation in the EMU may be granted only to those countries which meet the criteria set in the Maastricht agreement. The entry criteria must not be impaired by the firm time schedule agreed in Maastricht. The credibility of the European Central Bank would be supported if member states granted full independence to their national central banks very early in the transitional period.

Interest rates would not be an appropriate monetary policy goal for the ECB neither from a theoretical nor from a practical point of view. An interest rate-oriented monetary policy could easily come under pressure to pursue a short term anti-cyclical approach. Exchange rates, likewise, could not be regarded a suitable monetary policy goal. The close medium term relationship to inflation rate and GDP makes the money stock the best suitable goal for ECB monetary policy. A quantified money stock target would also protect monetary policy against its instrumentalization in favour of short term economic policy.

The monetary policy instruments applied by the national central banks will have to be harmonized at least to a certain extent. Minimum reserves should be needed for the liquidity steering by the ECB. They stabilize money demand on the money markets and provide a firm base for the ECB to forecast the liquidity needs of the European banking system as a whole. Minimum reserves will also contribute to keep decentralized the liquidity management of the EC-wide acting commercial banks and will, thus, counteract the establishment of one or a few big financial centers in the EMU area. Open market transactions in the way of repurchse agreements will certainly play an important role as they are already being used by most national central banks. They should not be based on public debt securities alone but also on corporate debt including, for instance, bills of exchange.

A high degree of decentralization should be realized in implementing monetary policy. The ESCB statute as well as the principle of subsidiarity require the transfer of all tasks to the national central banks they can properly perform, whereas the ECB shall have to confine itself to the "necessary guidelines". Large room of manoeuvre would be given to the national central banks if the ECB only pre-sets a certain target range for the call money rate which had to be maintained by own transactions of the national central banks. In this case big international financial centers with broad and well managed money markets might eventually attract a great volume of money market transactions from other places. In order to secure that all national central banks will participate in providing the banking system with liquidity it could be helpful to make a distinction between the supply of central bank funds for covering basic and current liquidity needs of the banks. Covering basic needs the ECB could set refinancing quotas for the national central banks to be used by their own liquidity transactions. The necessary supply of the central bank funds in excess of the quotas would have to be arranged by open market transactions. An "operational desk" of the ECB would only be necessary to carry out such finetuning money market operations. A more centralized implementation of the European monetary policy would make national central banks to something like ECB branches with purely technical tasks and this would hardly meet the interest of the national central banks.

References

Deutsche Bundesbank (1990) Monthly Report, October, p 41
Deutsche Bundesbank (1992) Monthly Report, February, pp 50-52
Gebauer W (1988) A Term Structure Approach to German Monetary Policy. Geld und Währung Working Paper no 7, Frankfurt
Hesse H, Roth G (1992) Die Zinsstruktur als Indikator der Geldpolitik? In: Kredit und Kapital, 25 Jhg, Heft 1, p 18
Issing O (1992) Perspektiven einer einheitlichen Europawährung. In: Deutsche Bundesbank, Auszüge aus Presseartikeln, no 33, May 7
Richter R (1992) Über Papierstandards, Währungsunion und das Ende der D-Mark. Lecture at the University of Frankfurt, February 14

Towards a Common Monetary Policy in the Transition: The Role of the Ecu and Required Reserves*

Daniel Gros
Centre for European Policy Studies, Bruxelles

I wish to thank Lorenzo Bini-Smaghi and José Vinals for stimulating discussions. The ideas expressed in this paper have been deeply influenced by the joint work with Niels Thygesen that has stretched over a number of years.

1 Introduction

Two successive European Councils set the date for the beginning of stage II and launched the Intergovernmental conference on EMU. Monetary union within this decade (and century) looks therefore increasingly likely. However, it is somewhat surprising that most of the work so far has concentrated on the final stage of EMU and not on the practical questions that arise during the transition.

The Delors report did not give any indication how the transition should be managed except to insist that during stage II the ultimate authority for (national) monetary policy should remain in national hands.[1] The preparatory work of the central bank governors has also concentrated on the final stage. Their draft statutes for the European System of Central Banks (ESCB) prepared by the central bank governors are likely to be incorporated in the forthcoming Treaty amendment. The most important elements of the final stage of EMU seem therefore to be in place.

It is thus time to begin to think about the practical problems that will arise in the transition. Discussion about the transition is particularly important in the area of monetary control since stage II represents an unknown new intermediate stage between the current EMS and the final stage of full monetary union. During stage II a common monetary authority already exists, but the ultimate authority for (national) monetary policy remains at the national level. This is different from the EMS where national authorities also retain ultimate authority, but where in the absence of a common monetary institution the exchange rate mechanism is run on mixture of informal cooperation and leadership by the strongest. It is also different from the final stage when no national authority in monetary matters remains.

---

* CEPS Working Documents are published to give an early indication of the work in progress within CEPS research groups and to stimulate reactions from other experts in those fields. Unless otherwise indicated, the views expressed are attributable only to the author in a personal capacity and not to any institution.

[1] See committee for the Study of Economic and Monetary Union (1989).

This paper therefore analyses how a common monetary policy could be organized during stage II. It focuses on the role of a system of reserve requirements because other mechanisms of monetary control that are used at the national level cannot be used at the European level during stage II when national currencies still exist and financial markets retain some national characteristics. The European Central Bank will not be able to rely on a stable demand for clearing balances by commercial banks since most clearing will presumably be done at the national level (and in national currencies). Moreover, the European Central Bank will also not be able to control the supply of currency in circulation because the common single currency will be introduced only in the final stage.

The paper assumes the Ecu will be the common currency in the final stage of EMU, the Ecu is therefore the obvious unit of account for the ESCB and also the obvious unit of account for the reserve requirements to be discussed below. This does not imply any presumption that the Ecu will (or should) become a parallel currency. The success of the Ecu as a parallel currency has no implications for the system proposed here. The well known objections against the parallel currency approach (see for example Pöhl (1989)) do not apply to the use of the Ecu proposed here.

The paper is, however, based on the premise that a wider use of the Ecu would be desirable to prepare the markets for the final stage, when the Ecu substitutes national currencies. See Steinherr (1990) for a discussion of other measures that could be taken to prepare the Ecu for its future role as the common currency.

The paper starts in section 2 by briefly summarizing the arguments for using a system of reserve requirements in stage II. It then turns to a discussion of two ways in which the ESCB could operate a system of required reserves. Section 3 describes the two systems:

i) A three-tier system under which the European Central Bank (ECB) (which is at the centre of the entire system called ESCB) would force national central banks to maintain reserve accounts in a special account. These reserves would be a proportion of certain national monetary aggregates and would be denominated in 'official' Ecus. Under this system the position of the ECB vis-à-vis national central banks would be similar to the position of national central banks towards commercial banks. This scheme is elaborated in Ciampi (1989).

ii) A two-tier system under which the ECB would impose a uniform Community reserve requirement on commercial banks that would be independent of national reserve requirements. The reserves would also be denominated in Ecu. This scheme is elaborated in Gros (1989a).

Section 4 then discusses a technical problem that would be common to both systems and section 5 discusses the comparative advantages of each system. Section 6 concludes.

2 Required Reserves During the Transition Towards EMU

Required reserves are not indispensable for an efficient monetary policy as shown by the example of countries that do not have a system of required reserves on commercial banks. For example, in the United Kingdom monetary policy relies on the demand of commercial banks for clearing balances and marginal accommodation of demands for liquidity. These instruments are sufficient to achieve control over domestic interest rates in the short run and the money supply in the long run.

However, this method of monetary control can not be used during the transition to EMU at the European level because as long as national currencies and national financial markets continue to exist most clearing will continue to be done at the national level. This implies that the demand for clearing balances will be in national currencies and go to national central banks.

The same line of reasoning applies to the accommodation of short term liquidity needs. For short term liquidity relief commercial banks could in principle go to other national financial markets. However, the foreign exchange transactions that would be needed to do this make this alternative in practice too expensive because of transactions costs. For example, a bid-ask spread of only 0.1% makes it uninteresting to go to another national financial market unless the weekly interest rate differential exceeds 500 basis points (assuming exchange rates are expected to remain constant). Commercial banks will therefore continue to rely on national central banks for short-term liquidity relief as long as national currencies exist.

The ECB could, of course, just intervene in the Ecu market and buy and sell Ecu denominated securities. Given the transaction costs that arise in the bundling and unbundling of Ecus the ECB could probably have considerable influence on Ecu interest rates in the short run if it did intervene in the Ecu market. However, it is difficult to see what purpose (other than short term interest smoothing) could be achieved by this.

Moreover, the ECB would be able to intervene in the Ecu market only if it can either create its own liabilities or has a line of credit with national central banks. In the latter case an intervention by the ECB, say an acquisition of Ecu denominated paper, would be equivalent to an expansionary policy in all member countries. In this case the ECB would therefore interfere directly with national monetary policy. In the former case (i.e. when the ECB can issue its own liabilities) the ECB would be able to create money and could possibly undercut the monetary policy of the country that constitutes the anchor for the exchange rate mechanism. This would not be acceptable for those who wish to maximize the chances that the system aims at price stability.

Another possibility that is often mentioned (see for example De Larosière (1989)) is to give the ECB the means to intervene in the foreign exchange markets vis-à-vis third currencies. However, while it is possible for a small open economy to define a monetary policy in terms of the exchange rate this would not be appropriate for the Community as it nears EMU because the Community is a big economy whose trade with the rest of the world accounts to less than 15 % of

GDP. It would therefore be difficult to provide an anchor for the Community monetary policy by relying only on foreign exchange interventions.

The British proposals for an 'evolutionary approach' (see HM Treasury (1989) and (1990) can also not be considered a viable alternative because it is highly unlikely that the markets would actually use the hard Ecu (which is in reality just a fixed basket Ecu).

A system of required reserves is therefore the most promising policy tool for the ECB during the transition.[2]

3 The Alternatives: Three-tier and Two-tier Systems

As mentioned in the introduction a system of reserve requirements at the European level could take two forms.

Ciampi (1989) proposes that the ECB could take a similar position vis-à-vis national central banks as the latter have vis-à-vis commercial banks. This would lead to a three-tier system under which the ECB would force national central banks to maintain reserve accounts in a special account. Figure 1 shows the organizational structure of this scheme.

The reserves to be held by national central banks with the ECB would be equal to a proportion of certain national monetary aggregates and would be denominated in 'official' Ecus. The latter requires that the automatic credit facilities of the EMS would have to be discontinued (unless the circuit for the new 'reserve Ecu' was isolated from the existing official Ecu).

Ciampi (1989) also mentions that the reserve requirement could be based on the liabilities of national central banks (i.e. the monetary base) or part of their assets, i.e. domestic credit. The former option would allow the ECB to control indirectly the overall monetary base in the Community. The latter option would require the ECB to coordinate interventions vis-à-vis third currencies if it wants to retain control over all sources of monetary base expansion. However, this latter option will not be considered any further in this paper because the part of domestic credit in reserve money varies too much across countries. In the case of the UK applying a reserve requirement on domestic credit (of the Bank of England) would not make sense because this item is negative.

An alternative, analyzed in more detail in Gros (1990), would be to allow the ECB to impose a uniform Community reserve requirement on commercial banks. This possibility is already foreseen in article 19 of the draft statutes elaborated by the central bank governors and the draft treaty submitted by the Commission for the IGC on EMU.[3]

---

[2] Bruni (1990) emphasizes the same point. It should also not be overlooked that the fact that most countries do have some form of reserve requirements, suggests that they are a convenient tool formonetary policy at the national level as well.

[3] This does not imply that the governors endorse the idea of using reserves on commercial banks during

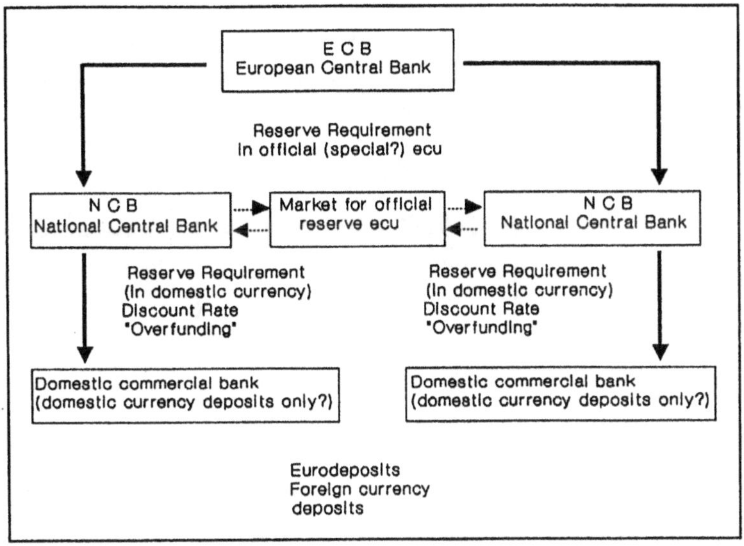

Figure 1. The 3-tier system

It is crucial for European reserve requirement to be independent of national reserve requirements, because only in this case it would constitute an independent policy instrument for the ECB.

Commercial banks would be able to satisfy this reserve requirement only by acquiring deposits with the ECB. These deposits might be called 'Ecu federal funds' in analogy with the federal funds banks in the US need to satisfy the reserve requirement imposed by the Fed. Since the ECB can always control its liabilities it would then be able to control the overall rate of monetary expansion in the Community in the same way a national central bank can control monetary expansion in the domestic banking system by limiting the supply of reserve money.

The reserve coefficient could be kept very low to minimize the tax it imposes on deposits within the Community. If the example of the US is a good guide a flat (average equal to marginal) reserve requirement of 1% should not lead to a significant displacement of deposits (it would involve an interest rate loss of only 8 basis points at an interest rate of 8%). But at the same time given that the total commercial bank deposits in the Community amount to over 2 600 billion Ecu,

during the transition. The governors might have had principally the final stage in mind for which they wanted to keep the option of using this instrument. Article 19 of the draft statutes mentions that these reserves might have to hold with national central banks. However, it is not important where commercial banks would have to hold their reserves. This is just a question of accounting as long as all decisions regarding the reserve requirement are taken by the ECB.

a 1% reserve requirement would lead to total reserves of over 26 billion Ecu, enough to provide a solid basis for a common monetary policy.[4]

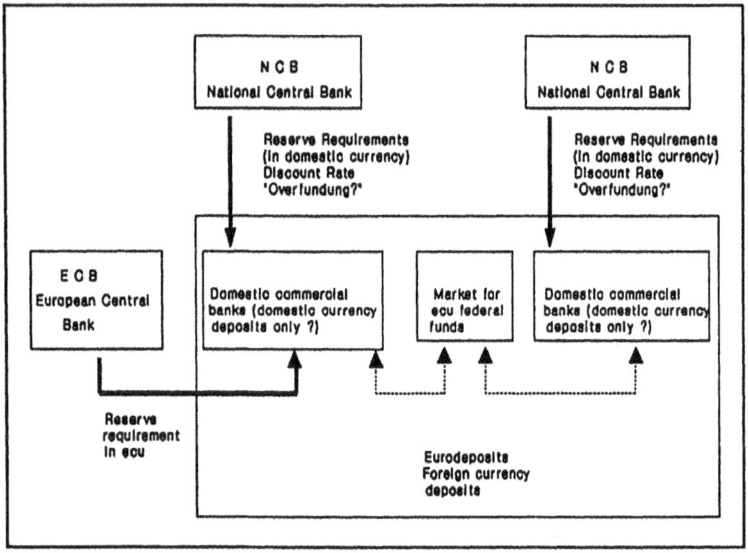

Figure 2. The 2-tier system

Figure 2 shows the organization structure of such a system under the assumption that the reserves have to be held with the ECB.

A feature that is common to both systems is that they can only provide an *additional* anchor for the common monetary policy. In the present EMS this anchor is provided by a mixture of dominance of the strongest currency and informal coordination. The introduction of a system of required reserves can only put an upper limit on monetary expansion, it therefore cannot be a constraint for any individual country (or even the average of all countries) if it desires to implement a more restrictive policy.

The comparative advantages and disadvantages of the two systems are discussed in section 5 below after a short digression on a technical problem that is common to both systems.

[4] The seigniorage the ECB would gain from a reserve coefficient of this order of magnitude would not be very large. If market interest rates are 8% the ECB would earn about 2 billion Ecu per annum on the 26 billion Ecu of securities it can buy with the proceeds from the required reserves. For this reason the fiscal implications of required reserves are not stressed in this paper. For more details on this issue see Bruni (1990) and Gros (1989).

4 Exchange Rate Changes and the Overall Demand for Reserves

Both systems would have to overcome a technical problem that arises because of the residual exchange rate changes within the bands that are still possible in stage II. Any intra-EMS exchange rate change would reduce the Ecu amount of the reserves to be held against deposits in the currency that is depreciating (this applies to the two-tier system; under the three-tier system the same effect applies to the reserves national central banks have to hold with the ECB). The Ecu amount of the reserves held against deposits in the currencies that are appreciating would, of course, increase, but it is not clear which effect will be stronger.

The net effect of exchange rate changes on the overall demand for reserves depends on the relationship between Ecu weights and the shares of national monetary aggregates as shown by the following simplified two currency representation of a reserve system that could be either of the two-tier or three-tier type:

The Ecu is defined as a basket with fixed amounts of DM (α) and FF (β):

$$(4.1) \qquad Ecu \equiv \alpha DM + \beta FF$$

The DM/FF exchange rate is denoted by e:

$$(4.2) \qquad DM \equiv eFF$$

The definitions (1) and (2) imply that the Ecu/DM exchange rate is given by:

$$(4.3) \qquad Ecu = (\alpha + \beta/e)DM$$

The required reserves, which are expressed in Ecu, are equal to a proportion, π, of the Community-wide total of the relevant monetary aggregate, M_{Ecu}. This aggregate could be the sum of all commercial bank deposits in the Community (in this case these equations represent the two-tier system) or the sum of national reserve monies (in this case these equations represent the three-tier system):

$$(4.4) \qquad RR = \pi M_{Ecu}$$

Denoting the two national reserve money supplies (or deposits with the national banking systems) by M_D and M_F, respectively, and using the DM/Ecu exchange rate, equation (3), this can be rewritten as:

$$(4.5) \qquad RR = \pi (\alpha + \beta/e) [M_D + eM_F]$$

A first question is whether (intra-Community) exchange rate changes affect the overall amount of reserves. Differentiating equation (5) yields:

$$(4.6) \qquad dRR = \pi\ [\alpha M_F - \beta M_D/e^2]\ de$$

The overall amount of reserves changes with the exchange rate if the expression in square brackets is different from zero. After some tedious algebraic manipulations (see Appendix) equation (6) can be rewritten in a more revealing form using the weight of the DM in the Ecu, denoted by $s_{Ecu,D}$, and the weight of deposits with the German banking system in the overall Community money supply, denoted by $s_{M,D}$. In elasticity form this yields:

$$(4.7) \qquad dRR/RR = (s_{Ecu,D} - s_{M,D})\ de/e$$

which establishes that the overall amount of reserves demanded by the Community banking systems is affected by the exchange rate only if the Ecu shares differ from the relative weights of the national money supplies. A one percentage change in the DM/FF exchange rate leads to a change in the demand for reserves equal to the difference between Ecu share of the DM and the weight of the German money supply in the overall Community aggregate.

Table 1. Ecu weights and shares of national monetary aggregates

	Monetary aggregate				
Share of:	Base Money	M1	M3	Domestic Credit	Ecu weights
Belgium	2.4	2.5	2.3	2.8	7.9
Denmark	0.9	3.2	2.1	1.6	2.5
Germany	30.7	22.5	27.1	39.7	30.1
Greece	2.0	0.6	1.3	0.7	0.8
Spain	15.9	7.7	7.7	8.6	5.3
France	12.7	18.5	15.2	12.0	19.1
Ireland	0.7	0.3	0.4	0.4	1.1
Italy	24.1	24.5	22.5	13.0	10.2
Netherlands	4.0	4.5	5.8	6.3	9.4
Portugal	1.3	1.0	1.3	0.9	0.8
United Kingdom	5.4	14.7	14.3	14.1	13.0
Sum of absolute difference with Ecu share	53.7	38.8	34.0	33.9	0.0
Memorandum item: Community total in billion Ecu	418.5	1053.9	2747.3	3419.9	

Source: Own calculations based on International Financial Statistics 1989 yearbook. N.b.: Weight of Germany increased by 20 % to account for the effects of reunification

How important is this effect in reality? It depends on the exact definition of 'money' used. Table 1 therefore shows the Ecu weights (as of the end of 1989) and the share of the major national monetary aggregates in the corresponding Community totals (the monetary aggregates are valued at average 1989 exchange rates).[5] This table shows that the 'monetary' weight of some countries varies considerably according to the aggregate used and that there are considerably discrepancies between the 'monetary' and Ecu weights.

These differences are mainly due to the large differences in required reserves since the major differences arise between the Ecu weights and the monetary base weights. For example, the Italian monetary base accounted for 24% of the overall monetary base of the Community (because of the 25% marginal reserve requirement on commercial banks) whereas the weight of the Italian lire in the Ecu was only 10%. Under the three tier reserve scheme based on reserve money a 1% depreciation of the lire vis-à-vis all other currencies would lead to a reduction in the overall amount of Ecu reserves of 0.14 %.[6]

The United Kingdom, which does not have required reserves on commercial banks, is an example of the opposite effect. Its weight in the monetary base of the Community was only 5% whereas the weight of the pound in the Ecu was 13%. A one percent depreciation of the pound would therefore increase the overall demand for Ecu reserves under the three tier system by 0.8%.

In general the correlation Ecu weights / shares of national monetary aggregates is less weak for the broader based monetary aggregates as can be seen in the last row of this table: the average absolute difference between monetary base and Ecu weights was 5.4% whereas the average absolute difference between domestic credit weights (the broadest monetary aggregate considered here) and Ecu weights was 3.4%.

Figure 3 tries to give an indication of the order of magnitude of the effect of exchange rate changes. Each line in this figure refers to a different base for the reserves and shows how the total amount of reserves would have varied in 1989 given actual 1989 monthly exchange rates. The line labelled base money (BM) therefore indicates the evolution of the total amount of reserves (in official Ecu) national central banks would have to hold with the ECB if the reserves were levied on the monetary base. The line labelled domestic credit (DC) does the same for the hypothesis that the reserves were levied on domestic credit. The line labelled M3 can represent both systems. For a two-tier system it indicates the effect of exchange rate changes on the overall demand for 'Ecu federal funds' and for a three-tier system it indicates the effect of exchange rate changes on the demand for official 'reserve Ecu' under the hypothesis that national central banks

---

[5] In this table the values for the German monetary aggregates have been increased by 20% to account for the increase that can be expected from unification. At the end of 1990 the part of M3 held in eastern Germany was about 14%, with a rapid recovery this proportion should rise to about 20 by 1994. The Ecu weights were not affected by this, reflecting the assumption that the Ecu weights will not be changed in 1994 and that there will be no major revaluation of the DM.

[6] This is obtained by multiplying (0.10 - 0.24) times 0.01 and converting it back into percentage terms by multiplying by 100.

have to hold reserves with the ECB that are proportional to the national broad money supply.[7]

Figure 3 suggests that exchange rate changes could affect the overall amount of reserves significantly. In some cases the monthly percentage changes exceed 4% at an annual rate. However, movements up and down tend to cancel out over time as long as the central rates are not changed. This effect should therefore be mainly a source of short run 'noise' without implications in the long run. Moreover, since during stage two exchange rates should vary less than in 1989, the effect should be less important than suggested by this data.

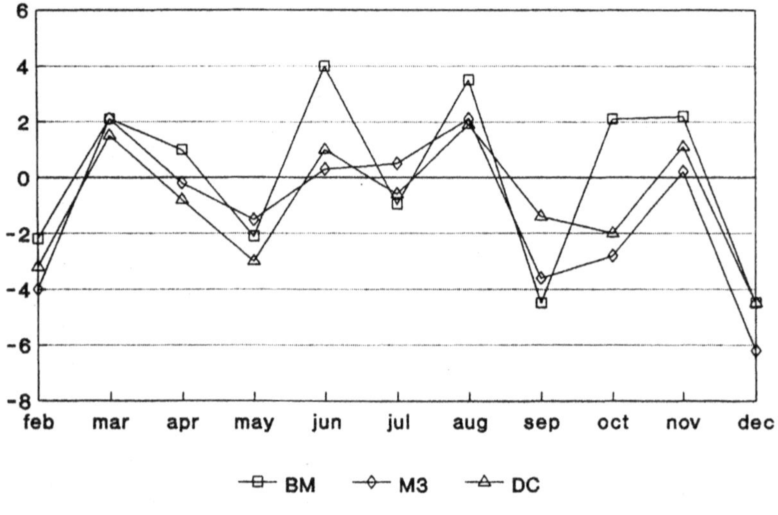

Figure 3. Total EC DC, M3 and BM in percentage changes using monthly currency/Ecu exchange rates from 1989 (Germ. +20%)

This effect should, however, not impair the ability of the ECB to conduct a stable policy based on a system of reserves since the net effect of exchange rate changes can be easily calculated in advance. The ECB could therefore neutralize this source of noise by simply changing the supply of reserves to accommodate automatically the effects of intra-Community exchange rate changes.

---

[7] Thygesen (1989) also argues in favor of basing the reserve requirement on a broader aggregate, he proposes total domestic credit of the banking system.

5 Three-tier Versus Two-tier Systems Compared

Although it would not be impossible to combine the two systems it is useful to consider the problems that could arise if either system were implemented on its own.[8]

One attraction of the three-tier system is that it anticipates the hierarchical structure between the ECB and national central banks that will arise once full EMU has been reached. If the reserves are levied on the monetary base the reserve coefficient could be raised over time until it reaches 100%. At this point national central banks would become just the equivalent of wholly owned subsidiaries of the ECB (Bini-Smaghi (1990)).

A three-tier system would, however, have the disadvantage that it would not eliminate the undercounting of the Community money supply that arises because national definitions of the main monetary aggregates often do not comprise foreign currency deposits and almost never comprise cross border deposits. For example, despite the Belgian-Luxembourg monetary union a deposit by a Belgian resident with a bank in Luxembourg is not counted in Belgium because it is not with a Belgian bank, nor is such a deposit counted in Luxembourg because it is a deposit of a non-resident. Another example is the United Kingdom which uses explicitly the aggregate 'Sterling M4' which excludes deposits in foreign currency. It is apparent that imposing the reserve requirement directly on commercial banks would allow eliminate this issue and would allow the ECB to control the total amount of all liquid monetary assets that can be expected to finance expenditure within the Community.

The overall importance of this undercounting is difficult to estimate since there is no systematic data on the currency breakdown of foreign currency deposits and of the country of origin of cross-border deposits. The scarce data that is available suggests that this phenomenon is not yet very important. Bini-Smaghi and Vori (1990) show that in the big member countries the ratio of foreign currency deposits to domestic deposits is below 10%. Since deposits in Community currencies are generally below one half of all foreign currency deposits, foreign currency deposits are still relatively small in relation to national money supplies.

Cross-border deposits (i.e. a deposit that is denominated in the currency of the bank, but whose owner is a non-resident) seem to be more important. However, most of this international activity is interbank business and has therefore have a no direct impact on the size of the liquid assets that are held by the non-banking sector. For that reason cross-border deposits are still relatively unimportant. For example, at the end of 1989 in Germany sight liabilities of domestic non-banks were equal to 263 billion DM whereas sight liabilities to non-bank non-residents were equal to only 23 billion DM. For time liabilities the share of non-residents was even lower. This implies that for the broader monetary aggregates these deposits of non-residents, which are not considered relevant for domestic monetary

---

[8] This section is based on Gros (1990).

policy because their relationship with domestic spending is not clear, are probably also of minor importance.

However, even though the problem of 'undercounting' the European money supply is at present not a serious one, it is clear that its importance only can increase with the increasing integration in financial markets. So by entering stage II it will probably be an important factor.

A three-tier system with reserves proportional to the national monetary base would have to deal with the implications of differences in national reserve requirements and therefore national multipliers. This problem has two dimensions:

i) If there is a shift in monetary base between countries with different multipliers the overall monetary aggregates would be affected: a shift from a country with a low multiplier (high reserve requirement) to a country with a high multiplier (low or no reserve requirement) would increase the total amount of deposits within the Community unless the ECB reacts to any of those disturbances.
ii) National central banks could conduct an expansionary national monetary policy by reducing the domestic reserve requirements. In order to keep control over the Community total the ECB would again have to react to this development.

This suggests that a reserve requirement on the national monetary base would lead to difficulties unless national reserve requirements have been harmonized. This is different under the two-tier system since the total of deposits in the entire Community cannot increase as long as the ECB does not increase its liabilities vis-à-vis commercial banks (i.e. as long as it does not supply more 'federal funds'). The two-tier system could therefore be implemented even before national reserve requirements have been harmonized.

The residual changes in exchange rates that are still possible in stage II are likely to pose another problem to a three-tier system even if they do not affect the overall amount as discussed in the previous section. Under the three-tier system the central bank of a currency that is depreciating would have excess reserves and would therefore be in a stronger position than the central bank of the currency that is appreciating. This would not be a problem if one could rely on the emergence of a smoothly functioning market in these 'official reserve Ecu'. But since central banks are not strictly profit maximizers and since only four central banks would dominate this market it is not likely that a central bank that experiences an appreciation of its own currency would be able to buy the 'official reserve Ecus' it needs.

In contrast, under the two-tier system there would be a market among commercial banks that would redistribute the 'Ecu federal funds' smoothly if exchange rates change (or if there is currency substitution).

This market for the 'Ecu federal funds' provides another argument for the two-tier system. Through its operations on this market the ECB would have, from the start, a direct contact with a Community-wide market. It would therefore immediately start to acquire the expertise that it will anyway need in stage III, when it acquires the exclusive responsibility for monetary policy. The interest rate on the market for 'Ecu federal funds' would also provide a convenient signal about the stance of the common monetary policy.

Finally, there seems to be no legal basis for the three-tier system. Article 19 of the draft statutes for the ESCB gives the ECB the power to impose reserve requirements on commercial banks, but not on national central banks. The ECB would therefore not be able to use sanctions to make sure that national central banks actually stay within the constraints imposed by the required reserves.

6 Concluding Remarks

This note has emphasized the usefulness of a system of reserve requirements to provide an anchor for the common monetary policy during the transition to full EMU. Since reserve requirements are a tax on deposits they are not the ideal instrument of monetary control in general, and, as the experience of countries without reserve requirements shows, this instrument is not indispensable for an effective monetary policy. A sound monetary policy can also be based on the demand of the public for cash and the demand of commercial banks for clearing balances with the central bank. However, these two instruments cannot be used as a base for a *common* monetary policy in stage II (probably even during stage IIIa, i.e. before the introduction of a common currency) because cash would still be in national currency and because the clearing in national currencies would still be done at the national level.

Imposing a small, uniform reserve requirement on all deposits held with a commercial bank in the Community would give the European Central Bank a convenient instrument with which it could always put an *upper limit* on total monetary expansion in the Community. The asymmetry in this system would provide a guarantee that it could never be used for a policy that is more expansionary than that of the most stability orientated member.

Appendix

Dividing equation (4.6) by equation (4.5) yields:

$$\text{(A.1)} \qquad \frac{dRR}{RR} = \frac{\alpha M_F - \beta M_D/e^2}{(\alpha + \beta/e)(M_D + eM_F)}\, de$$

adding and subtracting αM_D to the nominator (and multiplying by e/e) yields:
after some simplifications this yields:
The first term in the square brackets is the weight of the DM in the Ecu, $s_{Ecu,D}$,

(A.2)
$$\frac{dRR}{RR} = \frac{\alpha e M_F + \beta M_D - \alpha M_D - \beta M_D/e}{(\alpha + \beta/e)(M_D + eM_F)} \frac{de}{e}$$

(A.3)
$$\frac{dRR}{RR} = [\frac{\alpha}{\alpha + \beta/e} - \frac{M_D}{M_D + eM_F}] \frac{de}{e}$$

and the second term represents the weight of the German money supply in the overall money supply of the Community, $s_{M,D}$.

Q.E.D.

References

Bini-Smaghi L (1990) Progressing towards European Monetary Unification: Selected Issues and Proposals. Temi di discussione del Servizio Studi No 133, Rome, Banca d'Italia, April

Bini-Smaghi L and Vori S (1990) Competition, Hegemony and Monetary Unification, mimeo, Rome, Banca d'Italia, July

Bruni F (1990) Il Regime della Riserva Obbligatoria e l'Integrazione Europea dei Mercati Finanziari, mimeo Univeristà Commerciale Luigi Bocconi, Milan, November

Ciampi CA (1989) An Operational Framework for an Integrated Monetary Policy in Europe. In: Collection of papers annexed to Delors Report, pp 225-232

Committee for the Study of Economic and Monetary Union (1989) Report on Economic and Monetary Union in the European Community (the Delors Report), Office of Publications of the European Communities, Luxembourg

De Larosière J (1989) First Stages towards the Creation of a European Reserve Bank - the Creation of a European Reserve Fund. In: Collection of papers annexed to Delors Report, pp 177-184

Gros D (1988) The EMS and the Determination of the European Price Level, Centre for European Policy Studies, CEPS Working Document No 34 (Economic), Brussels

Gros D (1989a) Seigniorage in the EC: The Effects of the EMS and Financial Market Integration, Washington, International Monetary Fund, IMF/WP/89/7, January

Gros D (1989b) Paradigms for the Monetary Union of Europe, Journal of Common Market Studies, Vol XXVII, No 3, March, pp 219-230

Gros D (1990) The Ecu in the Common Monetary Policy, ECU Newsletter No 32, April, pp 14 - 19

Gros D and Thygesen N (1988) The EMS: Achievements, Current Issues and Directions for the Future, Centre for European Policy Studies, CEPS Paper No 35, Brussels

Gros D and Thygesen N (1990) Concrete Steps towards Monetary Union. In: Centre for European Policy Studies, CEPS Paper No 44, Brussels

HM Treasury (1989) An Evolutionary Approach to Economic and Monetary Union, London, November

Kneeshaw JT and Van den Berg P (1989) Changes in Central Bank Money Market Operating Procedures in the 1980s, Bank for International Settlements, Economic Papers, No 23, January

Lamfalussy A (1989) Macro-coordination of Fiscal Policies in an Economic and Monetary Union in Europe. In: Collection of papers annexed to Delors Report, pp 91-125

Pöhl KO (1989) The further Development of the European Monetary System. In: Collection of papers annexed to Delors Report, pp 131-155, September

Russo M and Tullio G (1988) Monetary Policy Coordination within the European Monetary System: is there a Rule? Ch 11 in: Francesco Giavazzi, Stefano Micossi and Marcus Miller (eds) The European Monetary System, Banca d'Italia, Centro Interuniversitario di Studi Teorici par la Politica Economica and Centre for Economic Policy Research, Cambridge University Press, Cambridge, pp 292-320

Steinherr A (1990) Roles for the ECU in the Process of Achieving European Monetary Union, mimeo, Luxemburg European Investment Bank

Thygesen N (1989) A European Central Banking System - Some Analytical and Operational Considerations. In: Collection of papers annexed to Delors Report, pp 157-176

Fiscal Policy Implications of the European Union*

Pompeo Della Posta
Dipartimento di Scienze Economiche, Facoltà di Economia e Commercio, Università di Pisa, and Department of Economics, European University Institute, Firenze

1 Introduction

The issue of fiscal policy in the future European Union as envisaged in the Delors Report first and more precisely defined in the Maastricht Treaty has already received the attention of many international economists. The most different prescriptions of economic policy arise from their analyses. The attempt to clarify the field, looking for a general, common framework from which to derive the different results by imposing one assumption or the others, is not an easy one, because quite often their economic frameworks have nothing to share with each other: Mundell-Fleming static models appear together with dynamic and intertemporal ones; one country and two or more country models; game theoretic approaches with different solution concepts; speculative attacks models, public finance approach and political equilibrium analyses. The result is a divergent span of opinions about the introduction of binding fiscal rules. The game theoretic approach, however, seems to provide the general framework sought for, so that many of the results obtained by the different authors can be read as the result of separate games played by the same domestic fiscal authority with different players.

Following the approach taken by the Commission of the European Communities (1990) in analyzing the issue of fiscal policy, I am going to consider and evaluate the different arguments in favour of *fiscal discipline* those for *autonomy* and those for *coordination*, by summarising the contributions given so far while making my own points. No clearcut conclusion arises, given the many possible "states of the world". There are countries for whom the imposition of fiscal constraints is not necessary, because their reputation and credibility (due for example to the way their political system is institutionally organized) allow them the autonomous use of the fiscal instrument to respond efficiently to negative shocks. But there are others which seem to have misused their fiscal autonomy. There are instances in which a coordination of fiscal policies seems to be the first best, but others in which autonomy is optimal and even more instances in which the best form of coordination is the imposition of binding rules. The only reasonable aim of this

---

* The paper has been written during a three months stage at the Directorate General for the Economic and Financial Affairs of the Commission of the European Communities, in Brussels. I wish to thank my Conseiller, Alain Morisset and the economists working in his division for the useful discussions. For the same reason I would like to thank Lucio Renzo Pench. Obviously, none of them can be held responsible for my mistakes.

paper is to try to shed some light on the reasoning behind the various policy prescriptions proposed for the running of fiscal policies in the future European Union. While doing so, though, the arguments in favour of the imposition of binding rules seem to prevail over the others.

Paragraph 2 summarizes critically the main arguments in favour of the imposition of fiscal discipline, autonomy and coordination. Paragraph 3 tries to disentangle the conclusions reached in the previous one by using game theory as a common framework. The different possible games played by a domestic Treasury are considered: with a domestic Central Bank, with a supranational monetary authority, with a foreign Treasury and with the private sector. Most of the conclusions reached by the authors who have dealt with the issue of fiscal policy in a monetary union can actually be interpreted as the result of one game or the others. In paragraph 4, I consider the prescriptions contained in the Maastricht Treaty and I criticize and comment on them. Appendix A contains a modification of a tax-smoothing model proposed by van der Ploeg, to show that the presence of a "copycatting" effect in a European Monetary Union (EMU) makes the relation between average tax rates and fiscal expansion relatively more expansionary compared to the case in which such effect is ignored. Appendix B contains a very simple analysis of the possible effects of the Maastricht rules on interest rates and debt/GDP ratio. The conclusions summarize the main points of this article.

2 Discipline, Autonomy and Coordination

2.1 Discipline: Arguments in Favour of the Imposition of Binding Rules

The idea of imposing budgetary rules for the countries adhering to the European Community lies already in the "1974 Convergence Decision" taken by the European Council, which called for establishing Community guidelines for the main aggregates of budgetary policy. However, such an idea was going more in the direction of allowing a supranational body, the Council, to meet on a periodic basis to revise the national budgets, rather than fixing once and for all binding and unmodifiable rules as prescribed by the Maastricht Treaty.[1]

The main argument in favour of the imposition of binding rules has to do with the risk of *financial instability* as a result of unsustainable positions. Giovannini

[1] Padoa Schioppa (1987) opposes constitutional and economic policy arguments to such an idea. The ministers composing the Council are the same who have national responsibilities and in many countries the budgetary authority is the Parliament so that no fiscal policy commitments can really be taken by ministers meeting in the Council. From the economic policy point of view the objection has to do with the difficulties in fine-tuning the fiscal policy given its substantial differences with respect to the implementation of the monetary policy. As we will see, Tanzi (1989) raises the same doubts as to the possibility of using fiscal policies for fine tuning.

and Spaventa (1991) point it out: when the expenditure (tax) gap, i.e. the difference between the current level of expenditure (tax) and the level necessary to guarantee the solvency of the country is such that the repayment of the debt is not feasible within a finite time horizon, then the domestic crisis may propagate to other countries. But the two authors don't even believe that the intertemporal budget constraint be operationally of any help because of the difficulties in predicting the future time path of the primary surplus.[2] In their view then, the externality produced by structural fiscal imbalances is the worrying one rather than the one resulting from aggregate demand, as we will see: they don't find any problem in the effects of a fiscal policy expansion on interest rates or inflation (as Wyplosz (1990) does, for example) but rather in the fact that high public debt may be unsustainable because it cannot be repaid by higher taxes, given the high degree of indexation in Southern European Countries and the instability of inflationary expectations, both preventing the introduction of higher indirect tax rates.

Looking at the performance of some countries adhering to the EMS, they conclude that no fiscal constraints have been felt by EMS member countries. Moreover, the complete liberalization of capital markets, far from threatening the domestic Treasuries, might in fact favour the financing of the debt through the *appropriation of community savings* as long as the exchange rate is reasonably stable and there persist interest rate differentials. Higher real interest rates and lower seigniorage imply that future generations will have to bear the burden of the debt. Monetary and exchange rate fields are unlikely, also in the future, to provide sanctions and incentives leading to fiscal discipline, so they propose to correct politicians' preferences (the Alesina type of argument) through the adoption of institutional changes and/or set a no-entry clause to increase the cost of debt financing.

As a matter of fact, it cannot be ruled out that markets might accept blindly to subscribe to fragile financial situations up until the moment in which, in the absence of a lender of last resort, an abrupt change of the market perceptions causes the drying up of any financing possibility and therefore a financial crisis. This is why the imposition of binding rules would be a correct measure to be introduced.

Ballabriga et al. (1991) show, using cointegration analysis, that *many European countries have already violated their intertemporal budget constraint* and calculate the expenditure gap and/or the tax gap necessary to gain a sustainable position. Given the violation of the intertemporal budget constraint, the imposition of fiscal guidelines finds a sound rationale. However, although recognizing a limited reliability of the market mechanism, they do not deny the role of short term fiscal policy stabilization, so some room for manoeuvre should be left into the hands of the fiscal authorities. In terms of sustainability, the effects of a larger financial area, as it has been already observed, makes a large outstanding stock of public

---

[2] Their critic is probably countered by the prescriptions, contained in the Maastricht Treaty, relative to the adoption of medium term convergence plans to be subject to the Commission monitoring. The submission of convergence plans should allow the markets to anticipate the future time path of macroeconomic variables and to evaluate the sustainability of the debt.

debt more likely to be absorbed at "tolerable" interest rates. Such an effect then, is likely to wipe out the fact that in a hard currency regime the need to keep an homogeneous monetary growth imposes a constraint on fiscal policy, if unsustainable fiscal positions want to be avoided. Their conclusion is that a wide array of both fiscal deficits and debt/GDP ratios is allowed by the market even in presence of the strict monetary requirements of a hard currency regime, so that the resulting risk of instability calls for the imposition of fiscal rules.

Bradekamp and Deppler (1989) see in the *elimination of the currency premium on interest rates*, when moving to a system of irrevocably fixed exchange rates, a weakening of the fiscal discipline. This would result in a once-and-for-all step increase in the amount of debt which the public would be willing to hold and a reduction in the debt service burden. According to them, then, an interest rate reduction should result independently of any convergence plan.[3] Furthermore an *increased solidarity* due to the participation to a common exchange rate system might imply the temptation for fiscal adventurism. The only reason for not fearing such a possibility, apart from imposing strict rules, lies in the open threat expressed by the market when capital is free to flow out of the domestic country at any time. In the system envisaged by the Maastricht Treaty, for example, such a threat should be enough to convince any undisciplined country that it is not the case to take the risk, given both the independence of the European Central Bank and the presence of a no bail-out clause. As a matter of fact, it is not clear why such a clause would be necessary once the independence of the European Central Bank is firmly declared, and above all once binding fiscal rules are introduced.

Jaans (1989) is very critical towards the move from EMS to EMU, seeing the *disappearance of both the intra-community foreign exchange market and the domestic balance of payments* as a main cause of concern. As a matter of fact, fiscal expansion causes in the short run, for a given level of output, an excess demand, inflationary tensions and pressures on the exchange rate, all pointing towards a deterioration in the current account positions. The removal of these two constraints, then, implies the relaxation of a clear and effective "spontaneous" market mechanism capable of assuring the orderly functioning of the economic system, and hinders the capacity to identify fiscal misalignments and to take the necessary corrective measures pointed out by market pressures.

I have to observe that even during the years of existence of the EMS the above mentioned constraints don't seem to have been binding as shown by the explosive public debt performance of some European countries. Still, such an observation doesn't imply that the removal of intra-European foreign reserves and current account might not make things even worse or that the debt explosion during the EMS period might have been caused just by the lack of such binding fiscal rules, given the already insufficient bite of the external constraints. A logical consequence of the arguments suggested by Jaans (1989), although not mentioned by him, is that once the EMU is chosen as an option for the future development of the EMS, the only way to substitute for the role played by market mechanisms

---

[3] In appendix B I present, instead, a simple model in which interest rates react to announced stabilization plans.

is to impose binding rules on the fiscal authorities, which is what both the Delors Report and the Maastricht Treaty propose.

Tanzi (1989) takes a position in favour of fiscal rules as opposed to cooperation. A policy of *fine-tuning would not be successful* because forecasts are generally not reliable and they are not jointly agreed. Even when these requirements are satisfied, the validity of the forecasts has a shorter time span than the time required for the implementation. Furthermore, the economic objectives to be achieved through coordination are not necessarily agreed not only between two or more different countries, but even within a country itself, where the monetary authority and the fiscal authority might well follow different objectives. While monetary policy is run by officials, for example, fiscal policy is decided by governments who have to be re-elected by the current generation of citizens and whose possible blame coming from future generations is likely to be discounted very heavily, in fact, it's likely to be ignored. This explains why, in the EMS experience, what has been achieved in the monetary field could not be achieved in the fiscal field as well. Coordination of fiscal policies may be very difficult to organize, so it might well take the form of binding rules. From a theoretical point of view, however, Tanzi (1989) recognizes a negative bias of fiscal policy as a result of the high degree of openess of the economy, which would call for some international coordination to promote fiscal expansion.

The very nature of the fiscal policy decision making though, provides a strong rationale for imposing budgetary rules, as pointed out by Corsetti and Roubini (1992). Verifying that tax smoothing behaviour does not explain the creation of fiscal deficits, they conclude that *the creation of public debt is only produced by political distorsions*. Ruling out any economic foundation behind fiscal deficits, they claim that the only way to control such a political bias is to impose binding rules to "tie the hands" of the fiscal authority after monetary policy has been tied just by joining a fixed exchange rate system with free capital mobility.

One additional rationale for the imposition of binding fiscal rules seems to me *the need to assure the adhesion of the virtuous European countries*. They might ask themselves why should they take any risk of possible future financial instabilities due to the excessive exposure of some of the undisciplined countries adhering to the monetary union. So, even if the probability that a high debt situation might cause confidence crises has a small positive value, such a value might just be enough to induce "virtuous" countries to refuse their participation. The imposition of binding rules, then, might have the simple but fundamental role of reassuring the strong countries that the "weak ones" will have to become virtuous themselves and that no risks at all will arise in joining in a monetary union together with them. Accepting binding fiscal rules would just be an investment in the reputation of the domestic Treasury.

Credibility problems, then, also call for the imposition of binding rules. An undisciplined fiscal behaviour has a low but still positive probability to cause a confidence crisis into the domestic country. Even in presence of a no bail-out clause, the countries of the community might not be in a position to let the country alone to stand the confidence crisis, because of its negative externality on the whole community. So, assuming a lower cost of the community intervention with respect to the community cost of the bankruptcy of a single country, even in presence of a no bail-out clause such a commitment will be violated, i.e. it is not credible. Recognizing such a non credibility might induce domestic fiscal authorities to behave in an unconstrained way. The only way to make the no bail-out condition credible is to impose strict fiscal rules to exclude at the outset the possibility of a confidence crisis.

Among other things, fiscal discipline rests, as it has been observed, on the idea that there might be an *undue appropriation of savings* from other community countries favoured by the higher interest rates offered by the high debt/undisciplined ones. To avoid such an appropriation, the high interest rates are likely to spread all over Europe, causing however the risk of hampering growth.[4] Still, there exists a third possibility, already mentioned: the markets might not be able to discriminate the debt situations of different countries adhering to the same monetary union so the initial low interest rates for both high debt and low debt countries would result. In such a case, then, the appropriation of community savings by undisciplined governments would still take place and even at lower costs. The resulting picture, therefore, is not positive for the disciplined governments participating in a monetary union together with more lax ones: independently of the functioning of the market, the expected loss is surely positive when foreign countries run divergent fiscal policies leading to divergent debt positions. The only possibility for not producing a negative externality obtains when the markets are capable of assigning the correct risk premiums to high debt countries, so that risk averse financial investors will not be attracted by the higher nominal interest rates and virtuous countries will not be obliged to raise their interest rates to face the competition of the "vicious" ones. But this view is neither shared by the Delors Report nor by the Maastricht Treaty, where the role of market perceptions in providing strong and compelling signals is seriously questioned.

2.2 Flexibility: Arguments in Favour of Autonomy

Krugman (1990) simply discards the problem of fiscal discipline as a non-problem: there isn't any theoretical reason, according to him, to claim that fiscal policy should be constrained when a domestic country decides to join a fixed exchange rate system.

Wyplosz (1990) believes in the *ability of the market to signal the risk of default* due to a positive difference between the unsustainable and the sustainable debt level: the real interest rate will reflect such a difference so as to impose a constraint on fiscal expansion. Moreover, in a monetary union, the domestic monetary policy is lost so that in the absence of a strong, conspicuous federal budget capable of intervening when temporary shocks hit the economy, *the*

---

[4] Fiscal repression allows a domestic economy to avoid the high interest rates that the high debt requires in an open economy. The imposition of capital controls, however, protects also the foreign countries from the negative interest rate externality otherwise coming from the less disciplined ones.

domestic fiscal instrument remains the only available.

Given the loss of the monetary instrument in a fixed exchange rate system, Van der Ploeg (1990) also stresses the need for maintaining national fiscal policy autonomy for *internal aggregate demand support.*

To support their arguments one can observe that the fiscal expansion of the 80s' in Benelux, for example, seems to be the effect of an automatic stabilizer to soften the social cost of an externally originated recession. So, preventing such a possibility may be very costly in terms of social welfare.

Masson and Melitz (1990) use the results given by the simulations performed using MULTIMOD, the econometric model of the IMF, to conclude against the imposition of binding rules. They assume a two arguments objective function for each of the two open economy countries composing their model. The two countries (they have in mind Germany and France) are assumed to assign different weights to their targets (prices and current account). Assuming also that the economy is hit by different kinds of symmetric shocks they prove the need for some fiscal autonomy to allow the minimization of the two different loss functions: *fiscal autonomy is necessary to avoid a compelled homogeneization of national preferences.* Their conclusions, although well grounded in their model, lack of a simple element: debt is not an argument of the objective function so that no merit can be assigned to a stabilization calling for fiscal discipline.

2.3 Coordination: The Role of Externalities

Externalities from one country to another call for policy coordination, although they are not quantitatively relevant when countries are small.[5] Bradekamp and Deppler (1989) suggest to distinguish between the externalities pre-existing to the fixed exchange rate regime and those having to do with such a system. Only the latter should call for policy coordination, although I don't really see why it should be so. They distinguish between two main sources of externalities: *a fiscal expansion in one country would draw partly on other country's savings and would cause higher real interest rates in both countries*, crowding out private investments. In the long run high real interest rates might negatively affect the potential growth rate so as to reduce the welfare of future generations. The higher interest rate might also cause an appreciation of the common exchange rate vis-à-vis third country currencies and might oblige the other countries within the currency area to stand adjustment costs, for example in the labour market to avoid unemployment, not internalized by the domestic country.

The need for coordination results also from the *strategic beggar-thy-neighbour policy in response to exogenous symmetric shocks* hitting two countries in a flexible exchange rate regime. Each of them will try to follow a fiscal expansion and a tight monetary policy[6] to appreciate the currency and export inflation. Without

[5] In that case Backus et al. (1988) (quoted in Bradekamp and Dappler (1989)), show that decentralized and uncoordinated policymaking is efficient.

[6] As we have seen, Masson and Melitz (1990), instead, examine the case of fixed exchange rates in

coordination the exchange rate won't move and the fiscal-monetary mix will be distorted. With fixed exchange rates such an incentive disappears but still there are externalities involved because of the effect on third currencies. The current account problems, for example, that in a non-MU are relative only to the expanding country, in a MU belong to the whole union, so this externality needs to be internalized to control the resulting expansionary bias.

Van der Ploeg (1990) makes the same point as de Grauwe (1985) as we will see: he stresses strongly the need for budgetary coordination on the grounds that *EMU will impose a restrictive bias on domestic fiscal policies*, rather than an expansionary one. The European Treasuries will find themselves in a prisoner's dilemma situation when deciding who should provide the public good "fiscal expansion" to be benefitted all over Europe: no one will want to concede and the most likely outcome, in absence of coordination, would be a Pareto-inferior Nash equilibrium. So, if on one hand the move from EMS to EMU will eliminate the beggar-thy-neighbour attempt to appreciate the currency in response to a symmetric shock so as to export inflation, on the other hand the competition among European treasuries might well lead to an under-dimensioning of the public sector. Obviously, with full price flexibility and/or labour mobility, no problems of government intervention would arise. In presence of such rigidities, however, there is a need for a federal fund to redistribute income and take care of socially unacceptable regional imbalances. The realization of such a transfer scheme might actually be interpreted as a way to guarantee the success of the fixed exchange rate system. Moral hazard problems are considered less relevant than the ones the transfer scheme would solve. In van der Ploeg's view, then, the possibility of a tight fiscal stance is produced by the lack of incentives in running expansionary policies to counter a common adverse supply shock for both the leader of the EMS and the followers: a fiscal expansion, as seen above, would cause a generalized *higher level of interest rates that will crowd out the initial employment effect* so as to discourage in the first place the implementation of expansionary policies. However, a domestic fiscal expansion might well cause a positive employment effect on a foreign country when the *interest rate externality* is outweighted by the *current account externality*. While other economists interpret the move from EMS to EMU, as we have seen, as the elimination of the current account constraint on the optimization performed by a domestic country so as to give to it an expansionary bias, van der Ploeg sees it as a further reason for constraining budgetary positions: a fiscal expansion, although not causing balance of payments problems any more, might still *favour the current account and therefore the employment of a foreign country implying a possible reduction of domestic employment.*

Van der Ploeg (1990) also observes that given the adoption in a EMU of a common inflation rate, lower than the optimal one for high debt countries, taxes will have to increase to compensate for such a revenue loss. On the other hand, he proposes also a simplified tax-smoothing approach to show that EMU leads to

---

which two countries, although having different objective functions, find an optimal policy mix.

an inefficient revenue-mix of taxes and inflation to cover fiscal expenditure, given the low inflation rate imposed by the leader country. From first order conditions, results a negative relation between optimal tax rate and fiscal deficit: a contractionary fiscal bias will result.

Two critics can be moved to such a stylized tax smoothing model and to the conclusions reached there. The first one is that the empirical validity of the public finance approach, according to which tax rates and inflation rates are random walks and move together to smooth out distortionary taxation, is rejected by recent works (see Corsetti and Roubini (1992), for example). The second one is that a simple modification of the model, considering also the need for a domestic country not to impose a divergent tax rate with respect to the lower foreign one in order to avoid the erosion of the domestic tax base, reduces the deflationary bias of fiscal policies with respect to the non competition case. The simple modification of the van der Ploeg's (1990) model is contained in appendix A.

One further reason in favour of the coordination of fiscal policies lies in the fact that *the European Community budget isn't large enough to be used countercyclically*: coordination among member states will be required to face asymmetric shocks given that the central budget of the community is very limited in size (only 2% of the community GDP).

Lamfalussy (1989) pushes strongly in favour of the coordination of fiscal policies without really distinguishing it from the concept of fiscal discipline obtained by limiting the scope of discretion at national level. He lists four reasons for coordination, not all of them convincing. The *need for an appropriate fiscal policy for the union as a whole* is probably the less objectable given its political content. Another point is the *need for convergence in budgetary positions during the transition*. Less convincing are the arguments, already pointed out by Bradekamp and Deppler (1989), relative to the *need to avoid disproportionate use of community savings by a single country* and the possible *bias towards lack of fiscal restraint*. His argument for claiming a common fiscal policy however, seems to rest on the need for the whole community to have an additional instrument beyond the monetary policy. It is not clear though, why this instrument should be taken away from the hands of the national authorities which, being so, would be the ones without instruments available. It looks to me that Lamfalussy is just ignoring the need for a fiscal authority, no matter at what hierarchical level, to be able to soften the impact of external shocks: discretion at national level might well be limited by imposing binding rules, but only if the federal authority is able to intervene substantially to ensure regional equity, which is not the case in the future EMU given the still limited federal budget compared to the European GDP, as Lamfalussy seems not to consider. It should be noted that my reasoning leads to opposite conclusions relative to the ones reached by Lamfalussy: in his view the use of the aggregate federal budget to correct the outcome of independent national policies, is alternative to the limitation of the scope of discretion at the national level in the absence of any federal instrument. Moreover, preferring a centralized federal budget to decentralized, national ones, *contradicts the principle of subsidiarity*, strongly invoked in the Treaties of the European Communities.
The difference between the view taken by Van der Ploeg (1990) and the one taken

by Lamfalussy (1989) lies in the different assumption about the size of the domestic economy running an expansionary fiscal policy compared to the rest of the Monetary Union. When the size is negligible no generalized higher interest rates are observed, while a larger country is very likely to affect the common interest rate. Relevant is also the belief relative to the functioning of the market mechanism: when markets are working efficiently, by signalling the existence of default risks (implicit or explicit), therefore charging positive risk premiums on the interest rate to be paid by high indebted countries, such an expectation might prevent the implementation of expansionary fiscal policies as maintained by Van der Ploeg; on the other hand, when not much confidence is given to the capability of the market to signal the existence of country-specific risks, one should not have any reason to conclude that fiscal policy is deflationary-biased. The divergent policy-prescriptions proposed by Van der Ploeg and by Lamfalussy follow consequently their assumptions and/or believes.

Padoa Schioppa et al. (1987) also favour coordination of fiscal policies but, as it is for van der Ploeg (1990), for *fears of a deflationary bias* without coordination. So the reason is definitely opposite to the one leading Lamfalussy (1989) to propose budgetary rules or coordination because of a possible inflationary-bias. However, although critical towards the idea of imposing binding rules considering both the limited size of the European federal budget and the experience of the existing federal states, they conclude that "if monetary integration were to move to a qualitatively more advanced level, budgetary policy at the community level might have to extend beyond the limited potential of coordination" (p.86) implying perhaps the need for a strong federal government to intervene at the regional level to guarantee equity.

Wyplosz (1990) studies the effect of a monetary union on the externalities produced by a domestic fiscal expansion. He considers a time horizon in which price changes become possible as a result of government policies. In his analysis possible effects of a temporary fiscal expansion are both an increase of the interest rates (due to demand pressure) and an increase in the domestic relative prices (due to demand pressure and for a given output). Permanent fiscal expansions, on the other hand are supposed to produce ambiguous results. Strangely enough he sees as a possible effect of the competition for the provision of public goods and services in a monetary union a higher than optimal government size, although he recognizes that the tax competition should have opposite effects on the size of the government i.e. lower taxes should imply lower government spending.[7] Looking at the experience of the United States, he concludes that a monetary union should increase the convergence towards the lower tax rates, induced by factors' mobility and governments' competition to maximize the tax base, what he calls "copycatting". At the same time interest rate equalization should result and the relative price effect should also be at work. He observes that many European countries with high debt are already running a primary surplus and therefore

[7] We will see that the conclusion reached using Van der Ploeg's (1990) model in presence of "copycatting" is just opposite: a lower average tax rate implies a relatively more expansionary optimal fiscal policy.

concludes that *the budget constraint is binding*. My obvious observation is that this is not the case for a country like Italy, for example, and above all that, as shown by Ballabriga et al. (1991), the intertemporal budget constraint has already been violated by many European countries. Following his conclusions, then, Wyplosz (1991) favours flexible forms of coordination like multilateral surveillance or a larger size of federal budget, capable of assuring domestic countries against the risk of negative shocks. Padoa Schioppa (1990) as well, agreeing with the British position, finds both *market pressures and multilateral surveillance capable of preventing fiscal indiscipline.*

Vander Wal et al. (1992) stress the role of a *separate coordinator acting at a hierarchically superior level to maximise the welfare of the lower level agents*. Such a situation is supposed to represent the layered structure of the European Community in which the role of the coordinator is played by the Commission, leading the countries composing the European Community towards the necessary convergence for Phase Three of the Delors report. Although the idea is a nice and intuitive one, the result doesn't seem to be substantially different from the one in which countries act cooperatively, to minimize a common weighted objective function with higher weights assigned to the preferences of the "toughest" ones. Their results are also biased by the absence in the objective function of any social cost linked to the stabilization and repayment of the existing public debt. Adding such an argument when considering a country like Italy, for example, would make convergence much more costly than in their estimated results.

Although there exists instances in which coordination of fiscal policies might actually turn out to be counterproductive, the possibility to control such cases relatively easily would lead us to conclude in favour of coordination. However a few questions still need to be answered: what is the current situation of the public finances in European countries? How is it possible that no market mechanism has prevented the build up of excessive public debts? What are the risks from such a high debt situation? And above all, what is the way out to a situation in which although there may be no risks, other countries may feel that there are some? Isn't the imposition of binding rules the only way to reassure more conservative community participants that nothing wrong will happen? This is probably the key point in evaluating the content of the Delors report and of the Maastricht Treaty.

3 Strategic Games Between a Domestic Treasury and Different Players

The game theoretic approach may provide a useful, general framework to interpret the different conclusions about the imposition of binding fiscal rules. The hypothesis is that the different fiscal policy prescriptions in a monetary union may also depend on the game explicitly or implicitly assumed and above all on the assumed players of such a game. One can consider the game played by the domestic Treasury, respectively, with the domestic Central Bank (Tabellini (1986),

(1988), Giovannini and Spaventa (1991), Della Posta (1992)), with the foreign Treasury (de Grauwe (1985), van der Ploeg (1990)), with a European Central Bank (de Grauwe (1990)) and with the private sector[8] (Cukierman (1989), Giovannini (1990), Della Posta (1991)).

3.1 Treasury versus Central Bank

The point made by Giovannini and Spaventa (1991) can be interpreted as the result of a strategic game between *Treasury and Central Bank*, where both authorities want to minimize their loss function one of whose arguments is credibility; so the game is about who will provide this public good. If the Central Bank does, then the fiscal authority can act in a loose way, feeling confident that the expectations of exchange rate stability together with some positive interest rate differentials will induce financial investors to subscribe the domestic public debt bonds. As a matter of fact, a tough monetary policy, by assuring higher interest rates, helps encouraging bonds subscribers who appreciate the advantage of such favourable rates if they are not compensated by expected exchange rate devaluations. The only problem with this interpretation is that, looking at the pre-EMS and at the first years of its existence, a looser monetary policy did not imply a stronger fiscal authority concerned with credibility: the argument has not a two-way validity. "Monetary dominance" (as defined by Tabellini (1988)), then, doesn't seem so effective in reducing government spending. The idea is that monetary dominance, far from imposing a behavioural constraint on the fiscal authority, might even strengthen the fiscal policy autonomy, thanks to the externality produced in terms of credibility. My considerations are perfectly consistent with the conclusion reached by Tabellini (1988) (together with the ones by Giovannini and Spaventa (1991)), that, for some European countries belonging to the EMS, the gradually decreasing degree of fiscal dominance has not caused any lower fiscal expansion over the period that he considers. Della Posta (1992) proposes an open economy version of the Tabellini model: the numerical results obtained by computer simulations, although still preliminary, show that when moving from a closed economy to an open economy a gradual rise of the end-of-period public debt level is observed: opening up the economy imposes a tighter optimal monetary policy while leaving the optimal fiscal policy substantially unchanged.

3.2 Treasury versus European Central Bank

De Grauwe (1990) sees two conflicting incentives on the fiscal authority of a country joining a fixed exchange rate system. On one hand the expectation of a *no-*

---

[8] Not relevant here is the game between a domestic Central Bank and the private sector (Kydland and Prescott (1975), Barro and Gordon (1982), Backus and Driffil (1985)) or between domestic Central Banks belonging to a fixed exchange rate system on one side and private sector on the others (Rogoff (1985)).

monetization clause (by a supranational monetary authority) produces fiscal restrictions; on the other hand the *moral hazard* problem given by the possibility to rely on the help of the Community might induce fiscal laxity. The former, according to de Grauwe is assumed to prevail. His conclusion is based on the observation of the experience of the existing federal countries where, although no fiscal rules have been introduced, no divergent fiscal positions have resulted. Anyway, the experience of the EMS shows that the key factor to assure the viability of the system is monetary rather than fiscal policy. Belgium and the Netherlands, for example, have been able to peg to the DM by shadowing the German monetary policy, while leading divergent fiscal policies; the contrary happened to France.

On one hand, then, the moral-hazard problem might arise, as pointed out by Giovannini and Spaventa (1991), among others, in the strategic game between domestic Treasury and Central Bank; on the others, as de Grauwe (1990) observes, the same problem might arise in the game between the *domestic Treasury* of a lax country and a *supranational monetary authority* representing the whole community. As it should be evident, believing in one case implies that the other one is also possible. Why should a domestic fiscal authority take advantage of the reputation offered by a strong domestic Central Bank but give up the benefits resulting from the reputation offered by a European Central Bank? As a matter of fact this fear, be it grounded or not, has some content in reality, so that the introduction of binding fiscal rules might find its most fundamental rationale, as we have already observed, in the need to get the adhesion of the stronger countries who would refuse otherwise their participation: the result of the recent Danish referendum might be a clear example of the need to assure a sound economy that no risks of instability arise when participating to a fixed exchange rate system together with more lax countries. Fiscal constraints, then, imply a direct investment in the credibility of weak countries through which one potential source of time inconsistency is removed and stronger countries may believe that no risks arise in joining together with the initially weaker ones.

The passage from a domestic Central Bank to a European Central Bank, though, might make things worse for the domestic Treasury. The high reputation of the domestic Central Bank, which translates into tight money and high interest rates, may encourage the inflow of foreign capital. However, when a European Central Bank is established, no interest rate differentials are likely to result because it won't be possible any more to adopt tighter domestic monetary policies. I find this point particularly relevant: great attention is paid to the risk of community savings appropriation by undisciplined countries as a result of a deeper and a wider financial market; it should not be ignored, however, that the passage from domestic Central Banks to a European Central Bank may remove one involuntary support for the fiscal indiscipline: the strong domestic Central Bank reputation but, above all, a domestic high interest rate policy, capable of assuring the financing of the government debt.

An interesting point made by Padoa Schioppa (1990) is given by the conclusion of *substitutability* between monetary and fiscal discipline: the higher the monetary discipline, the lower the required fiscal discipline to assure the viability of the system. A strong monetary constitution endowing the European System of Central Banks (ESCB) with a sufficient degree of independence from national governments, is sufficient to allow the free availability of the fiscal instrument to pursue the domestic targets. He concludes that it would be preferable to allow the Community to run temporary deficits or surpluses on its own budget rather than endowing it with authority on national budgets. This point brings us back to Giovannini and Spaventa (1991) and to Tabellini (1986). It looks like they all agree on the fact that monetary rules are in practice *substitutes* rather than *complements* of fiscal rules. However, while the last three authors point out that the credibility gained through a strong monetary authority allows the fiscal authority to behave in an undisciplined way, so that the two former authors take a position in favour of binding rules, Padoa Schioppa concludes that the strong commitment of the Central Bank is enough to assure and justify the flexibility of the fiscal instrument to respond to the occurrence of adverse shocks. He sees with favour such an autonomy of the fiscal authority but, by doing so, he ignores the possibility of a distorted use of the fiscal instrument as the experience of some European countries shows instead. Van Wijmbergen (1985) follows the line of research opened by Sargent and Wallace (1981) to conclude that fiscal balance should precede the imposition of strict monetary rules that might otherwise even exacerbate the credibility problem due to the expectation of a future taxation or monetization of the debt. In an intertemporal framework, then, monetary and fiscal rules become *complements*: only on a temporary basis one might believe that fiscal expansion can be financed through the market while keeping tight the money creation. At some point the debt will have to be repayed and the expectation of the necessary monetary creation might cause serious problems to the stability of the system: the monetary discipline imposed de facto by a fixed exchange rate system has to be complemented by fiscal discipline, to be imposed through the introduction of binding rules, given the ineffectiveness of the market mechanism.

3.3 Domestic Treasury versus Foreign Treasury

De Grauwe (1985) interprets, rather in opposition with the common believes, the first years of the EMS as characterized by a tight fiscal stance due to the *strategic game played between the fiscal authorities of different countries*. The intuitive idea is that a fiscal expansion, given a low capital mobility, crowds out the external sector of the expanding country, so that there is a typical case of prisoner's dilemma where each country hopes to benefit of the expansion of the others while "shirking" himself. The outcome is a Nash equilibrium at a lower welfare level than in the Stackelberg case in which one of the two players would take the leadership and would adopt an attitude of benign neglect towards its own balance of payments situation as in the case of the USA during the Bretton Woods system. I don't find this story particularly convincing, given the public debt performance of countries like Italy, Greece or Portugal (to ignore Ireland and Belgium). To be fair, however, France, that would like to promote a coordinated plan of fiscal expansion to reduce the European unemployment, hesitates to do it independently, mainly for the above mentioned reasons: what may be true for one country doesn't have to be necessarily true for others. According to his analysis, then, an exogenous shock affecting the national balance of payments will produce as a result a generalized tight fiscal stance which, while leaving unchanged the balance of payments, will reduce the welfare. The obvious solution to such an under-dimensioning of the fiscal stance would be the coordination of fiscal policies. As we have seen, the same point is made by van der Ploeg (1990).

3.4 Treasury versus Private Sector

The game between the domestic Treasury and the private sector may cause the risk of unstable financial situations when the parity is not declared irrevocably unmodifiable, as pointed out by Giovannini (1990), Cukierman (1989) and Della Posta (1991).[9] Running expansionary and divergent domestic fiscal policies may cause on one hand the reaction of the labour market which, anticipating a devaluation to balance the current account deficit, causes an inflationary pressure on wages (Cukierman (1989)) and, on the other hand, the reaction of the financial markets which , anticipating the possible devaluation, asks for higher interest rates and starts a speculative attack on the currency of the divergent country (Giovannini (1990)). In particular, the financial markets will realize the time inconsistency which arises when exchange rate parities are declared while running divergent fiscal policies, so that reoptimization of the government objective function at a later stage produces as a result a different optimal exchange rate. The resulting speculative attack is performed by forward looking financial markets which anticipate and force the devaluation (Della Posta (1991)).

Once more the conclusion is that to avoid the risk of such speculative attacks the fiscal authorities should follow a tight behaviour. If they are not capable of doing so, or if they don't recognize the risk that financial markets might change rapidly their attitude towards high debt countries, then binding fiscal rules should be imposed to guarantee sound public finances.

Obviously, while the running of divergent fiscal positions may cause the expectation of a devaluation, the anticipation of a fiscal consolidation is likely to produce the opposite effect, so that, in order to avoid an undesirable revaluation of the exchange rate, an interest rate reduction is likely to result, as shown in appendix B.

[9] The analyses of the three authors refer in particular to the design of the transition to the EMU, given in the Delors Report.

4 Critics to Maastricht and Effects of the Expected Convergence

It is interesting to observe how the proposed passage from the EMS to EMU changes the forms of solidarity among member states. In the Nyborg agreement (1987) it was established for Community countries in temporary difficulties the availability of a special reserve fund, the Very Short Term Financing facilities (VSTF) so as to being able to resist any speculative attacks performed by the market. Grilli and Alesina (1988) had stressed the importance of such a measure, necessary if the monetary authorities want to be able to decide independently if and when to use the exchange rate instrument to restore (partially) the loss of competitiveness due to higher inflation differentials. Once the Central Bank has the availability of such reserve fund, it should be in a position to surprise the market, implementing a random devaluation without causing any dangerous portfolio shifts.[10] In an EMU, however, by definition intra-European reserves will have to disappear and they will only be kept at the European Central Bank level for transactions with third countries outside the monetary union area. The solidarity previously directed towards the provision of foreign reserves to avoid the risk of speculative attacks on the foreign exchange market, then, might well be transformed into the provision of a "lender of last resort" function, to guarantee domestic and foreign bond holders against the risk of confidence crises that might occur in heavily indebted countries. The moral hazard aspect of such a measure is counterbalanced by the assurance offered to bond holders. So, on one hand, by imposing a no-bail-out condition, the role of the market wants to be reinforced, by allowing the correct signalling of the existence of risk premiums on indebted countries. On the other hand, the important function of a lender of last resort is neglected leaving open the door for any, not necessarily rationally produced, outcome. Denying the need for a lender of last resort, however, appears consistent with the whole package designed in the Maastricht Treaty according to which no problems would arise in the first place given the limits every country will have to abide by, if it wants to join in the Third Phase. This is why the selection for the access to the full EMU cannot be only a formal one, influenced by reasons of political opportunity or of historical "merits" (like being the country where Michelangelo or Leonardo were born!): admitting a country with a fragile financial situation in the absence of a lender of last resort to assure the markets and rule out the risk of runs and panics, might turn out to be particularly unfortunate. My considerations, then, go towards the conclusions reached by Giovannini and Spaventa (1991) with their no-entry clause.

A strong comment about the conclusions reached in the Delors Report which obviously apply also to the Maastricht Treaty, is made by Buiter and Kletzer (1990) who don't find convincing the imposition of binding fiscal rules and see

---

[10] The devaluation of the Italian lira decided during the month of September 1992 (before the submission for publication of this paper, presented in June at the workshop) shows how the provision of the VSTF has been unable to defeat the speculation and how the solidarity between "strong" and "weak" Central Banks disciplined in the Nyborg agreement could not be maintained.

such a prescription as the result of the typical conservative approach of central bankers towards government deficits. They also criticize the fact that no lower bounds for fiscal deficits are mentioned, as if it was normal to be worried for over-dimensioned budget deficits, but not for under-dimensioned ones.

Many different forms of time inconsistency arise from the set-up of the Maastricht Treaty: a perfect functioning of the market is highly desirable, so as to charge appropriate risk premiums for the most undisciplined countries. But the higher the interest rates to service the debt, the more difficult it will be for such countries to repay their debt and to follow a stable convergent path. At the same time very high interest rates would be the signal of a run on the debt of a country: the outcome is certainly produced by well functioning markets but its desirability can be questioned. It is very likely then, that the initial threat to let the market operate so as to signal the presence of unstable situations be reneged at some point, when the application of such a threat might turn out to pose problems to the whole community. The no-bail out clause then, might be interpreted by weaker countries as non credible, as I have already observed, because they know already that it won't be possible to let one country belonging to the Union go alone against the punishment of the market: it won't be possible, in the need, to refuse solidarity although it is clearly ruled out at the outset. This is why the no-bail-out clause has to be preceded by more strict entry rules just to avoid the possibility to find oneselves in such a situation.

Time inconsistency type of issues are signaled, as observed above, by the presence of risk premia on the interest rates required by the market. The rules solution, time consistent by definition (no debt explosion and no speculative attack from the private sector) should be the intermediate one between the optimal but time inconsistent (debt explosion, but no speculative attack) and the sub-optimal time consistent (where the markets anticipate the debt explosion, so an appropriate risk premium is charged). Therefore, different levels of public debt matter a lot for the time inconsistency issue (see Van der Ploeg (1990) and Gros (1991)).

It has been argued that in a flexible exchange rate system the current account represents an effective constraint on expansionary fiscal policies. The current account deterioration, however, might well be caused by investments, not necessarily inflationary and not responsible for any long run solvency problems. It can be inferred then that the loss of such a constraint when moving from a flexible to a fixed exchange rate system should not be seen as serious because the constraint itself should not have been taken seriously when in place. For the same reason I can argue that the focus on budget deficit or on debt is not necessarily appropriate being the actual levels caused by many different reasons: a qualitative, intertemporal rather than a quantitative, static analysis would be necessary to judge when a fiscal position is unsustainable. This is the point made also by Ballabriga et al. (1991) who recognize the need for a deeper evaluation of the fiscal position of a country: although difficult in practice to evaluate, the crucial thing would be the satisfaction of the golden rule according to which actual net borrowing should not exceed the net investment expenditure. They also evaluate the possible effects of fiscal expansion on real interest rates to be spread all over

Europe, concluding that there doesn't seem to be enough evidence that large fiscal imbalances reflect into higher interest rates and even if they do, this happens just temporarily on short term interest rates. Giovannini and Spaventa (1991) also ask themselves whether the budget deficit might be the best indicator for aggregate demand externalities and conclude that in fact it is not: the pressure on real exchange rates depends on the nature of the aggregate demand increase (on domestic or foreign goods) and on the degree of substitutability between goods. So, once more one can conclude that the imposition of binding rules on budget deficits and government debt doesn't have too much meaning.[11]

One further problem with the Maastricht Treaty is that there is no reason why rules should be equal for every country, ignoring the different starting points of them. By averaging out the current situation so as to find the "ideal" rules, it has been ignored that if on one hand the more undisciplined countries might find clear and useful guidelines to orientate their convergence to safer finances, on the other hand more virtuous countries might feel encouraged to run more expansionary fiscal policies, given that they already meet the requirements contained in the Treaty. Nothing is wrong with this, in fact it might well be a desirable feature of the future EMU in which some flexibility to counter the cycle would be accorded to those countries who still have some room for manoeuvre, but not to the others. A possibility, however, is that the financial markets assign some positive probability to a fiscal expansion and therefore impose higher interest rates, to be compensated for the risk of higher future taxes and/or monetization. If the financial markets react to the imposition of fiscal targets then, it makes sense to expect that for high debt countries the risk premium will be suddenly reduced at the (credible) announcement of the start of a convergence programme. At the same time domestic markets might even discount the positive probability of a foreign fiscal expansion, given the leeway that it has. Therefore, markets might spurt virtuous buying attacks on countries who are rebalancing their situation (see appendix B for a simplified model).

On the contrary Wyplosz (1990) sees as a possible effect of an expected stabilization plan higher, rather than lower interest rates r: $r = r^* + a(B_0 - B^*)/B_0$ i.e the foreign interest rate (r^*) has to be compensated for the higher expected *taxes* due to the difference between the actual level of the debt (B_0) and the level at which the stabilization plan will bring it through tax increase (B^*). In the opposite direction goes the effect deriving from considering lower financial wealth, lower wealth effect and therefore lower demand pressure which will reduce interest rates. In his analysis, then, EMU is likely to lead to a specific increase in public bond rates. However, it will be the less so, the more difficult it becomes to tax resident households and corporations: EMU implies a tighter budget constraint being the government subject to the tax competition effect and therefore having to reduce government expenditure. From this point of view, then, there should be no need to impose fiscal rules. Money creation rules should be enough.

By imposing binding rules on fiscal policy so that, for example, one of the

---

[11] See also Casarosa (1986) for a deep analysis of the reasons why the public debt/GDP ratio cannot be taken as a reliable indicator of government's behaviour.

conditions to move to Phase Three will be a ratio debt/GDP not higher than 60%, the objective of inflation convergence might be seriously undermined, given the independence of domestic monetary authorities from any centralized European bank in Phase Two. There might be incentives for domestic Treasuries to push the respective domestic central banks to monetize part of the debt in order to reach the target of 60% of debt/GDP. However, I am not really convinced that such a possibility has to be taken seriously, above all looking at the history of the EMS where domestic Central Banks have steadily moved towards a greater independence from the fiscal authorities estabilishing more and more their strong reputation for anti-inflationary preferences. On the other hand one should not forget that even the Bundesbank, the "toughest" Central Bank in Europe, had to accept the conditions imposed by the political view leading to the German reunification.

The trade-off between fiscal convergence and inflation convergence arises also because on one hand a higher indirect taxation might be necessary in southern countries given the lower revenues compared to EEC, but on the other hand that might increase inflation, given the high degree of indexation and inflationary expectations (as seen above in Giovannini and Spaventa (1991)).

In Corsetti and Roubini (1992), the tax smoothing view of fiscal policy is rejected for developped as well as for developping countries: transitory shocks to output and government spending fail to explain the movement of public debt in a large set of countries and inflation rates do not appear to be correlated (or co-integrated) with tax rates. So, large fiscal deficits and public debt accumulation are due to political determinants rather than to intertemporal optimization. A fully state contingent tax smoothing policy would be first best and dominate both the discretionary political equilibrium and the balanced budget rule. But it is not enforceable because of observational errors and potential cheating on the part of ruling government. As we have seen, a second best equilibrium would be a "fiscal rule with escape clause": tax smoothing would be allowed only when the shock is above a given threshold: in presence of systematic uncertainty, reputational mechanisms might not be sufficient to enforce any of these alternative cooperative rules of fiscal discipline. They suggest the imposition of explicit sanctions to mimic a punishment strategy à la Barro and Gordon rather than an innocuous and ineffective monitoring operated by the Commission. So they raise a double critic: the Maastricht Treaty contains too rigid targets on the inflation unadjusted and cyclically unadjusted overall fiscal balances of the EC countries whose implementation however, would be subject to a "political" evaluation rather than backed by effective sanctions.

The experience of the stabilization plans of Ireland and Denmark tells how important it has been for their success the reaction produced by the financial markets: from this point of view it is relevant not only the timing of the stabilization plan with respect to some reference targets deemed as clear signals of an irreversible change in the dynamics of the government, but it is also crucial the expectation of what instruments will be modified (budget cuts, higher taxation, monetary creation). This is the direction followed by Bertola and Drazen (1991) to explain the reaction of markets to stabilization plans. It should be noticed how in an EMU money will not be allowed to diverge and market competition will also imply the impossibility to impose divergent indirect tax rates and not too divergent direct tax rates so that the only remaining element to control, in order to stabilize the economy reducing the government indebtedness is expenditure cuts. This opinion is partly shared by Buiter and Kletzer (1990): not only the limited scope for tax adjustments, but also the impossibility to have recourse to the inflation tax suggest that the only possibility to meet the convergence criteria is either to reduce expenditure or just default on the debt. If the market assigns a positive probability to the latter event, it will require to be compensated by the imposition of a risk premium which will make more and more difficult to meet the repayment of the debt and therefore will make more likely the default. On one hand, then, the market may anticipate the default, for example because the stabilization plan is not credible, so it charges a risk premium; on the other hand it might well believe in the promise of the government to cut expenditures so as to lower the level of the interest rates. Given the equalization of real interest rates, no inflation tax and assuming that even divergent budget surpluses are difficult to implement, one way to reduce the debt level would be to perform a higher rate of growth of the economy. But this is rather difficult to achieve and might even contradict the objective of price stability.

With the adoption of irrevocable fixed exchange rates, expected depreciation and exchange risk premiums will disappear so as to lead to nominal interest rates equalization on assets of the same nature, maturity and specific risk. According to a study conducted by the Commission of the European Communities (1990), the only difference between a fixed exchange rate system and a single currency system, is that the rate of conversion between currencies of different countries is not one for one because of the existence of transaction costs. I find more relevant the distinction based on the observation that in a fixed exchange rate system the irrevocability of the parities can always be questioned by market forces because of the relatively limited economic cost of leaving the system. Again, credibility is the crucial thing and markets may still be able to assess the credibility of one currency by charging correspondingly some risk premiums. Much more difficult it would be to assume an abandonment of the agreement after a single currency is accepted. It seems to me, however, that the most important difference between a single currency system and a fixed exhange rate system is represented by the role of foreign reserves: in the latter, allowing or not for the possibility of devaluations, foreign reserves are necessary to peg the domestic exchange rate vis-à-vis the others belonging to the system, while such role disappears when the irrevocability of the parity is sanctioned by the adoption of a single currency. The literature on speculative attacks explains quite well what the risks are of declaring and fixing a given exchange rate when the "fundamentals" do not converge: foreign reserves are bound to be depleted. No such problems would arise in a system in which the money is unique and reserves would keep a role only with respect to third countries outside the monetary union.[12]

---

[12] The study of the Commission of the European Communities (1990) lists the advantages of the single currency: no transaction costs, transparency of prices, economies of scale, credibility, visibility and

5 Conclusions

The paper examines the reasons in favour of coordination, autonomy or discipline of fiscal policies in the European Union so as to evaluate the related prescriptions contained in the Delors Report and in the Maastricht Treaty.

Although the issue is complex and there exist good arguments to support any of the three possible cases, it looks to me that the reasons behind the imposition of binding fiscal rules prevail over the others, above all considering that in some countries (although not in others!) the adoption of a given fiscal stance is more often determined by political distorsions rather than by the need to face temporary adverse shocks.

The game theoretic approach provides a useful tool to interpret the different conclusions about the restrictive or the expansionary bias of fiscal policies when moving to a monetary union and to argue in favour or against the imposition of binding rules.

The two simple models proposed in appendix A and B lead to conclude that on one hand the move to EMU makes fiscal policy relatively more expansionary if compared to EMS and on the other hand that the imposition of binding, therefore credible rules may generate a virtuous process through which high debt countries accelerate their convergence path through an interest rate reduction. At the same time it might turn out that countries with unemployment problems but well within the limits imposed by the Maastricht Treaty will feel authorised to run expansionary fiscal policies: a gradual convergence of the debt/GDP ratio towards the known and credible target might result, together with the nominal interest rate equalization.

Appendix A: The Relative Expansionary Bias of Fiscal Policy in a Fixed Exchange Rate System with Tax Competition

Using a slightly modified version of the tax smoothing model proposed by Van der Ploeg (1991), I am going to show that when the foreign average tax rate (t^*) is lower than the domestic one (t), and a "copycatting" effect is assumed i.e. t tends to converge to the lower t^* in order to prevent factors to emigrate to more friendly fiscal environments (see also Wyplosz (1990)), the contractionary fiscal bias, obtained as a result of the above mentioned model, gets reduced. Let the following objective function to be minimized over time:

external benefits.

(A.1)
$$\int_0^T [b_1t^2+b_2p^2+b_3(g-g^d)^2+b_4(p-p^*)^2+b_5(t-t^*)^2]e^{-r\tau}d\tau$$

s. t.

(A.2)
$$\dot{d}=rd+g-t-pm$$

where t is the average tax rate, p is the domestic inflation rate, g is public spending, g^d is its desired level, m is the monetary base and starred variables refer to foreign ones. The only substantial modification relative to the model proposed by Van der Ploeg (1990) is relative to the inclusion of the last element, expressing the need for the domestic government not to diverge from the foreign average tax rate. Considering only domestic tax rates, public spending is negatively related to them: the higher the tax rate, the lower the optimal public spending; however, when at the limit the domestic tax rate converges to the lower foreign one, fiscal policy becomes relatively more expansionary.
Deriving the first order conditions so as to calculate the optimal tax rate, inflation rate and public spending one gets:

(A.3)
$$\frac{\partial H}{\partial t}=e^{-r\tau}[b_1t+b_5(t-t^*)]=\lambda$$

(A.4)
$$\frac{\partial H}{\partial p}=e^{-r\tau}[b_2+b_4(p-p^*)]-\lambda m=0$$

(A.5)
$$\frac{\partial H}{\partial g}=e^{-r\tau}[b_3(g-g^d)]+\lambda=0$$

(A.6)
$$\frac{\partial H}{\partial d}=-\dot{\lambda}=r\lambda$$

(A.7)
$$\frac{\partial H}{\partial \lambda}=\dot{d}=rd+g-t-pm$$

From (A6) we get the value for the shadow price:

(A.8)
$$\lambda_t=\lambda_0e^{-rt}$$

to substitute in (A3), (A4) and (A5) to have:

(A.9)
$$t=\frac{b_5 t^* + \lambda_0}{b_1 + b_5}$$

(A.10)
$$p=\frac{m\lambda_0 + b_4 p^*}{b_2 + b_4}$$

(A.11)
$$g=g^d-\frac{\lambda_0}{b_3}$$

and isolating λ_0 from (A9) and substituting into (A10) and (A11):

(A.12)
$$p=\frac{m[(b_1+b_5)t-b_5 t^*]+b_4 p^*}{b_2+b_4}$$

(A.13)
$$g=g^d+\frac{b_5 t^*-(b_1+b_5)t}{b_3}$$

implying that the foreign tax rate has its effects also on the optimal inflation rate and on the optimal government spending. When, due to the copycatting effect, the domestic average tax rate has to converge to the assumed lower foreign average tax rate (A13) becomes:

(A.14)
$$g'=g^d-\frac{b_1 t^*}{b_3}$$

where for $t > t^*$, it follows that $g' > g$.

So, considering the tax competition between two different countries and assuming as a likely outcome the foreign lower tax rate to prevail, it follows that optimality conditions suggest a relatively more expansionary fiscal stance compared to the case in absence of "copycatting", although the negative sign still links the optimal tax rate and the optimal budget deficit. This is only to say that the conclusion reached by van der Ploeg (1990) about the restrictive bias of fiscal policies when moving from EMS to EMU is far from being demonstrated: not only his model doesn't contain any significant distinction showing how fiscal policies become more restrictive when moving to EMU, but if one takes account of the possible change, due to the "copycatting" effect, then the assumed restrictive bias gets relatively relaxed.

Appendix B: The Effect of the Expected Convergence on Disciplined and Undisciplined Countries

As pointed out by the Commission of the European Communities (1990), the convergence and the move to Phase Two and to the EMU imply systemic and policy changes, the former being the institutional changes due to the introduction of the ECU, to the creation of a ESCB, to a completed single market and to the introduction of budgetary rules; the latter reflecting the firmer commitment to price stability and the adhesion to budgetary guidelines. Behavioural changes in turn will result from the systemic and policy changes i.e. a shift in expectations should result if the market believes in the irrevocability and the firmness of such changes. The economic impact would result in microeconomic efficiency, macroeconomic stability and regional equity.

Following this suggestion, the simple model I propose assumes that the government bond market reacts to expected variations of interest rates. More precisely, higher expected future interest rates tend to slow down the current demand to favour a heavier investment in the near future. Such a slow down of the bond demand increases the interest rate immediately, thus producing negative effects on the government finances. A specular argument applies to the case in which lower expected future interest rates make the demand for bonds increase immediately so as to cause an anticipation of the interest rate reduction. Intertemporal arbitrage is the mechanism behind the market reaction: financial investors modify their behaviour by comparing the current with the expected future interest rates. An alternative to such an intertemporal arbitrage is to invest on a very short horizon although even in that case the market will still operate by differentiating the short from the long interest rate. Announced and credible convergence plans and more in particular the imposition of binding fiscal rules might imply the expectation of future interest rates different from the current ones. A lower expected future debt level will imply a lower expected interest rate because of a reduction of the risk premium on it and vice versa, independently of the way such a reduction is expected to be obtained (expenditure reduction or higher taxes). Therefore, it is likely that the fiscal rules contained in the Maastricht Treaty have some expectational effects on the European interest rates. If the convergence plans of the more indebted countries are credible, then, a gradual interest rate reduction that will help the convergence process should result. On the other hand, more virtuous countries which are well within the bounds but which suffer, for example, unemployment problems (I have in mind the French case), might feel tempted to perform a fiscal expansion: there is the possibility that the fiscal limits given to the Community countries become the point of attraction of both the disciplined and the undisciplined countries.

Let the demand for domestic bonds be determined by the following equation:

(B.1) $$B^D_t = a_0 + \eta[B^D_t - E(B^S_{t+1})] + a_1 i_t$$

where B^D_t is the demand for domestic bonds at time t, $E(B^S_{t+1})$is the expected supply of bonds in period t+1, as indicated by the convergence plan and i_t is the nominal interest rate at time t. When $B^D_t = B^S_t = E(B^S_{t+1}) = B$ it follows that:

(B.2) $$i_t = \frac{B - a_0}{a_1}$$

For a foreign country the same thing, with starred variables, apply so that, assuming identical structure for the two countries:

(B.3) $$i_t - i^*_t = \frac{B - B^*}{a_1}$$

i.e.

$$i_t = i^*_t + \frac{B - B^*}{a_1}$$

where $(B-B^*)/a_1$ is the risk premium on the domestic interest rate due to the different debt level. Now, if $B^D_t \neq E(B^S_{t+1}) = B'$ where B' is the announced debt level resulting from the implementation of the convergence plan, it follows that:

(B.4) $$i^S_t = \frac{(1-\eta)B^D_t + \eta B' - a_0}{a_1}$$

where i^S_t is the interest rate obtained when a stabilization plan is credibly announced. The size of the interest rate jump obtained as a result of the announcement is:

(B.5) $$i_t - i^S_t = \frac{B^D_t - B'}{a_1}$$

so that when a lower future debt level (or debt/GDP ratio) is announced as a result of a convergence plan or as a result of binding rules like the ones established in the Maastricht Treaty, a lower interest rate will be obtained thereby making easier the convergence itself.

There is no reason why the same behaviour should not be realised when a higher debt level is expected. Obviously, I am not claiming that any country whose debt/GDP ratio is below the level indicated in the Maastricht Treaty as the maximum allowed will take advantage of the possibility to perform a fiscal expansion (limited anyhow by the maximum allowed deficit/GDP ratio), above all if motivated, for example, by heavy unemployment problems. I am only pointing out the existence of such a possibility, as a result of the rules which are in place. In presence of social problems, the citizens belonging to a "virtuous" country might well ask themselves why they should not have a more flexible fiscal stance given that their country is well within the limits imposed by the Community rules. The expectation of a fiscal expansion, then, would cause specular effects, with an initial interest rate jump and a gradually increasing debt/GDP ratio accompanied by higher interest rates. One possible picture for Europe is then a gradual convergence, from above and from below, towards the debt/GDP target indicated in the Maastricht Treaty and a contemporaneous gradual convergence towards the same interest rate, as figure 1 illustrates[13].

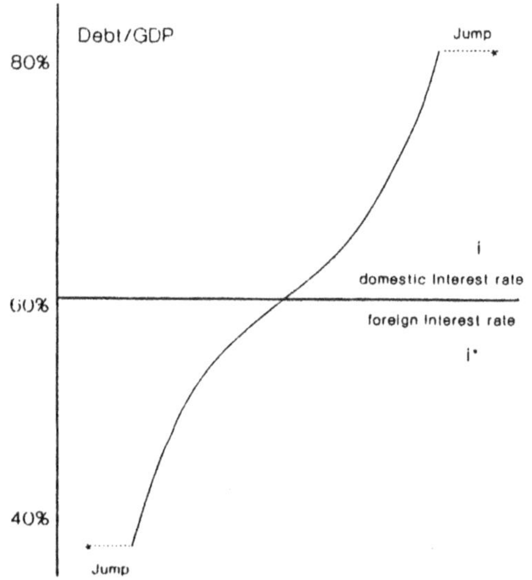

Figure 1. Interest rate effect of a credible 60% debt/GDP target

---

[13] The trajectory leading both the high debt and the low debt country towards the 60% debt/GDP target is obtained assuming that the closer one country gets to the target, the higher the probability, assigned by the market, that the target will be reached, so that the effect on the interest rates is gradually increased. As it is evident, this simple model deserves some further investigation, which is what I am planning to do in my future research.

References

Backus D and Driffil J (1985) Inflation and Reputation, American Economic Review, June

Ballabriga F, Dolado J and Viñals J (1991) Fiscal Deficit Guidelines in the Transition to EMU. Paper prepared for the "Second International Macroeconomics Programme Meeting" hosted by the Bank of Spain, Madrid, June 7-8

Barro RJ and Gordon DB (1983) Rules, Discretion and Reputation in a Model of Monetary Policy, Journal of Monetary Economics No 12, pp 101-121, July

Bertola G and Drazen A (1991) Trigger Points and Budget Cuts: Explaining the Effects of Fiscal Austerity. Discussion Paper CEPR no 599, December

Bredekamp H and Deppler M (1989) Fiscal Constraints of a Hard Currency Regime. IMF (mimeo)

Buiter WH and Kletzer KM (1990) Reflections on the Fiscal Implications of a Common Currency, Discussion Paper CEPR no 418, May

Casarosa C (1986) Il significato economico del rapporto fra debito pubblico e PIL: un'analisi critica, Politica Economica, No 2

Corsetti G and Roubini N (1992) Tax Smoothing Discretion vs. Balanced Budget Rules in the Presence of Politically Motivated Fiscal Deficits: the Design of Optimal Fiscal Rules for Europe after 1992, Paper prepared for the Conference on "The Transition to Economic and Monetary Union in Europe", organized by the Banco de Portugal, January 16-18, Estoril, Portugal

Commission of the European Communities, Directorate General for Economic and Financial Affairs (1990) One Market, One Money. European Economy, no 44, October

Cukierman A (1989) Discretion, Precommitment and the Prospects for a European Central Bank. Fixed Parities vs. a Commonly Managed Currency. Paper presented at the Bank of Israel and the David Horowitz Institute Conference on "Aspects of Central Bank Policymaking" held in Tel-Aviv, January 1990

de Grauwe P (1985) Fiscal Policies in the EMS - A Strategic Analysis, ch VII in International Monetary Systems op. cit.

de Grauwe P (1990) Fiscal Discipline in Monetary Unions, International Economics Research Papers CES Katholicke Universiteit Leuven, Department Economie, no 72

Della Posta P (1991) Time Inconsistent Fixed Exchange Rates: the Risk of Speculative Attacks in Phase Two of the Delors Report. Paper presented at the Students Workshop at the EUI, Firenze, May

Della Posta P (1992) An Open Economy Dynamic Game Between a Monetary and a Fiscal Authority: Analytical and Numerical Results. Paper presented at the Students Workshop at the EUI, Firenze, January

Giovannini A (1990) The Transition to Monetary Union, CEPR Occasional Paper, No 2

Giovannini A and Spaventa L (1991) Fiscal Rules in the European Monetary Union: a No-Entry Clause, Discussion Paper CEPR no 516

Grilli V and Alesina A (1987) Avoiding Speculative Attacks on EMS Currencies: a Proposal, Center Discussion Paper No 547, Economic Growth Center, Yale, Yale University, December

Gros D (1990) Seigniorage and EMS Discipline. In: de Grauwe P and Papademos L (1990) (eds) The European Monetary System in the 1990s, Longman, London and New York

Jaans P (1989) The Basic Difference Between the Frameworks for Policy Decision-Making Provided by the EMS and EMU. In: Report on Economic and Monetary Union in the European Community, Collection of Papers, Commission of the European Communities, April

Krugman P (1990) Policy Problems of a Monetary Union. In: de Grauwe P and Papademos L (1990) (eds) The European Monetary System in the 1990s, Longman, London and New York

Kydland F and Prescott EC (1977) Rules Rather than Discretion: the Inconsistency of Optimal Plans, Journal of Political Economy, June

Lamfalussy A (1989) Macro-coordination of Fiscal Policies in an Economic and Monetary Union in Europe. In: Report on Economic and Monetary Union, Collection of Papers, Commission of the European Communities, April

Masson P, Melitz J (1990) Fiscal Policy Independence in a European Monetary Union. CEPR Discussion Paper No 414, April

Padoa-Schioppa T et al (1987) Efficiency, Stability and Equity. A strategy for the Evolution of the Economic System of the European Community, Oxford University Press

Padoa Shioppa T (1990) Fiscal Prerequisites of a European Monetary Union. Paper presented at the Bank of Israel and David Horowitz Institute Conference on "Aspects of Central Bank Policymaking" held in Tel-Aviv, January

Rogoff K (1985) Can International Monetary Cooperation be Counterproductive? Journal of International Economics, No 18, pp 199-217, North Holland

Sargent T and Wallace N (1981) Some Unpleasant Monetarist Arithmetic. Federal Reserve Bank of Minneapolis Quarterly Review, Fall

Tabellini G (1986) Money, Debt and Deficits in a Dynamic Game, Journal of Economic Dynamics and Control, No 10, pp 427-442, North-Holland

Tabellini G (1988) Monetary and Fiscal Policy Coordination with a High Public Debt. In: Giavazzi F, Spaventa L (eds) High Public Debt: the Italian Experience, Italian Macroeconomic Policy Group, CEPR, Cambridge University Press

Tanzi V (1989) International Coordination of Fiscal Policies: Current and Future Issues. In Monti M (ed) Fiscal Policy, Economic Adjustment and Financial Markets. IMF, Centro di Economia Monetaria e Finanziaria, Papers presented at the seminar held in Milan on January 28-30

Van der Ploeg F (1990) Macroeconomic Policy Coordination during the various Phases of Economic and Monetary Integration in Europe. In: Commission of the European Communities, Directorate General for Economic and Financial Affairs (1990) The Economics of EMU, European Economy, Supplement to no 44, October

Vander Wal D et al (1992) On the Road to EMU. A Hierarchical Coordination Approach, mimeo, Paper presented at the seminar held at the Commission of the European Communities DG II on March 23

Van Wijnbergen S (1985) Fiscal Deficits, Exchange Rate Crises and Inflation, Discussion Paper CEPR no 87

Wyplosz C (1990) Monetary Union and Fiscal Policy Discipline. In: Commission of the European Communities, Directorate General for Economic and Financial Affairs (1990) The Economics of EMU, European Economy, Supplement to no 44, October

The (Term) Structure of Interest Rates as a Predictor of Real Economic Growth: An Econometric Analysis for Germany

Klaus J.W. Schmidt
University of Frankfurt

"A third reason economists are interested in the term structure is that it may provide information about the expectations of participants in financial markets. These expectations are of considerable interest to forecasters and policymakers. Market participants' beliefs about what may happen in the future influence their current decisions; these decisions, in turn, help determine what actually happens in the future." (Russell 1992, p. 37)

1 Introduction

1.1 The Information Content of Financial Markets - Theoretical Considerations

In this article, I investigate interest rate based forecast models for German real economic activity, measured in annual growth rates of real GNP. One might ask why financial variables can be viewed as leading indicators of the business cycle. On financial markets economic agents allocate their consumption intertemporally; thus, the prices on financial markets - interest rates - are regarded as intertemporal prices of purchasing power, which are not only determined by present, but also by (expected) relevant future economic conditions such as the future path of real economic activity. Furthermore, financial markets can react much faster to business cycle relevant information (e.g. from fiscal- or monetary policy) and adjust their prices accordingly, long before the impact is reflected in the business cycle. Therefore, *market* prices on financial markets are supposed to contain economic agents' expectations about future economic activity, and hence, if those expectations are systematically correct, can provide a look into the future.

Traditionally, stock market indices have been used as leading indicators. In that context, the price of stocks is expressed theoretically as the capital value of all future dividends, which are assumed to be linked to economic activity ('fundamentals'). Empircal research, however, has shown that the 'fundamental' stock prices often are disturbed by irrational 'noise'. Refering to the German stock market, Harvey (1991) e.g. states: "The stock market appears to be forecasting recessions in 1971, 1974, 1977, 1979, 1984 and a severe recession in 1988. Only three of these six recession forecasts were realized." (p.708).

In the contemporary literature (cf. deBondt/Bange 1991, Davis 1990, Estrella/Hardouvelis 1991, Friedman/Kuttner 1991, Hardouvelis 1988, Harvey

1991, Jaeger 1992 and Shah/Wadhwani 1990) therefore, one can observe an increased interest in the predictive ability of interest rates on the 'riskless' bond and money markets. These articles suggest that it is not sufficient to consider one interest rate - or the interest rate *level* - alone, but rather the term *structure* of interest rates, expressed as the difference between a long- and a short-term interest rate ('slope of the yield curve', SPREAD).

At least three theoretical arguments are frequently used to motivate this approach: (1) Consider that a recession is advancing in the not too distant future: consequently, the economic agents expect a decrease of economic activity and, hence, a possible loss in their income. They will therefore try to hedge their income and buy long-term assets, which deliver a pay-off during the expected recession, and finance their purchase by selling short-term assets. Thus, the price of long-term assets would rise (the long-term interest rate would fall) and the price of short-term assets would fall (the short-term interest rate would rise), i.e. the yield curve would become flatter or even inverse (the SPREAD would become smaller or even negative). Thus, a flatter yield curve is indicative for a recession in the near future. This argument reaches back to Irving Fisher (1907) and is used by Harvey (1991, p.702f). In addition, the sole restructuring of savings economic agents can reduce real expenditures to finance additional savings, causing an additional decrease of the long-term interest rate. Because of the partial loss of total demand, this reinforces the danger of a recession ('self-fulfilling prophecy'). (2) The next argument refers to the expectations theory of the term structure (a good explanation is given in Shiller 1990): according to that theory, the nominal long-term rate is an average of current and expected future nominal short-term rates, such that expected holding period returns are equalized. Thus, a flattening of the yield curve would indicate a drop of future nominal short rates, and it is presumed that this drop is associated with a decline in real economic activity. Estrella/Hardouvelis (1991, p.555) argue in such a way; own prior research (Schmidt 1991) suggests, that a changing slope of the yield curve predicts future *changes* of short rates correctly. Moreover, it should be mentioned that Kessel already showed in the mid sixties (cf. Kessel 1965) that there are typical slopes of the yield curve during the business cycle. (3) The last theoretical argument is built on the expectations theory as well: it is presumed, that a tightening of monetary policy - i.e. rising short rates - preceeds the recession. If the economic agents believe that the central bank thereby can successfully reduce the future inflation rate, the Fisherian inflation premia, incorporated in the nominal long-term rate, will be reduced. Consequently, the yield curve will become flatter or even inverse. This argument is used by Gebauer (1989) where the term structure is dealt with as an indicator for monetary policy.

1.2 Previous Evidence

All of the three theoretical arguments describe forces which tend to flatten the yield curve before a recession. Estrella/Hardouvelis (1991) and Harvey (1991), who have made the most interesting contributions in that context, find strong evidence in favour of that approach. Moreover, Jaeger (1992) shows, that the information content of the SPREAD hitherto has been largely ignored by professional forecasters in nearly all important industrial countries. Dealing with quarterly US data Estrella and Hardouvelis examine the predictive power of the SPREAD in great detail for different time horizons, for the real GNP as a whole and for its components. Moreover, they investigate whether the SPREAD has predictive power above other variables and compare its forecast performance with survey forecasts (Estrella/Hardouvelis 1991):

"We present evidence that the slope of the yield curve can predict cumulative changes in real output for up to 4 years into the future and successive marginal changes up to a year and a half into the future. The slope of the yield curve has extra predictive power over and above the predictive power of lagged output growth, lagged inflation, the index of leading indicators, and the level of real short-term interest rates. The slope outperforms survey forecasts both in-sample and out-of-sample, and it predicts all the private sector components of real GNP: consumption, consumer durables, and investment."(p.574f)

Harvey's analysis for Germany is not as extensive as the work of Estrella and Hardouvelis. He considers only one forecast horizon and does not disaggregate real GNP. His model - also based on average quarterly data - only contains the SPREAD and a CONSTANT as explanatory variables, but his finding is similarly enthusiastic (Harvey 1991):

"An accurate forecasting model may help reduce any uncertainty. Accuracy is measured in many different ways. Traditionally, accuracy is measured by the difference between forecast values and actual values. This paper demonstrates, that the interest rate based model has substantially lower forecast errors than the forecasts of the Deutsches Institut für Wirtschaftsforschung. The interest rate based model also outperforms the consensus forecasts of five major research institutes. Accuracy is also measured by the ability to pick up the turning points in the business cycle. The term structure model has correctly signalled all the turning points in the last 20 years. The term structure model also has the ability to pick up more subtile (non-recessionary) turning points."(p. 716f)

A SPREAD-model very similar to the models of Harvey and Estrella/Hardouvelis will be revised and discussed in section 2; if they are as good as stated, they are a natural benchmark, with which other forecasting models have to be compared. Moreover, this seems to be necessary, because Estrealla/Hardouvelis and Harvey only address the out-of-sample performance of their models to demonstrate their advantages, but do not test the specification of them as rigorously; at least they do not report many test statistics. Hence, the models might or might not be misspecified, or - to use a term of the LSE-approach in econometrics[1] - congruent with the available information. If not, there is a pontential for an

[1] The acronym LSE stands for 'London School of Economics', where this econometric approach has its roots. It will be discussed briefly in section 2. A good overview is given by Eitrheim/Nymoen (1988) and Gilbert (1986). A textbook presentation on the topic is provided by Charemza/Deadman (1992). Hendry and Ericsson (1991) illustrate the LSE-approach with an example. Along with numerous theoretical articles, Hendry also developed PC-GIVE (cf. Hendry, 1989) which was used in the empirical part of the present article.

improved model which is superior.

Figure 1 provides visual evidence confirming the predictive ability of the SPREAD: the solid line - denoted 'y' - is the annual growth rate of German real GNP, expressed in annualized percentage points. The dotted line is the SPREAD, defined as the difference of the yield to maturity of all public bonds and the 3 month money market rate.[2]

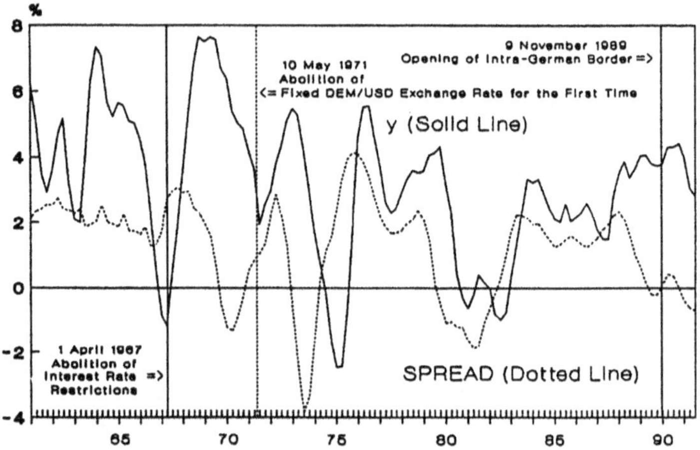

Figure 1. Spread and growth rate of real GNP. Germany, FR, 1961(1)-1991(3); 3-quarter moving averages. The SPREAD is defined as the difference of the yield to maturity of public bonds and the 3-month money market rate.
Datasource: Deutsche Bundesbank.

The predictive power of the SPREAD is quite striking: roughly one year in advance of every great recession in the last 20 years - namely in 75 and in the beginning of the 80s - the slope of the yield curve flattened drastically and finally inverted, thus indicating a recession. Furthermore, smaller movements of real GNP are also indicated by preceeding movements of the SPREAD.

Before 1967, however, the predictive ability of the SPREAD seems to be quite poor. This is not very surprising though, as until April 1, 1967 interest rates were restricted in Germany. Hence, if interest rates cannot be treated as market prices, they will not contain the economic agents' information about the future development. Therefore, the second quarter of 1967 is the first sample

[2] Harvey uses the interest rate for overnight money as the short-term rate. Own prior investigations show, however, that forecasts are superior using the 3-month money market rate. 3-quarter moving averages were used to smooth the curves in order to stress tendencies optically. Clearly, the regressions in section 2 are carried out with the original values.

observation in the subsequent econometric analysis. But one must consider that Germany had a fixed exchange rate against the USD from 1967 to 1971. On May 10, 1971 the DEM/USD exchange rate was temporarily released for the first time after the agreement of Bretton-Woods, thus being the earliest possible point in time from which on the German short-term interest rate could move rather independently from the monetary policy in the USA. This fact is marginalized by considering the SPREAD alone.

For Harvey, the exchange rate regime shift in 1971 seems to be a severe problem; consequently, he starts his regressions with the first quarter of 1971 (cf. table 1 in Harvey 1991, p. 709). I can not concur with him in that respect and account explicitly for the regime shift using a DUMMY variable. On the other hand, I agree with Harvey in that one should not use data which is distorted by the German unification process (cf. Harvey 1991, p. 715). Not because I think that the models might not be able to cope with that 'problem', but simply because of the poor quality of the data; it is obvious that interest rates, which are denoted in a certain currency, contain information concerning the whole currency area, i.e. Germany as a whole, whereas reliable GNP data is only availabe for West Germany. As Harvey, I therefore choose the fourth quarter of 1989 as the last observation point.

2 Econometric Evidence

2.1 Basic Concepts

The empirical investigation is methodologically based on the LSE-approach in econometrics. The LSE-approach explicitly distinguishes between theoretical and empirical models: here, we deal with the latter. For empirical models a very basic concept is the 'data generating process' (DGP), a set of (partly unknown) mechanisms, which actually generated the observed data. The DGP is characterized by the joint density function of all relevant variables, and on principle can be a dynamic, non-linear system with time-varying parameter structure. According to Hendry, one of the main LSE-econometricians, empirical "modelling is seen as an attempt to characterize data properties in simple parametric relationships that are interpretable in the light of economic knowledge, remain reasonably constant over time, and account for the findings of preexisting models" (Hendry/Ericsson 1991, p.18). Empirical models are, in other words, attempts to characterize the DGP: 'good' and 'bad' models can be distinguished by their ablility to capture its main features.

Therefore, every model can be thought of as being derived from the DGP by a sequence of reductions and transformations. Because this sequence may entail a loss of information, that loss has to be judged by "a taxonomy, that partitions the universe of information into disjoint sets: a) economic theory, the b) past, c) present, and d) future data of one's own model, e) the measurement system of the data, and f) the data of alternative models" (Hendry/Ericsson 1991, p.19). Referring to this taxonomy six properties of good models are frequently reported (cf. Hendry and Ericsson 1991, p.19): (1) The static long-run solution of a model should be *theory consistent*, i.e. the model has to be interpretable in the light of economic knowledge. Cointegration of the relevant variables is a necessary condition for theory consistency. (2) The model should have *white noise (innovation) errors*, because of their statistical (validity of the estimation method and the diagnostic tests, suitability of the functional form and the dynamics) and theoretical implications (neglectible influences on the theoretically postulated relations). (3) The regressors should be at least *weakly exogenous* for the parameters of interest. (4) The model should have *constant parameters*, because parameters should be the invariant elements of a model. Recursive estimation methods and Chow-tests are tools to investigate parameter constancy. Those tests are tests on valid exogeneity assumptions too, as weak exogeneity is implied by super exogeneity (and thus by models having constant parameters). (5) The model should be *data admissible*, i.e. the model should not generate negative values of inherently positive economic variables. (6) The model should *encompass* - i.e. account for the findings of - previous models. It should (variance and/or forecast) encompass rival models and parsimoniously encompass larger models within which it is nested.

A model which satisfies those criteria is called 'congruent (with the available information)' and can be viewed as an 'adequate representation of the DGP'. The implications of congruency can be tested. The diagnostic tests developed for this purpose have the desired properties of congruency as their null hypothesis, which should not be rejected for 'good' models. Notice that those tests are no independent sources of information as each of them is constructed under the assumption that the other null hypotheses are valid. If one null hypothesis can be rejected, the other tests' outcome may be distorted. Thus, rejecting one null hypothesis is sufficient to reject the model as a whole. In particular, it cannot be assumed that the alternative hypothesis is valid (cf. the remarks to 'autocorrelated residuals' below). The battery of tests has two functions: (1) destructive, to evaluate existing models; and (2) constructive, to design 'good' models.

Exactly this will be done in the following two sections of this chapter: Firstly, the simple SPREAD-model as proposed by Harvey (1991) and Estrella/Hardouvelis (1991) will be tested for congruency. Secondly, an alternative model will be developed, which can be compared to the SPREAD-model, using the *general-to-specific modelling strategy*. This modelling strategy is an attempt to formalize the constructive role of econometrics in order to find an efficient way to 'good' models. As already stated above, every model can be thought of as being derived from the DGP by a sequence of reductions and transformations. For example, the joint density function is separated in a conditional density function (the model) and an unconditional (the exogenous process), parameters are restricted, and so on. Hence, every empirical model is nested within the DGP. In order to capture the main features of the DGP, it is therefore extremely important to reduce 'correctly', i.e. without a significant loss of information.

It would appear to be an expression of 'brilliance, infinite creativity or extreme luck' (Hendry) if a simple empirical model - as the SPREAD-model - is congruent at the first attempt. Often it is rather the other way around, finding some misspecifications in simple models (e.g. autocorrelated residuals). 'Correcting' such misspecifications (e.g. by the Cochrane/Orcutt-procedure) is not suitable, because one cannot assume that the alternative hypothesis is valid if the null hypothesis is rejected (e.g. autocorrelated residuals are often indicative for dynamic misspecification and/or omitted variables instead of autocorrelated 'true' error terms).

Such problems can be avoided by starting the process of modelling from a fairly general model with many variables and lags, because such a model contains less restrictions imposed on the DGP compared to a simpler model and, therefore, is more likely to be congruent. A very good model to start with is an autoregressive-distributed lad model (ADL), because it contains many types of models frequently used as special cases (cf. Charemza/Deadman 1992, p.84; Hendry 1989, p.6):

$$a(L)Y_t = \sum_{k=1}^{K} b_k(L)X_{kt} + D_t + u_t \;. \tag{2.1}$$

Y_t is the endogenous variable, X_{kt} are the k exogenous variables, u_t is the 'white noise error' and t the time index; a(L) and $b_k(L)$ are polynomials of a given order n in the lag-operator L.[3] The deterministic part D_t may contain a CONSTANT, a deterministic TREND, and saisonal or other DUMMIES.

If the estimated ADL-model is congruent, it should be simplified by marginalizing variables and/or lags, transforming variables, imposing restrictions, and so on. Whether the reduction is valid or not can be tested.[4] Moreover, the simpler model also has to be tested for congruency. If it still proves to be congruent, it can be simplified further. The testing procedure has to be repeated after each reduction step. A 'wrong' reduction will influence the properties of the residual. Therefore the diagnostic tests on the residual's properties are very important. The residual represents the theoretical error term, i.e., everything in the data which is not explicitly allowed for by the model. Hence, in so far as the residual does not contradict to the properties, which are imposed on it a priori (white noise innovation), the reduction might be valid. The reduction sequence ends, when there are no more restrictions, which can be meaningfully imposed, or when the simpler model is no longer congruent. If the reductions are conducted 'correctly', the final simple model parsimoniously encompasses the ADL-model. The difference to the 'traditional' modelling approach now appears to be quite clear: instead of *simply assuming* that a simple model is correctly specified (and, hence, that the restrictions imposed on the DGP are valid), one only accepts a

---

[3] I.e., $a(L) = a_0 + a_1L^1 + ... + a_nL^n$, with $a_0 = 1$. The lag-operator itself is defined as $L^iX_t = X_{t-i}$, $i=1,...,n$. The polynomials $b_k(L)$ are defined in the same way, although their orders do not necessarily correspond.

[4] An appropriate test statistic is the F-form of a Lagrange-multiplier test (LMF); cf. Charemza/Deadman (1992), pp. 87-95.

simple model, if it is derived from a general and congruent one, which is quite 'near' to the DGP, by imposing restrictions *which proved to be valid* in appropriate tests.

2.2 The General ADL-Model

First of all I would like to explain the variables used in this investigation and test them for stationarity. Real economic activity is represented by the variable 'y', defined as the annual growth rate of real GNP in percentage points per annum: $y_t = \ln(Y_t/Y_{t-4}) \cdot 100$, whereby Y_t is the seasonally adjusted quarterly observation of real GNP (1980=100, billion DEM) in the Federal Republik of Germany from t=1967(Q2) to 1989(Q4) (S4, tab. 1)[5]. Variables, which are commonly claimed to determine the structure of interest rates in a broad sense, are used as explanatory variables. The inflation rate is defined according to 'y' as $\pi_t = \ln(P_t/P_{t-4}) \cdot 100$, whereby P is the GNP deflator (calculated from S4, tab. 1). RS is the 3 month money market rate on the Frankfurt interbank money market (MR, tab. V.6), and RL is the yield to maturity of all public bonds (S2, tab. 8b). The DEM/USD exchange rate (S5, tab. 5b) as additional variable proved to be insignificant;[6] the exchange rate regime shift addressed above can best be allowed for by a DUMMY - BW for Bretton Woods - which is 1 until 1971(Q1) and 0 otherwise. Interest rates were only available as monthly averages; quarterly averages were calculated as the simple arithmetic mean of the corresponding monthly values. Agreeing with Estrella and Hardouvelis (1991, p.558) I use quarterly averages for the investigation (instead of point-in-time data), because it seems plausible, that real economic activity is more closely associated with averages.

All variables have been tested for unit roots using an ADF(4)-test with a CONSTANT. The results are -3.81** for y, -2.14* for π, -3.64** for RS, and -2.97** for RL. Exact critical values are not available for those tests; Charemza/Deadman (1992, tab. 3, pp. 325-330) provide critical values based on simulation, which are -2.95 for 1% error probability (marked by '**') and -2.01 for 5% error probability (marked by '*').[7] The null hypothesis of a stochastic trend can be rejected for all variables with at least 5% error probability. I therefore proceed under the assumption of stationarity of all variables. Hence, it is not necessary to test for cointegration and standard estimation methods can be used.

---

[5] The data sources are the monthly reports (MR) and the statistical supplements, series n, (Sn) to the monthly reports of the Deutsche Bundesbank, with n=1,...,5.

[6] Further explanatory variables were considered, but proved to be insignificant in the presence of interest rate variables in the regression equation. In particular, this is true for: (A) the growth rates of the monetary aggregates M1, M2 and M3 (MR, tab. I.2.b) as additional monetary variables, and (B) the growth rate of the wages-per-employee index (S4, tab. 11) and the growth rate of the received-orders-in-manufacturing-industries index (MR, tab. VIII.4) as additional real variables.

[7] The ADF-tests in this article are based on 86 observations, whereas Charemza/Deadman only provide critical values for 75 and 100 observations. The critical values reported above were obtained by linear interpolation.

Both models considered in the subsequent sections - the simple SPREAD-model proposed in the literature and the alternative model developed below using the general to specific modelling strategy - are nested in a general ADL-model. For that reason I want to present it in the beginning:

$$(2.2)\quad y_{t+5} = \sum_{i=0}^{5} a_i y_{t-i} + \sum_{i=0}^{5} b_{1i} RL_{t-i} + \sum_{t=0}^{5} b_{2i} RS_{t-i} + \sum_{i=0}^{5} b_{3i} \pi_{t-i} + b_4 BW_t + C + u_t$$

The dependent variable is the future growth rate of real GNP from quarter t+1 to t+5 (the annual period following the current quarter t).[8] The autoregressive part contains the current and up to 5 quarters lagged growth rates of real GNP, the distributed lag part contains the inflation rate, long- and short-term interest rates, again the current and all up to 5 quarters lagged values. BW is the Bretton-Woods DUMMY, as explained above, and C is a CONSTANT. No restrictions except the lag length are imposed a priori. Table 1 contains the estimated parameters of model (2.2) and the most important diagnostic tests for congruency.

The summary statistics and diagnostic tests reported here and for the subsequent estimations are: the t-values in brackets below the estimated parameters, the mean value (M.V.) and standard deviation (S.Dev.) of the regressand, the standard error of regression (σ), the multiple coefficient of determination (R^2), its value adjusted for degrees of freedom (adj. R^2), the sum of squared residuals (RSS) together with the number of var(iables) and obs(ervations), the Durbin-Watson statistic for first order autocorrelation (DW), the Schwarz information criterion (SC), and an F-test of the joint significance of all slope coefficients. For tests, which are reported in the F-form, the degrees of freedom are given in paranthesis and - after the outcome of the test - the error probability is given in brackets. One would have to accept this error probability if one wishes to reject the null. Asterisks denote significant test statistics (* 5%, and ** 1% error probability, respectively). The following tests refer to the desirable properties of the residuals: no residual autocorrelation up to order 4 (AR1-4 F), normality (Normality Chi^2), two tests for homoskedasticity (ARCH 4 F and X_i^2 F), and a t-test[9] for a zero mean value of the innovation. Two tests for appropriate functional form (RESET F and X_i*X_j F) and two tests for parameter constancy (Forecast Chi^2, Chow F) terminate the diagnostic check.[10] Some test outcomes may not be available due to too few degrees of freedom. Notice that the estimation period can differ from 1967(Q2) to 1989(Q4) because of the creation of leads/lags or differences.

---

[8] This specification has been chosen to sustain comparability with Harvey (1991).

[9] For this test, the models were estimated recursively over the last 11 years.

[10] The last 8 years ('forecast period') have been reserved to conduct the tests for parameter constancy. The forecast Chi^2 should not be considered as a strict test, but rather as a hind for numerical parameter stability. If the test statistic exceeds 2 the model can not be recommanded for forecasts. Details of these and all other tests mentioned above are given in Hendry (1989) or, partly, in Charemza/Deadman (1992).

Table 1. Modelling y_{t+5} by OLS for 1969(Q3) to 1988(Q3) - ADL-model

Variable	coefficients (t-values) for lag i					
	0	1	2	3	4	5
y	-0.146 (-0.977)	0.136 (0.867)	0.077 (0.534)	-0.233 (-1.572)	0.164 (1.167)	0.163 (1.271)
RL	-0.821 (-1.524)	0.814 (1.151)	-0.175 (-0.244)	0.175 (0.251)	0.589 (0.817)	-0.664 (-1.326)
RS	-0.291 (-1.144)	-0.109 (-0.304)	-0.428 (-1.267)	0.059 (0.177)	-0.076 (-0.228)	0.500 (2.080)
π	-0.191 (-0.699)	0.375 (1.194)	0.275 (0.922)	-0.184 (-0.607)	-0.464 (-1.497)	0.300 (1.038)
BW	1.664 (1.781)					
CONSTANT	4.238 (2.196)					

Statistics and diagnostic tests

M.V. = 2.365	S.Dev. = 2.125	σ = 1.282
R^2 = 0.756	adj. R^2 = 0.632	RSS = 83.877 (26 var/77 obs)
DW = 1.69	SC = 1.55	F(25,51) = 6.31 [0.0000]

White noise (innovation) errors

AR 1-4 F(4,47) = 1.34 [0.2677]	Normality-Chi^2(2) = 0.76
ARCH 4 F(4,43) = 0.37 [0.8291]	Xi^2 F(39,16) = 0.43 [0.9842]
t(-) for zero innovation mean = not available	

Functional form

RESET F(1,50) = 0.01 [0.9316]	Xi*Xj F(-,-) = not available

Parameter constancy for 1980(Q4) to 1988(Q3)

Forecast Chi^2(32)/32 = 5.25	Chow F(32,19) = 1.16 [0.1335]

The tests do not reject any implication of congruency. Thus, the ADL-model is an appropriate starting point for the general to specific modelling strategy, especially since it obviously is overparameterized and contains insignificant variables and lags. Moreover, the forecast Chi^2 indicates that it should not be used as a forecast model itself, because it evidently exceeds 2.

2.3 Destructive Part: Evaluation of the SPREAD-Model

The SPREAD-model contains the SPREAD = RL-RS as the only explanatory variable (beside the CONSTANT and BW). An OLS-estimation yields the results described in table 2.

Table 2. Modelling y_{t+5} by OLS for 1969(Q3) to 1988(Q3) - SPREAD-model

y_{t+5} =	0.810	$SPREAD_t$	+ 2.304	BW_t	+ 1.339	+ u_t
	(8.049)		(3.863)		(6.143)	

Statistics and diagnostic tests

M.V. = 2.365	S.Dev. = 2.125	σ = 1.551
R^2 = 0.482	adj. R^2 = 0.461	RSS = 177.961 (3 var/77 obs)
DW = 1.16	SC = 1.01	F(2,74) = 34.38 [0.0000]

White noise (innovation) errors

AR 1-4 F(4,70) = 6.03 [0.0003]**	Normality-Chi²(2) = 0.55
ARCH 4 F(4,66) = 1.63 [0.1781]	Xi² F(3,70) = 0.25 [0.8627]
t(43) for zero innovation mean = -0.10	

Functional form

RESET F(1,73) = 2.87 [0.0943]	Xi*Xj F(4,68) = 0.19 [0.9432]

Parameter constancy for 1980(Q4) to 1988(Q3)

Forecast Chi²(32)/32 = 0.43	Chow F(32,42) = 0.43 [0.9923]

Parsimonious encompassing of ADL-model

Nested F(23,51) = 2.49 [0.0035]**

Although many tests have favourable outcomes, the null hypothesis of no residual autocorrelation can clearly be rejected. The probability of being wrong is extremely low (0.03%). This indicates that significant information has been lost during the (conjectural) reduction sequence from the ADL-model to the SPREAD-model. If the SPREAD-model were a valid simplification of the ADL-model, the following parameter restrictions must hold: the coefficients of the contemporaneous long-term interest rate RL_t and the contemporaneous short-term interest rate RS_t should be equal but opposite in sign (i.e. $b_{10} = -b_{20}$), and all other coefficients except those of the CONSTANT and BW should be zero. A

LM-test of this null hypothesis yields in the F-form $F(23,51) = 2.49^{**}[0.0035]$.[11] Hence, the null can be rejected with very low error probability, or, in other words, the SPREAD-model does not parsimoniously encompass the ADL-model.

Moreover, one has to bear in mind, that all the other tests besides that for residual autocorrelation are no longer valid as they are constructed under the assumption of no residual autocorrelation. Rejecting one null hypothesis is sufficient to reject congruency, as already stated in section 2.1. Consequently, the SPREAD-model is not congruent, further implications of congruency do not have to be tested. On the other hand, this means that there is a possibility for an improved model, which is to be developed in the subsequent section. Figure 2 finally provides the 'actual versus fitted' values plott of the SPREAD-model.

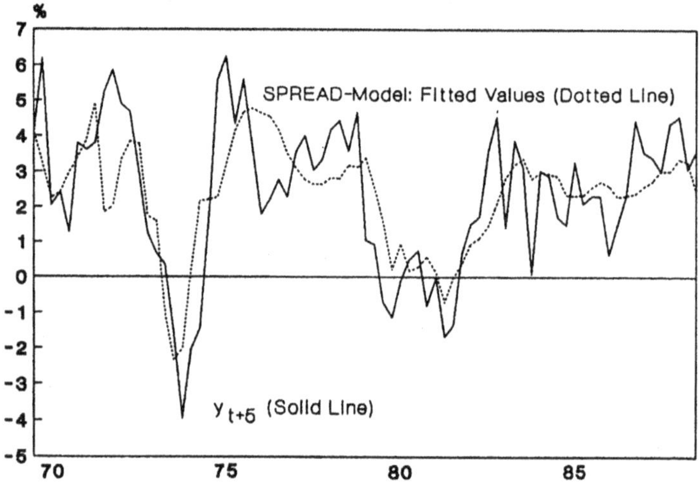

Figure 2. Actual versus fitted values - SPREAD-model

2.4 Constructive Part: Developing an Alternative Model

Starting from the ADL-model (2.2) the general to specific modelling strategy described in section 2.1 has been carried out. Because of the lack of space, I only report the final model, which I - to anticipate the main result of this section - call the 'Congruent model'. According to this model the following variables are indicative of a drawback of real economic activity in the subsequent year: an acceleration of the increase of the long-term interest rate compared to its last year value ($\Delta_1\Delta_4 RL_t$); a 2 quarters lagged increase of the short-term interest rate

---

[11] Reported as 'Nested F' in the tables.

($\Delta_3 RS_{t-2}$); an increase of the contemporanous short-term interest rate relativ to the 1 quarter lagged inflation rate ($RS_t - \pi_{t-1}$), this variable primarily reflects the influence of monetary policy; and the last year value of the inflation rate (π_{t-4}). The signs are theoretically plausible. The SPREAD does not appear in the model, because the corresponding parameter restriction imposed on the ADL-model is invalid: i.e. an increase of the long-term rate ceteris paribus has a different impact compared to a corresponding decrease of the short-term interest rate (in the SPREAD-model both are equal, because only the difference matters). Nevertheless term structure aspects have been taken into account, because both long- and short-term interest rates enter the model.

Table 3. Modelling y_{t+5} by OLS for 1969(Q3) to 1988(Q3) - congruent model

y_{t+5} =	-0.543	$\Delta_1\Delta_4 RL_t$	-0.368	$\Delta_3 RS_{t-2}$	-0.427	$(RS_t - \pi_{t-1})$
	(-2.398)		(-5.027)		(-6.283)	
	-0.255	π_{t-4}	+1.759	BW_t	+4.360	u_t
	(-2.928)		(3.549)		(9.236)	

Statistics and diagnostic tests

M.V. = 2.365	S.Dev. = 2.125	σ = 1.227
R² = 0.689	adj. R² = 0.663	RSS = 106.877 (6 var/77 obs)
DW = 1.62	SC = 0.67	F(5,71) = 31.42 [0.0000]

White noise (innovation) errors

AR 1-4 F(4,67) = 1.76 [0.1475]	Normality-Chi²(2) = 0.96
ARCH 4 F(4,63) = 0.52 [0.7239]	Xi² F(3,70) = 1.10 [0.3732]
t(43) for zero innovation mean = -0.62	

Functional form

RESET F(1,73) = 0.20 [0.6546] Xi*Xj F(4,68) = 0.75 [0.7511]

Parameter constancy for 1980(Q4) to 1988(Q3)

Forecast Chi²(32)/32 = 0.99 Chow F(32,42) = 0.93 [0.5748]

Parsimonious encompassing of ADL-model

Nested F(20,51) = 0,70 [0.8081]

Figure 3 reports the 'actual versus fitted' values plott of the congruent model.

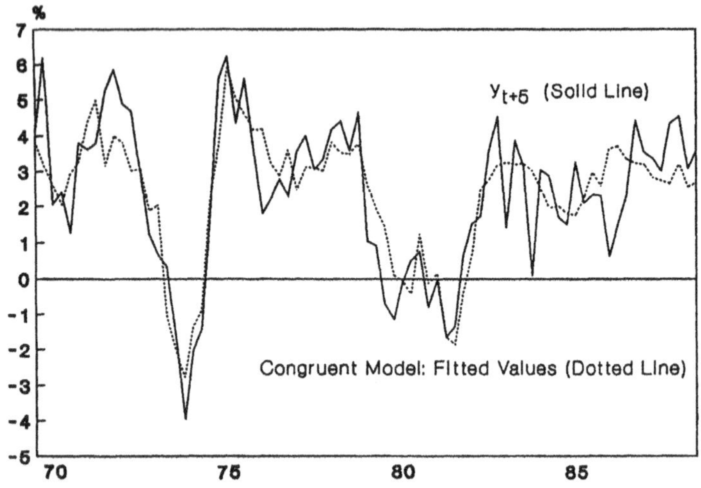

Figure 3. Actual vs. fitted values - congruent model

No diagnostic test rejects the null hypothesis at conventional significance levels. Thus, *white noise innovation errors* and - because of the data transformation, which was chosen - *data admissibility* are accepted as valid assumptions. Further implications of congruency are examined in the following.

Theory consistency: the dynamic congruent model implies a static long-run solution described by equation (2.3):

$$(2.3) \qquad y^* = 4{,}36 - 0{,}43RS^* + 0{,}18\pi^*$$

Equation (2.3) contains the long-run proportionalities between the variables considered, i.e., the proportinalities in the (unobservable) steady-state equilibrium. Because the variables do not change in the equilibrium, the terms with a difference operator 'Δ' and the time index 't' can be neglected. According to the LSE-approach the static long run-solurion should be consistent with economic theory. In the equilibrium the nominal short-term interest rate has a negativ and the inflation rate has a postive effect on the growth rate of real GNP. The small but positve effect of the inflation rate could be viewed as evidence for the validity of the Phillips-curve. The short-term interest rate in (3.2) however is a little surprising, although the sign clearly cannot be questioned. If the model is correct, the central bank is particularly reponsible for the business cycle, because short-term interest rates are under its control. This result contrasts the view that real economic activity mainly depends on investment in real capital which itself is determined by the long-term interest rate. As the yield of the long-term alternative (opportunity costs, supply cost of capital in Tobin's Q-theory), one would therefore expect the long-term interest rate to enter equation (2.3).[12]

A priori it is not known how a change of the short-term interest rate effects the long rate. According to the expectations theory of the term structure of interest rates, which is the most widely accepted theoretical explanation of the relation between long- and short-term rates, the long-term interest rate is nothing but an average of the current and expected future short-term interest rates. Hence, a single change at the short end of the yield curve changes long rates insofar as it influences expectations about future short rates.[13] In the long-run equilibrium, however, long- and short-term interest rates are equal to each other, because the short rate keeps constant. Hence, the short rate in (2.3) is consistent with that view, because it describes long-run relations. Moreover, taking it that way, equation (3.2) can explain why the SPREAD-model considered above - although not congruent - is a fairly good forecaster. It implicitly assumes the validity of the expectations theory as well, and, hence, similar long-run relations; merely the dynamics and the inflation effect are misspecified in that model.

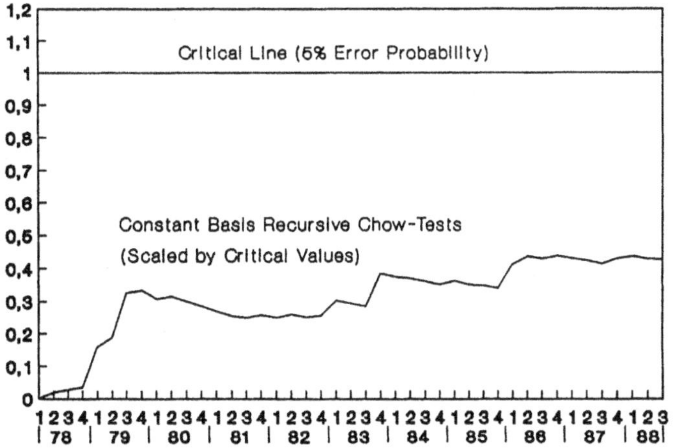

Figure 4. Constant basis recursive Chow-tests of the congruent model:1978(Q1) to 1988(Q3)

---

[12] This traditional view is also rejected by Filc (1992, pp. 12-17), who concludes that real economic activity can best be forecast by using short-term instead of long-term interest rates.

[13] As an implication of that relationship, the SPREAD is often suggested as an appropriate indicator for the stance of monetary policy.

Parameter constancy is one of the implications of congruency, which already has been checked by two diagnostic tests in table 3. Because it is especially important for forecast models, an additional powerful test has been carried out: a constant basis recursive Chow-test in order to detect eventual structural breaks. The model was estimated over a base period - 1969(Q3) to 1977(Q4) - in the first step; then the end of the estimation period was augmented by one quarter once per step and the model was reestimated. Finally, it was tested whether or not the parameters of the model estimated over each augmented period are constant compared to the base period. The test statistics were divided by their respective critical values at 5% error probability, such that '1' is the critical line in a graphical output (figure 4). Even this test does not reject the null hypothesis of parameter constancy for the congruent model. Moreover, an important implication of super exogeneity has been tested. Because weak exogeneity is necessary for super exogeneity, I conclude that the independent variables are (at least) *weakly exogenous* for the parameters of interest.

Encompassing: if the general to specific modelling strategy has been conducted correctly, the congruent model parsimoniously encompasses the ADL-model. As can be seen in table 3, a LM-test of this null hypothesis yields F(20,51) = 0.70 [0,8081]; thus it cannot be rejected. Although both the SPREAD-model and the congruent model are nested in the ADL-model, no one is nested within the other. Therefore they can be viewed as rival models of the same economic phenomenon, which can be compared by variance encompassing tests. A simple test is the J-test (cf. Davidson/McKinnon 1981): the fitted values of model A - $\hat{y}_A$ - are added to model B as an additional explanatory variable and its coefficient is tested for significance with an ordinary t- or F-test. If it is significant, model A (variance) encompasses model B. The J-tests yields the result, which is expected: the congruent model encompasses the SPREAD-model - F(1,73) = 49.381 [0.0000]** - but the SPREAD-model does not encompass the congruent model - F(1,70) = 0,584 [0.4475].

Table 4. Variance encompassing-tests

Model A: congruent model

Model B: SPREAD-model

A vs. B	Form	Test	Form	B vs. A
0.759	N(0,1)	Cox	N(0,1)	-9.256
-0.753	N(0,1)	Ericsson IV	N(0,1)	6.574
0.587	Chi²(1)	Sargan	Chi²(4)	29.926
0.584 [0.4475]	F(1,70)	Joint Model Probability	F(4,70)	11.882 [0.0000]

The J-test however is only an assymptotically valid test and not very powerful in small samples. Various alternatives, which are valid in small samples, are conducted by PC-GIVE (Cox', Ericsson's instrument variable and Sargan's test). The outcome of those tests are presented in table 4, together with a test for parsimonious encompassing of the joint model (the smallest model within which both models are nested). They uniformly confirm the result of the J-test. The tests are constructed such that model A encompasses model B if the test statistics on the left-hand side are insignificant et vice versa (cf. Hendry 1989).

In this section it has been shown, that the SPREAD-model proposed in the literature is misspecified, and that a congruent model can be developed, which appears to be superior in a great number of within-sample tests, as far as the model specification is considered. As it is the purpose of this article to find a model, which can be recommended for forecasts of future German real economic activity, the out-of-sample forecast performance of the model should be examined very carefully as well. After the final section we will know if the effort of the preceeding pages was worthwhile.

3 The Out-of-Sample Forecast Performance

To investigate the out-of-sample forecast performance of both models under realistic conditions, quarterly forecasts have been made for the period 1978(Q1) to 1989(Q4) using only information, which one could have had 5 quarters earlier, i.e. at that point in time 't', when the forecast was made (1976(Q4) to 1988(Q3)). In order to estimate the parameters of the models at 't', the actual growth rate of real GNP is available at best, which is related to explanatory variables observed 5 quarters earlier. Hence, it is necessary to stop the regressions 5 quarters before that point in time when the forecast is made in order to be realistic, even though all obeservations are available ex post.[14]

The subsequent investigation is based on the forecast errors, which are the difference of realisation and forecast. A very simple way of evaluating the forecast performance of models is to examine if their forecast errors are on the average lower than those of other forecasters. The mean forecast error is not appropriate for this, because positive forecast errors could compensate negative ones. Hence, the sign has to be eliminated. This can be done by taking either the absolute values of the forecast errors or their squares. Exactly this is the idea of mean

---

[14] Generating the out-of-sample forecasts, Harvey (1991, tab.2, p.709) used the subscript 't' for the parameters in his model instead of 't-5' as suggested by the considerations above. It can be presumed that recursive estimators have been used, which estimate the model using observations up to 't', such that the 'forecast errors' are equal to the one-step residuals, which are usually calculated by modern econometric software packages. This might be convenient, but not realistic, because y_{t+5}, which has to be forcast and therefore should not be implicitly treated as known, enters the recursive estimates as regressant.

absolute error (MAE) and the root mean square error (RMSE). They are defined as follows (cf. Fair 1986, p. 1984); let A = actual value, F = forecast value, n = number of forecasts, t = time:

(3.1)
$$MAE = \frac{1}{n} \sum_{t=1}^{n} |A_t - F_t|$$

(3.2)
$$RMSE = \sqrt{\frac{1}{n} \sum_{t=1}^{n} (A_t - F_t)^2}$$

Notice, that the RMSE weights large errors more heavily. Another very basic feature of a forecasting model is that it should not yield forecast errors which are larger than those of status quo forecasts, i.e., 'no-change' predictions. A measure for this is Theil's inequality coefficient U.[15] It is defined as follows; let $\Delta A_t = A_t - A_{t-4}$ actual change (here: compared to last year value; quarterly observations), $\Delta F_t = F_t - A_{t-4}$ forecast change:

(3.3)
$$U = \frac{\sqrt{\frac{1}{n} \sum_{t=1}^{n} (\Delta A_t - \Delta F_t)^2}}{\sqrt{\frac{1}{n} \sum_{t=1}^{n} \Delta A_t^2}}$$

Notice, that the numerator is the RMSE of the forecast changes of the model, and the denominator is the RMSE of predicting, that next year it will be like this year ($\Delta F_t = O$ for all t).[16]

MAE, RMSE and U can vary between zero (perfect forecaster) and infinity. U should at least be below one: otherwise it would not be worthwile to establish a model, because the simple no-change rule would yield lower forecast errors. Table 5 reports MEA, RMSE and U for the congruent model and the SPREAD-model.

'Quarterly frequency' of the forecasts means that the statistics are calculated using all forecast errors. For 'annual frequency' they are calculated using solely the forecast errors for the fourth quarters, i.e. those forecast errors made by forecasting the growth rates associated with a calendar year. All statistics indicate that the congruent model is superior having lower forecast errors on the average. Both models are considerably better than the naive no-change forecaster: their forecast errors are only about one half of the status quo forecasts.

---

[15] This formulation of Theil's inequality coefficient is taken from Theil (1966, p.28) and should not be mixed up with an earlier version (Theil, 1961, p.32) which is based on levels and can vary between zero and one. The earlier version proved to be defective (cf. Granger/Newbold, 1986, pp.278-280).

[16] In the case of status quo forecasts, all pairs $(\Delta F_t, \Delta A_t)$ lie on the vertical axis of figure 5.

Table 5. Forecast performance of interest rate based models 1978(Q1) to 1989(Q4)

	congruent model		SPREAD-model	
Frequency	quarterly	annual	quarterly	annual
MAE	0.95	0.81	1.02	0.83
RMSE	1.22	0.97	1.27	1.16
U	0.58	0.46	0.59	0.55

The statistics considered so far are rather descriptive, as they express the forcast power of a model in a summary measure. More sophisticated insights into the 'nature' of the forecast error can be drawn from a regression, as is explained by figure 5 (cf. Theil 1961, p.21).

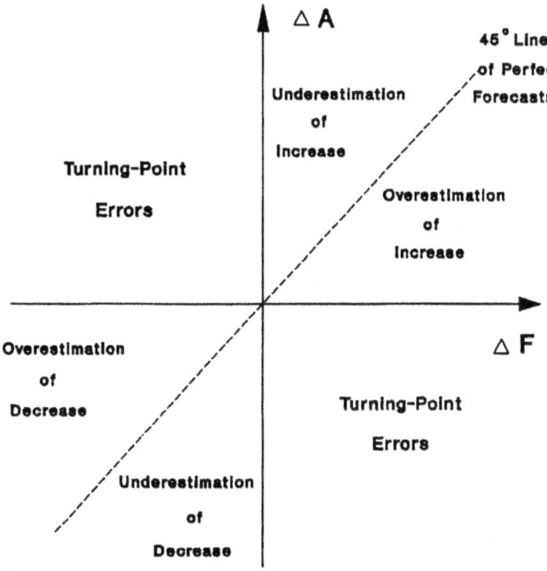

Figure 5. Actual versus forecast changes.

On the vertical axis $\Delta A_t = A_t - A_{t-4}$ denotes the actual change of the variable to be forecast (compared to its last year value). In the same way, $\Delta F_t = F_t - A_{t-4}$ denotes the forecast change on the horizontal axis. Every pair of forecast/realised change corresponds to a single point $(\Delta F_t, \Delta A_t)$ in the plane. For a perfect forecaster, all pairs (ΔA_t,ΔF_t) are on the 45°-line through the first and third quarter (i.e. $\Delta F_t = \Delta A_t$ for all t). Pairs in the second and forth quarter mark turning point errors (a decrease was forecast, whereas an increase took place, et vice versa). The other areas are described accordingly. Because it is practically excluded that forecasts are always correct, not all pairs may be on the 45°-line, but - for a good forecaster - they should be there on the average at least. This can be tested by regressing ΔA on ΔP and a CONSTANT (cf. Theil 1966, pp.26-36). Clearly, the slope coefficient should be insignificantly different from one, the intercept insignificantly different from zero: then, the estimated regression line would only differ insignificantly from the perfect forecast line. The forecast error can thus be devided into three parts: (A) the bias proportion (the intercept is significantly from zero); in that case the model on the average predicts to high or to low. (B) The regression proportion (the slope coefficient is significantly different from one): in that case the model under- or overpredicts changes. (C) the disturbance proportion (represented by the error term of the regression): this should be an unpredictable error, which cannot be avoided. (A) and (B) reflect systematic influences, which should be avoided by a good forecaster.

Table 6 contains the results of such a regression for both models. The regressions were only run for the quarterly frequency of forecasts, because otherwise there would be too few degrees of freedom.

Table 6. Modelling ΔA by OLS for 1978(Q1) to 1989(Q4)

	congruent model		SPREAD-model	
variable	coefficient	t-value	coefficient	t-value
ΔP	0.987	-0.123	1.343	2.522**
CONSTANT	-0.196	-1.021	-0.053	-0.286
Diagnostic tests of the residuals				
$R^2 = 0.676$		$\sigma = 1.262$	$R^2 = 0.698$	$\sigma = 1.218$
Normality $Chi^2 = 4.68$			Normality $Chi^2 = 1.07$	
AR 1-3 F(3,39) = 2.02 [0.1264]			Ar 1-3 F(3,39) = 0.79 [0.5088]	
ARCH 3 F(3,36) = 0.24 [0.8671]			ARCH 3 F(3,36) = 1.02 [0.3968]	
Xi^2 F(2,39) = 0.55 [0.5828]			Xi^2 F(2,39) = 0.51 [0.6072]	

Only the congruent model has the desired properties. The forecast error of the SPREAD-model suffers from a highly significant regression proportion, thus reflecting the lack of congruency. As the slope coefficient is significantly greater than one, the SPREAD-model tends to underpredict changes, i.e. it is conservative. Figures 6a and 6b present these rusults graphically: the dotted line is the 45°-line of perfect forecasts, the solid line is the OLS-line from table 6.

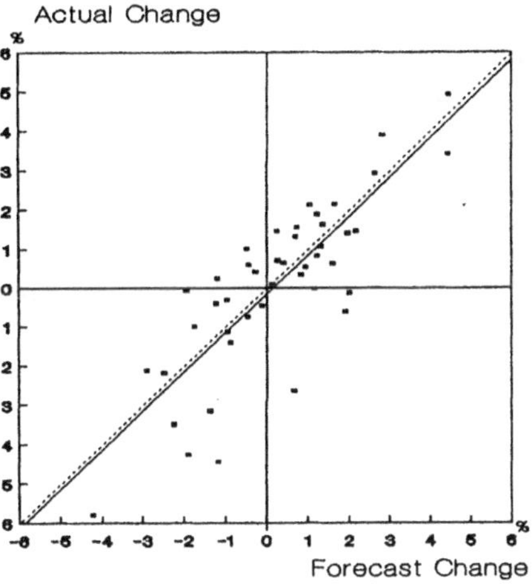

Figure 6a. Actual and forecast changes: congruent model

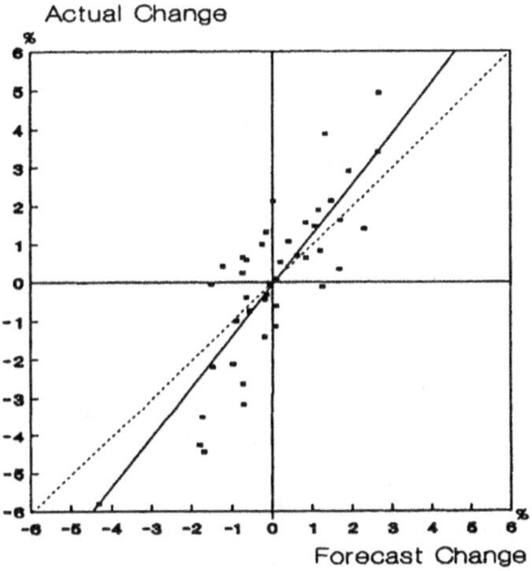

Figure 6b. Actual and forecast changes: SPREAD-model

Up to now the congruent model proved to be superior to the SPREAD-model. Hence, one would expect that the congruent model can account for the forecast errors of the SPREAD-model, but not vice versa. Similar to the J-test a test for forecast encompassing can be constructed (cf. Chong/Hendry 1986). Let 'F' be a compound forecast of the forecasts of the model A - 'F^A' - and B - 'F^B' - weighted with λ $(0 \leq \lambda \leq 1)$; 'A' is the realisation and 'u' is the compound forecast error:

(3.4)
$$F_t = (1-\lambda)F_t^A + \lambda F_t^B$$
$$\text{resp.} \quad A_t = (1-\lambda)F_t^A + \lambda F_t^B + u_t \,.$$

If model A were the 'true' model, then $\lambda = 0$ and $F = F^A$. This leads to the testable hypothesis described by equation (3.5), with $u^A = A\text{-}F^A$ being the forecast error of model A:

(3.5)
$$u_t^A = \lambda(F_t^B - F_t^A) + u_t \,.$$

Model B forecast encompasses model A if λ in (3.5) is significant. Applied to the models considered in this article, the test leads to an inconclusive outcome: the congruent model forecast encompasses the SPREAD-model with 1% error probability (t = 2,73**), but the SPREAD-model also forecast encompasses the congruent model, though only with 5% error probability (t = 2,01*). Hence, the SPREAD-model may contain some exclusive information, which has not entered the congruent model and which can partly explain the congruent model's forecast error.

Which conclusion can be drawn? In general it is evident that the search for a congruent model is worthwhile as it proved to be superior in all tests. The general-to-specific modelling strategy was an efficient tool for model design. But even the forecast ability of the SPREAD-model - although misspecified - could be confirmed. Having in mind the extreme simpliticity of the models presented here, their predictive ability in comparison to much more sophisticated and expensive methods (such as large scale macro models) is quite stiking. They are themselves an expression of the economic principle: they yield at least as good results as the alternatives, but at much lower costs. Clearly, the models also generated rather poor forecasts sometimes. One has to bear in mind that the models exploit the common knowledge incorporated in financial prices; hence, the models can only be as good as the expectations of economic agents, and there is no guarantee that they are always right. Moreover, the inconclusive outcome of the forecast encompassing tests points out the possibility of a further improved model, which may be subject to further research. Both models imply a theoretic framework, which is built on the interdependencies of central bank policy, short-term and long-term interest rates, inflation and real economic activity. It may be promising to investigate these relations more closely, even on a theoretical level.

4 Summary

The (term) structure of interest rates contains information about future real economic activity. The literature states in particular that a flattening yield curve normally is associated with a future decline of real economic activity. This general finding is (re)examined in detail, using average quarterly data for Germany from 1967 to 1989. To make sure that standard estimation techniques are admissible, the stationarity properties of all time series are investigated by unit root tests. In the following, a comparatively new econometric modelling approach is used, which attempts to overcome the shortcomings of traditional modelling: according to the 'LSE-approach', good models have to satisfy six criteria to be an adequate representation of the 'data generating process'. This can be evaluated by diagnostic tests. If a model passes all those tests, it is 'congruent (with the available information)'. Applied to a simple term structure model similar to that recently advanced by Harvey (1991), which only contains the SPREAD and a CONSTANT as explanatory variables - and on which he states that it outperforms the DIW forecasts and the consensus forecasts of five German research institutes - those tests reveal some specification errors and, hence, the possibility of an improved model. Thus, a congruent interest rate based model is developed along the lines of the 'general-to-specific modelling strategy' and it is shown, that it outperforms the SPREAD-model in out-of-sample forecasts.

References

Blake NS (1991) Modelling Trends in Macroeconomic Time Series. In: Federal Reserve Bank of Dallas: Economic Review, May, pp 19-33

Charemza WW, Deadman DF (1992) New Directions in Econometric Practice - General to Specific Modelling, Cointegration and Vector Autoregression, Aldershot (Edward Elgar)

Davis EP (1990) Credit Quality Spreads, Bond Market Efficiency and Financial Fragility, LSE Financial Markets Group Discussion Paper No 97, September

deBondt WFM, Bange MM (1991) The Role of the Capital Markets as Leading Indicators: Evidence from the United States since 1869, Wisconsin Working Paper 1-91-1, January

Chong YY, Hendry DF (1986) Econometric Evaluation of Linear Macro-Economic Models. In: Review of Economic Studies, Vol 53, pp 671-690

Davidson R, MacKinnon JG (1981) Several Tests for Model Specification in the Presence of Alternative Hypotheses. In: Econometrica, Vol 49, pp 781-793

Deutsche Bundesbank (Hrsg) (1983) Monatsbericht der Deutschen Bundesbank, January

Dickey DA, Fuller WA (1981) Likelihood Ratio Statistics for Autoregressive Time Series with a Unit Root. In: Econometrica, Vol 49, pp 1057-1072

Dickey DA, Jansen DW, Thornton DL (1991) A Primer on Cointegration with an Application to Money and Income. In: Federal Reserve Bank of St. Louis: Review, March/April, pp 58-78

Eitrheim Ø, Nymoen R (1988) LSE-Skolen i Økonometri, Arbeidsnotat av Norges Bank, Oslo, 10:1988

Engle RF, Yoo BS (1987) Forecasting and Testing in Co-Integrated Systems. In: Journal of Econometrics, March, pp 143-159

Engle RF, Granger CWJ (1987) Co-Integration and Error Correction: Representation, Estimation, and Testing. In: Econometrica, Vol 55, pp 251-276

Estrella A, Hardouvelis GA (1991) The Term Structure as a Predictor of Real Economic Activity. In: The Journal of Finance, Vol 46, pp 555-576

Faßbender H (1973) Zur Theorie und Empirie der Fristigkeitsstruktur der Zinssätze, Berlin (Duncker und Humblot)

Fisher I (1907) The Rate of Interest, New York

Fisher I (1922) The Purchasing Power of Money - Its Determination and Relation to Credit Interest and Crisis, 2 Ed, New York (Reprint by Augustus M Kelley)

Filc W (1992) Zinseskalation in Deutschland? - Devisenmarktanalyse für das zweite Vierteljahr 1992, Institut für Empirische Wirtschaftsforschung, Hagen

Friedman BM, Kuttner KN (1991) Why Does the Paper-Bill Spread Predict Real Economic Activity?, Working Paper No 3879, NBER, October

Gebauer W (1989) Zinsstrukturtheorie und Zentralbankpolitik In: Bub N, Dudewag D,Richter R (Hrsg): Geldwertsicherung und Wirtschaftsstabilität, Festschrift für Helmut Schlesinger zum 65. Geburtstag, Frankfurt (Fritz Knapp), S 71-86

Gilbert CL (1986) Professor Hendry's Econometric Methodology. In: Oxford Bulletin of Economics and Statistics, Vol 48, pp 283-307. Wiederabgedruckt in: Granger CWJ (ed) (1990) Modelling Economic Series, Oxford (Clarendon Press), pp 279-303

Granger CWJ (1986) Developments in the Study of Cointegrated Economic Variables. In: Oxford Bulletin of Economics and Statistics, Vol 48, pp 213-228

Granger CWJ, Newbold P (1986) Forecasting Economic Time Series, 2nd Ed, Orlando (Academic Press)

Hardouvelis GA (1988) The Predictive Power of the Term Structure during Recent Monetary Regimes. In: The Journal of Finance, Vol 43, pp 339-356

Harvey AC (1990) The Econometric Analysis of Time Series, 2nd Ed, New York (Philip Allan)

Harvey CR (1991) Interest Rate Based Forecasts of German Economic Growth. In: Weltwirtschaftliches Archiv, Bnd 127, pp 701-718

Hendry DF (1986) Econometric Modelling with Cointegrated Variables: An Overview, In: Oxford Bulletin of Economics and Statistics, Vol 48, pp 201-212

Hendry DF (1989) PC-GIVE (Generalized Instrumental Variables Estimators) - An Interactive Econometric Modelling System, Version 6.0/6.01, Oxford

Hendry DF, Ericsson NR (1991) An Econometric Analysis of U.K. Money Demand in Monetary Trends in the United States and the United Kingdom by Milton Friedman and Anna J Schwartz. In: The American Economic Review, Vol 81, pp 8-38

Hesse H, Roth G (1992) Die Zinsstruktur als Indikator der Geldpolitik? In: Kredit und Kapital, 25 Jg, pp 1-25

Jaeger A (1992) Zinssätze als vorauseilende Indikatoren der Konjunkturentwicklung. In: Monatsberichte des Österreichischen Instituts für Wirtschaftsforschung, J 65, pp 286-290, Mai

Kessel RA (1965) The Cyclical Behavior of the Term Structure of Interest Rates, Occasional Paper 91, NBER, New York

Russell S (1992) Understanding the Term Structure of Interest Rates. In: Federal Reserve Bank of St. Louis Review, Vol 74, pp 36-50

Sargan JD, Bhargava A (1983) Testing Residuals from Least Squares Regression for Being generated by the Gaussian Random Walk. In: Econometrica, Vol 51, pp 153-174

Shah M, Wadhwani S (1990) The Effect of the Term Spread, Dividend Yield and Real Activity on Stock Returns: Evidence from 15 Countries; LSE Financial Markets Group Discussion Paper No 98, September

Shiller RJ (1990) The Term Structure of Interst Rates. In: Friedman BM, Hahn FH (Eds) Handbook of Monetary Economics, Vol 1, Amsterdam (Elsevier), pp 627-722

Theil H (1961) Economic Forecasts and Policy, 2nd Ed, Amsterdam (North Holland)

Theil H (1966) Applied Economic Forecasting, Amsterdam (North Holland)

Tobin J, Brainard WR (1977) Asset Markets and the Cost of Capital. In: Balassa B, Nelson R (Eds) Economic Progress, Private Values, and Public Policy, Amsterdam (North Holland), pp 235-262

Wicksell K (1899) Penningeräntans inflytande på varupriset. In: Nationalekonomiska föreningens förhandlingar under förra halvåret 1898, Stockholm, pp 47-70

The Evolution of Ecu Markets

Alfred Steinherr
European Investment Bank, Luxembourg

This paper has three parts. Part I defines the Ecu, notes its technical features and describes the evolution of Ecu markets. Part II starts from the Maastricht Treaty and interprets the implications for the Ecu on the way to European Monetary Union (EMU). Part III attempts an outlook.

1 From the Origin to the Maastricht Treaty[1]

1.1 Origin and Definition of the Ecu

The Ecu is older than most people realize and is, in fact, a reincarnation of the European Unit of Account (EUA), created in 1974 as an accounting unit for the European Development Fund. This unit was then renamed the Ecu (European Currency Unit) when the European Monetary System (EMS) was established in 1979 and its fate was linked to progress on European monetary integration.

The EUA was supposed to represent a European average. This is why the Ecu contained all Community currencies, and the weights were to reflect the relative economic size of each country in relation to Community GDP, intra-Community trade and the EMS financial support system. These objective criteria were used in 1979 to determine the initial composition of the Ecu basket.

The concern to have a representative basket is also evident in the provision that the composition of the basket is re-examined and, if necessary, revised by the ECOFIN council every five years, or on request if a change in weight exceeds 25 per cent. The creation of the EMS and the change of name in 1979 must have introduced additional considerations since this provision was not used even though, at that time, some imbalances had emerged. (For example, in 1979 the Italian lira's share in the Ecu basket had been reduced to less than one-third of the D-Mark's.) However, in 1984, when the Greek drachma was added to the basket, and in 1989 when the Portuguese escudo and the Spanish peseta were included, some judgmental adjustments were made which offset the increased weight of the stronger currencies. This implies that since 1979 the economic criteria have served only as broad indicators.

---

[1] A more complete survey is supplied by Gros (1991).

In 1979 the actual shares of the two strong currencies, the D-Mark and the Dutch guilder, exceeded their economic weight (and correspondingly the shares of the weaker currencies were lower than their economic weights). According to economic criteria the share of the D-Mark should have been 25 per cent in 1979, but its actual share was 33 per cent; conversely, the lira's share should have been 13 per cent, but its actual share in 1979 was only 9.5 per cent. An important consideration has been the degree of participation in the exchange rate mechanism (ERM). Italy, with a wider intervention band, and the UK, which did not participate in the ERM until 1990, received smaller weights. The recompositions in 1984 and 1989 followed a similar pattern: the shares of the strong currencies (the D-Mark and Dutch guilder) always remained well above their weights according to official economic criteria. In this sense the Ecu was always stronger than the average value of the Community currencies.

The Ecu is defined on a basket of fixed amounts of (at present) 12 Community currencies. These amounts are fixed between recompositions and the weights can change only because of exchange rate movements.

The fixed-amount basket definition thus has the drawback that, at times of large currency fluctuations, it creates a need for periodic revisions if the basket is to reflect some representative average performance. It would have been possible to avoid this problem by adopting another basket definition, for example the fixed-weight basket. There are several different ways a fixed-weight basket can be achieved in practice. One solution would be to automatically increase the amounts of the depreciating currencies and to automatically reduce amounts of the appreciating currencies.

A further option, equivalent to the hard Ecu proposed recently by the UK, is the 'asymmetrical' (also fixed-weight) basket, which would not depreciate against even the strongest currency because quantities of the weaker currencies would be added automatically in the same proportion as they depreciate, whereas the amounts of the appreciating currencies would remain unchanged. These options were rejected at the time the Ecu was created because they would be too cumbersome for potential private market participants.[2]

However, one might even regard the automatic increase in the weight of the stronger currencies as an advantage. Given that the future currency of the Community has to be strong, it is desirable to see the weight of the weaker currencies fall over time. That is why it has often been proposed to freeze the composition of the Ecu.[3] This would leave the governments of the more inflationary countries with the alternatives of either seeing their currencies slowly disappear from the Ecu or adopting tougher anti-inflationary policies.

It can be argued that the Ecu is an amazingly complicated currency construction on at least three accounts.

First, because weights are a function of exchange rates one cannot simply assume constant weights for the computation of longer maturity interest rates. As long as interest rates on the basket component currencies differ, interest

---

[2] For a detailed discussion, see Girard, Pacheco and Steinherr (1991).

[3] see Steinherr et al (1985).

rate parity suggests that exchange rates are expected to move in line with interest rate differentials. Therefore weights change over time: those of strong currencies increase and those of weak currencies decline. As a result, the Ecu yield curve is flatter than the average of the basket weighted by current shares. This is illustrated in Figure 1 where it is assumed that the yield curve is flat in all component currencies.[4]

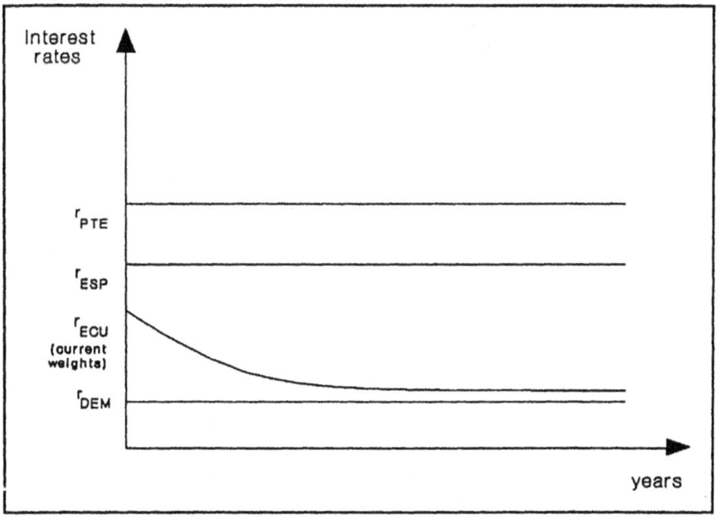

Figure 1.

Second, the recompositions at 5 year intervals tended to increase the weight of the weak currencies and thereby the basket interest rate. Ecu holders suffered a corresponding capital loss that increases inversely with the length of time to the next recomposition and proportionately with the remaining maturity beyond recomposition. To compensate for this expected loss, the Ecu rate had to increase above the basket-average. Girard and Steinherr (1989) computed a premium ranging from 30 basis points (5 years before) to 70 basis points (1 year before) the recomposition of 1989 for an Ecu bond maturing in 1997. In addition there is a risk premium of several basis points as the recomposition could not be forecast with certainty.

Third, it needs to be recognised that despite the definition of the Ecu as a basket, the two are not the same thing. For example, recomposition has an effect on the Ecu but not on the basket held as a diversified portfolio. Therefore, there is no strict risk-free arbitrage forcing returns on both to fall

[4] See Girard, Steinherr (1989) The Ecu: A Currency Unlike any Other, EIB Papers, June.

within a range set by transaction costs. Indeed, transaction costs of bundling or unbundling the Ecu can represent 15-20 basis points whilst the spread between actual and synthetic Ecu rates is often much higher.

Interest rate parity between the Ecu and the basket, within limits set by arbitrage transaction costs, would require stopping basket revisions and could be enforced either through intervention by a monetary authority or by making the Ecu and the basket legally equivalent as means of payment. Neither condition being satisfied, the Ecu is, in fact, independent of the basket.[5] This is an important consideration for the evaluation of the Maastricht objective in Part II.

To avoid confusion and cumbersome notations, it may prove useful to define the following notions of the Ecu. The EMS treaty created the official Ecu whose use was restricted to central banks and certain official transactions. Markets then developed in the private Ecu with the same basket definition. This basket definition can be used to compute an Ecu exchange rate and interest rate as a weighted average of the basket components. These rates are called the *basket* or *theoretical* rates, which differ from the rates determined by the market for the Ecu (*market* or *actual* rates) for reasons developed below. The future single European currency will also be called Ecu. Obviously it will not be basket-based any longer and is therefore referred to as the *abstract* Ecu.

1.2 The Ecu and the EMS

When the EMS was established, the Ecu was supposed to be at the centre of the system because it has four functions in the EMS. It is:

(i) used to calculate the grid of bilateral exchange rates for the ERM. However, since the choice of the numeraire used to calculate the grid is completely arbitrary, this is only an accounting convention.
(ii) the basis for the divergence indicator, which was created to indicate which currency is deviating from the average. This divergence indicator is supposed to trigger corrective action in the diverging country (in practice often Germany). However, in reality it is seldom used.
(iii) the unit of account for the operations of the European Monetary Cooperation Fund (EMCF).
(iv) the means of settlement for operations arising through the financing mechanisms of the EMS.

The Ecu could therefore have played an important role in the EMS. In fact, the use of the Ecu in the EMS has been limited to the operations of the EMCF, so that the official Ecu has been effectively used only to settle

[5] Steinherr et al (1991).

transactions among EMS-member central banks. Thus, whilst the EMS was a key for the development of the Ecu, the EMS would have functioned just the same without the Ecu.

The EMS agreement did foresee a very restricted use of the Ecu, i.e. the official Ecu. All EMS national central banks (whether or not they participate in the ERM) have to deposit 20 per cent of the approximate market value of their gold and dollar reserves with the EMCF (through automatically renewable three-monthly swaps) and receive corresponding amounts in (official) Ecu. These official Ecus can be held only by EMS member central banks and other officially designated institutions. The way in which these official Ecus are created shows that it is not really a currency or a reserve asset, but only a book-keeping device for exchanges of the underlying US dollar and gold reserves.

1.3 The Potential of the Ecu for the Borrowers, Bankers and Investors

The private Ecu is simply a contract in which the contracting parties have denominated payment obligations in Ecu and have accepted its official definition. This is the so-called 'open-basket' Ecu, which changes composition when the official composition changes. In practice, private markets have almost always used this open basket, instead of the closed basket under which the Ecu is defined as the sum of the amounts of the currencies in the basket at the time the contract is concluded. This implies that a five-year Ecu bond issue concluded before 1989, when neither the peseta nor the escudo were in the basket, has to be repaid with Ecus that contain two new currencies.

If financial markets had used the closed-basket definition, they would have eliminated the risk inherent in recompositions that can never be accurately predicted. However, with the closed basket, different Ecus would be created which would cause confusion in the markets. The open-basket definition was thus crucial to allow a unified Ecu market to emerge.

The Ecu took off only two years after the creation of the EMS. The first Ecu bond issues and bank deposits came in 1981, and the amounts involved were initially modest. Starting from almost nothing (Ecu 213 million issued in 1981), the market exploded as new Ecu bond issues amounted to Ecu 31.6 billion in 1991 or 10.6% of all international issues. See Table 1.

Table 1. International bond-issues

Proportion in per cent	1987	1988	1989	1990	1991
US-Dollar	36.2	37.2	49.6	34.6	30.2
Yen	14.8	9.9	9.3	13.4	13.7
ECU	4.1	4.9	4.9	7.8	10.6
Pound Sterling	8.4	10.6	7.7	9.2	8.7
Canadian Dollar	3.3	5.8	4.9	2.8	7.6
Swiss Franc	13.4	11.6	7.3	10.1	6.8
German Mark	8.3	10.4	6.4	8.0	6.7
French Franc	1.4	1.3	2.0	4.3	5.9
Australian Dollar	4.9	3.7	2.6	2.3	1.5
Other Currencies	5.2	4.6	5.3	7.5	8.3
Total	100	100	100	100	100

Source: OECD

The use of the Ecu in the banking sector follows a similar long run pattern as shown in Figure 2. An interesting feature of the Ecu banking market is the imbalance between assets and liabilities. Banks can have open positions in Ecu because they can cover themselves by taking the opposite position in the individual currencies that constitute the basket. Before 1989 the share of Ecu assets in total assets was much higher than the share of Ecu liabilities in total liabilities. The situation was corrected in 1989 to 1990, so that banks are now roughly balanced. They maintain however net claims vis-a-vis non-banks.

The use of the Ecu has not been restricted to these two basic market segments. Since 1985 a number of derivative markets have developed which enhance the usefulness of the basic instruments denominated in Ecu. The Ecu markets have also become more liquid and technically more complete, attracting different classes of investors. Although less spectacular than the initial growth of the Ecu in the bond and banking markets, this widening and deepening of the Ecu markets since 1985 is crucial for the future development of the Ecu as exchange rate variability becomes less important. One sign that the Ecu is overcoming the barrier of low transaction volumes, and therefore high costs, is that the turnover in Ecu securities increased constantly in the late 1980s until, in 1990, the Ecu accounted for over 10 per cent of the total turnover in the Euromarkets. The usefulness of the Ecu is further enhanced by the clearing system in Ecu (operated through the BIS) which is the only European-wide system to provide same-day settlement.

This brief survey suggests that the use of the Ecu in private international financial markets, which only started in 1981, increased very rapidly until 1985 and then increased more slowly, before accelerating again in 1989. The Ecu has thus become a significant Euro currency, albeit the only one without a domestic base. In 1991 the Ecu ranked third in international bank syndicated loans and international bond issues.

While the Ecu is widely used in financial markets, it is not yet an important vehicle for current transactions such as the invoicing of international trade. The Ecu is also not widely used as a unit of account in the private sector. This explains why most of the Ecu bank activity constitutes interbank business.

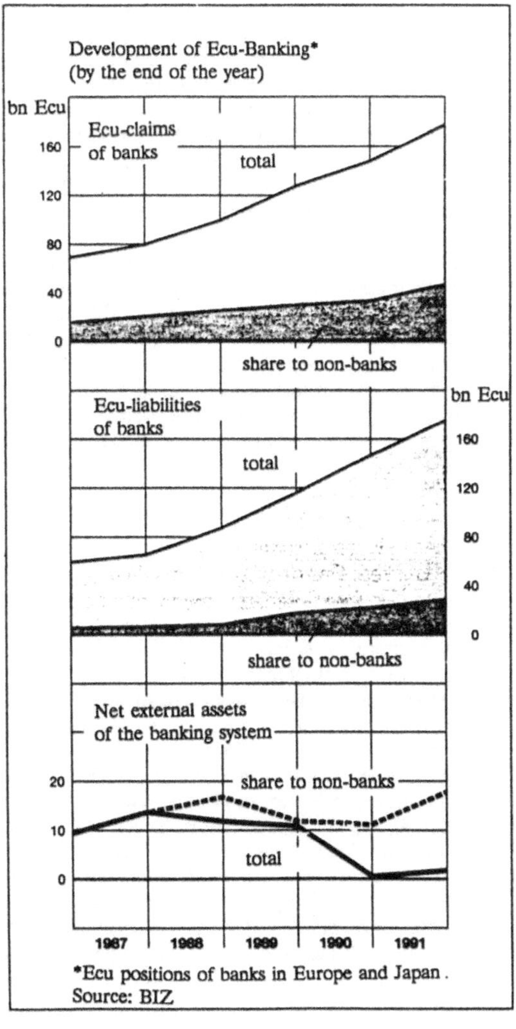

Figure 2.

What makes the Ecu so attractive for investors, bankers and borrowers? In the early 1980s, the main attraction of the Ecu was that it proved a convenient hedge against currency fluctuations. However, as intra-EC exchange rate fluctuations are reduced through the EMS, this aspect is losing some of its initial importance. The diversification argument , while important, should also not be overestimated. Exchange rate variability among the component currencies has already been reduced to about one-third of the level reached during the early 1980s, but the Ecu has apparently maintained its attractiveness in financial markets.[6] Other factors must therefore play a role.

One factor which might have been important in the past was that the Ecu received preferential treatment from the French and Italian authorities. Certain transactions that were prohibited under French and Italian capital controls could be carried out if the Ecu were used. However, this factor cannot have been important, for the use of the Ecu in these (and other) countries has actually increased even after full liberalisation of the capital markets in France and Italy. Similarly, it appears that the German prohibition of bank accounts denominated in Ecu, which was lifted in 1987, was also not very important as the use of the Ecu in the banking sector in Germany has remained very limited even after the elimination of this obstacle.[7]

The decisive factor favouring the Ecu at present must, therefore, lie elsewhere. The Ecu continues to be attractive even as exchange rates become stable, because of the prospect of full European Monetary Union (EMU), with the Ecu as the single common currency.

2 From Maastricht to EMU

At the European Summit in Maastricht on 11 December 1991 a decision was made on how to move to a single currency in the Community before the end of the century at the latest. The agreement also provides the details of the three-stage proposal of the Delors Committee on European Monetary Union (EMU). Institutionally, a European Monetary Institute (EMI) will be created at the beginning of Stage Two in 1994, preceding the European Central Bank as the core of the European System of Central Banks which will be created in 1997 at the earliest and by the second half of 1998 at the latest. The Treaty of Maastricht - or Union Treaty - was signed in early February and must be ratified by the Community's twelve national parliaments, a process that will probably take about a year. The probability that at least one country will be unable to ratify has always been quite high, albeit largely ignored. Denmark's negative referendum result has demonstrated the high risk of the approach.

[6] see Steinherr, Perée (1991).

[7] The restriction on the issuance of Eco-denominated bonds was only lifted in 1990. For a survey of the legal status of the Ecu, see Arthur Andersen.

2.1 How Will the Future European Currency Compare to the D-Mark?

Before discussing the feedback effects of the Maastricht decision on the actual Ecu and the path to EMU, it is useful to reflect on the final outcome when a single currency exists. The key question is doubtlessly how good a currency will it be or, more practically, how will it compare to the D-Mark?

This is, of course, the question with which the Germans are most concerned at present as they are requested to give up a currency that has been tested times and times again and has successfully held out against major shocks (oil shocks, unification, etc,) without durably losing its remarkable price stability performance or losing its rank among international currencies.[8]

There is considerable debate about the necessary and sufficient conditions for securing price stability in an economy without price and exchange controls. I consider that independence of the monetary authorities and their constitutional responsibility in pursuing the goal of price stability are necessary but not sufficient conditions. Other necessary conditions are fiscal restraint and a fairly even distribution of income across the monetary union. This is certainly a characteristic of the few countries with the most stable currencies (Germany, Japan, Switzerland).[9]

The Maastricht Treaty rightly insists on all these aspects, even if not necessarily for the right reasons. To start with the last argument, the question is whether D-Mark stability can be extended to a group of countries as diverse as those of the Community? The Treaty emphasises the need for an increase in structural funds to sweeten the perception of the tough requirements for convergence and thereby creates considerable moral hazard. To be able to enter EMU the convergence criteria need to be satisfied. These criteria do not comprise, however, previous convergence of living standards.

Pronounced differences in economic development do not make price stability impossible but are likely to cause trouble. In other terms, and in spite of all the measures promoted by the Commission, the Community is farther away from being an "optimal currency union" than are national states, particularly regarding the integration of labour markets.[10] In an integrated market with a single currency it will be increasingly difficult to restrain wage increases to productivity increases when identical workers in a neighbouring country earn significantly more. German unification illustrates this problem well. The size of fiscal transfers to the new states (Länder) of Germany is such (60% of income in the East) that it is neither sustainable nor replicable for the poorer

---

[8] See Issing O (1992) Europäische Währungsunion-Kriterien nicht aufweichen, Handelsblatt, 9.März, p 13.

[9] See Giovannini, Spaventa (1991). They argue that some member countries' current and projected budget deficits are inconsistent with the stabilisation of their debt/GNP ratios. EMU will multiply the opportunities for tax avoidance by mobile factors and therefore exacerbate structural imbalance. Unsustainable fiscal imbalances that affect the market value of government securities and hence the stability of financial markets could force the ECB to inject liquidity in order to avoid widespread financial crises and their effects on the real economy.

[10] See Mèlitz (1991).

countries of the Community. The pressure to be borne by the ECB may therefore be such that its formal independence may not withstand prolonged crises and sustained unemployment differentials. And it is good to remember in this context that Bundesbank independence is not as much due to constitutional provisions as to the support of the German people.

Furthermore, the remarkable Treaty agreement on simple majority voting in the Governing Council of the ECB is likely to stir up problems. It needs to be seen how large countries react when confronted with opposing views from representatives of small countries. Unlike in the Federal Reserve Open Market Committee where regional votes number 5 out of 12, in the Governing Council of the ECB regional votes number 12 out of 18 and more with new memberships. In the Council the weight of the representative of Luxembourg equals that of the Bundesbank's representative. Tolerance for unweighted, simple majority voting will certainly be tested when coalitions form which favour growth over price stability.

The compromise reached at Maastricht in interpreting the convergence conditions as guide-lines rather than as binding constraints is also worrisome to the pessimists. The future Ecu may well be the currency of countries with record public sector indebtedness (but recent trend reversals), high but falling public sector borrowing requirements (not adjusted for business cycle influences, as in the structural fiscal deficit), and widely diversified incomes. Some observers argue that the convergence criteria have no economic justification other than as threats and incentives. Whether the weaker countries can respond to them remains unclear. Others go further and argue that the fiscal rules in particular are undesirable and unenforceable. Such rules are too vulnerable to clever accounting techniques to be enforceable and should have distinguished between "structural" and "cyclical" deficits.[11] The basic structure therefore would appear weaker than the one on which the D-Mark was based, not mentioning Germany's long-term current account surpluses (tattered by unification), which compares with a deficit or a small surplus for EMU.

In terms of autonomy, the Treaty includes all one could have hope for (and even more!) and what paper can achieve. Not only the ECB, but all national central banks in the European System of Central Banks are required by Article 109E.3 to be made independent. Regarding government financing, the Treaty is even more restrictive than the Bundesbank laws: the ESCB cannot extend credits to government and the public sector (except public sector banks) and cannot bail-out a government in trouble. Formally, this constraint could be circumvented by acquisition of government debt in the secondary market (which is allowed for open market and liquidity operations). But it is to be hoped that independent members of the ESCB will not bow to government pressure and use this way of negating the spirit of the Treaty. It certainly cannot be expected that a Treaty delivers sufficient conditions for price stability. Maastricht delivered what was possible, unavoidably leaving

[11] See Dornbusch, Draghi (1991).

unanswered questions and doubts.[12] Credibility can only be established over time and by acts, and central bank independence by general popular support. If, one day, a majority of Europeans considered price instability a lesser evil than slow growth or high unemployment, then the ECB might prefer to respect this preference of the majority.

Therefore, it does not seem compelling to consider the future Ecu as "at least as good as the D-Mark", but its chances are excellent. Nor is acquisition of the actual Ecu an investment in the future European currency, as argued in the next Section.

2.2 Market Reactions

Political commentators and markets have interpreted the Maastricht agreement as a final victory for the actual Ecu. This sentiment has been translated into expanded demand for Ecu securities, as evidenced by decreasing market Ecu yields in relation to the theoretical basket yields (until the Denmark referendum). This favourable view is further sustained by the recent issue of Ecu 1.5 bn 30-year bonds by the government of France and the auction of the first Ecu 1 bn 3-year notes by the British Treasury. Both issues were enthusiastically received at prices close to (for the bonds) or below (for the notes) French franc yields. The 30-year French Ecu bond is peculiar in that its maturity date was set to coincide with that of an outstanding French franc bond which can be converted into the Ecu issue once France switches to the single European currency. In the view of some observers, the Ecu now has the potential of becoming, and even before 1997, the second largest international currency in financial markets, besides the US dollar.[13]

The attractiveness of the Ecu market is further illustrated by the fact that it now includes benchmark issues spanning the whole 3-month to 30-year gamut.[14] In this respect only the US, and to a lesser extent the British and French markets, offer a similarly liquid range. Up until now mean-variance based models of optimal portfolio allocation have resulted in shares of Ecu fixed-income securities far in excess of actual shares held.[15] The reason for this discrepancy between theory and practice has been attributed to the reduced choice of Ecu instruments, lack of political support behind the Ecu and uncertainty over the Ecu's future. On all three accounts one can now expect that Ecu market shares will get closer to those dictated by theory. So, even before EMU, the Ecu could become the most important currency in

---

[12] For example, if there is a major crisis in banking or in the payments system, will price stability remain lexico-graphically superior or will there be a trade-off?

[13] For an early assessment of this potential, see Bishop (1991).

[14] Top-rated Ecu-denominated securities are now available throughout the yield curve: 3 and 6 month bills and 3 year notes (UK); 4 year bonds (Belgium, Spain and Norway); 8 - 10 year bonds (UK, France, Italy and the EIB); 13 year bonds (Finland and France's SNCF); 20 year bonds (Italy and France, respectively).

[15] See Steinherr, Girard (1991).

international portfolios besides the US dollar.

From a currency point of view the D-Mark is the obvious rival to the Ecu. From an investment angle, a totally different picture emerges. As EMU implies ultimate convergence of interest rates, the high-yield currencies offer the greatest scope for capital gains. Borrowers, by contrast, are likely to favour the D-Mark and the Ecu. Hence, there will be increased pressure toward interest rate convergence in anticipation of EMU. Combining this argument with the political reluctance of Southern European countries to be seen as laggards, and the possible entry of hard-currency countries such as Austria (and Sweden) in the EC, leads G. Bishop to expect Stage Three to effectively begin on 1 January 1995.[16]

3 Outlook: EMU and the Ecu

The creation of the single market in financial services will allow the elimination of many of the restrictions that impose the use of the national currency for large investors, such as pension funds or life insurance companies. These restrictions are no longer appropriate because intra-EC exchange rate fluctuations are slowly being eliminated by the EMS, making the Ecu a low-risk investment. A huge new market, estimated by Bishop (1991) at Ecu 800 billion, will therefore open for the Ecu when regulations that impose the use of the national currency for the investments of insurance companies and pensions funds can also be fulfilled by an investment in Ecu. This was proposed in a recent EC framework directive.

A second growth phase for the Ecu could therefore start well before EMU is achieved. During this phase, exchange rate variability will be progressively eliminated, so that the Ecu will not be used because of its hedging qualities but because it will be a convenient instrument to tap a European-wide capital market. Ecu capital markets are already achieving a degree of liquidity and a spectrum of maturities only surpassed by US dollar markets.

EMU will not only affect the domestic (that is, European) role of the Ecu. EMU will also make the Ecu a major global currency, presumably on a par with the US dollar, for the economic potential of the EC exceeds that of the US.

What are the implications of a global role for the Ecu? First, the EC will earn some seigniorage, which is the profit that results from issuing currency. These seigniorage gains will be significant but less important than sometimes believed because they can be earned only on Ecu assets that bear no interest, i.e. sight accounts, bank notes and coins in Ecu.

Second, EMU should also lead to a large substitution away from US dollar in

---

[16] See Bishop (1992).

Ecu assets. These portfolio demand shifts would not yield any seigniorage revenues for the EC, but they could have an effect on the Ecu/dollar exchange rate. Large portfolio shifts could be expected from both the official and the private sectors. For example, if the Ecu achieves the same share as the US dollar in foreign exchange reserves, central banks all over the world will have to exchange the equivalent of about Ecu 120 billion of their dollar reserves into Ecu. Estimates of the shift in private international portfolios range from Ecu 150 billion to Ecu 300 billion.

Whether these portfolio shifts lead to a large appreciation of the Ecu against the dollar and other currencies depends on how fast international financial institutions react to provide sufficient Ecu-denominated instruments. At present, it seems likely that the EC will run an aggregate current account deficit during the transition to EMU. Such a deficit would represent a net supply of claims on the EC.

Thus pressures for appreciation of the Ecu might result from its growing financial role in official and private portfolios. But a large appreciation of the Ecu is not essential, especially if the Community proves willing to accept a collective current account deficit in a transitional period.

This upbeat outlook for the Ecu is therefore based on further progress towards EMU. Its role within the EC will be increasingly to represent an EC-wide capital market as exchange rate variability falls and the internal market programme creates a truly integrated European financial market. On the wider global scene, the breakthrough will come only with full EMU, i.e. when the Ecu becomes the single common currency. It should then become as important as the US dollar. However, from here to there, there are serious risks, as demonstrated by the devastating effect on market of the referendum in Denmark.

References

Allen PR (1990) The private Ecu markets: what they are, why they exist and where they may go. Journal of Banking and Finance, 14(5), November

Arthur, Andersen and Ecu Banking Association (1991) The Ecu - making it work in Europe. Arthur Andersen & Co and EBA, February

Bishop G (1990) Toughening the Ecu - Practical Steps to Promote its Use. Salomon Brothers, London, October

Bishop G (1991) ECUland - The Nineteenth Member of the EC?, London: Salomon Brothers

Bishop G (1992) EMU - 1995?, London: Salomon Brothers, February

Dornbusch R, Draghi M (eds) (1991) Public Debt Management: Theory and History, Cambridge University Press

Ecu Newsletter, Istituto Bancario San Paolo di Torino, Turin

Giovannini A, Spaventa L (1991) Fiscal rules in the European Monetary Union: A No-Entry Clause, CEPR discussion paper no 516, January
Girard J, Pacheco L and Steinherr A (1991) The Hard Ecu: Enrichment of the Basket Ecu with a Multiple Currency Option, EIB Papers
Girard J, Steinherr A (1989) The Ecu: A Currency Unlike any Other, EIB Papers, June
Gros D (1991) The Development of the Ecu. In: Johnson C (ed) Ecu - The Currency of Europe, London: Euromoney Publ
Gros D, Thygesen N (1991) European Monetary Integration: From the EMS towards EMU, Longman, London
Mèlitz J (1991) A Suggested Reformulation of the Theory of Optimal Currency Areas, CEPR discussion paper no 590, October
Padoa-Schioppa T (1988) The Ecu's coming of age. In: Nighoff M (ed) The Quest for National and Global Economic Stability. Kluwer, Amsterdam
Steinherr A et al (1985) Ecu Basket Revisions: Market Repercussions and the Reform Proposals, Ecu Banking Association, May
Steinherr A et al (1991) The Ecu - To Be or Not to Be a Basket - That is the Question, Ecu Banking Association, June
Steinherr A (1990) Roles for the Ecu in the process of achieving European Monetary Union. Unpublished paper for the Ecu Banking Association, European Investment Bank, December
Steinherr A, Perée E (1991) Investing in Ecu. In: Johnson C (ed) Ecu - The Currency of Europe, London: Euromoney Publ
Steinherr A, Girard J (1991) Ecu Financial Markets: Recent Evolution and Perspectives. In: Steinherr A and Weiserbs D, Evolution of the International and Regional Monetary System - Essays in Honour of Robert Triffin, London: Macmillan

Part III

External Issues

Economic Transformation and the Integration of Central and Eastern Europe in the European Community

Stefan Collignon
Association for the Monetary Union of Europe, Paris

1 Introduction

Who would not remember the joy and enthusiasm when the wall of Berlin finally came down in November 1989? A new world seemed to become possible. We dreamed of a new Europe of peace, democracy and prosperity. Three years later, this view has given way to a more sober assessment of reality. The Soviet Union has disappeared, but in its wake we find unrest and civil war. The crimes against humanity in former Yugoslavia have shamed the European Community, so proud of its committment to peace and so impotent to put it in practice. In Central Europe, the three fast-reforming countries, Poland, Hungary and Czechoslovakia, have made courageous steps to transform their political and economic systems. Here, the political transition to a democratic system has been a success. Democratically elected governments have come to power and look for the best ways of integrating their countries into a new and larger Europe. But the danger of political instability persists. Poland has seen in 1992 an extended period when the Government was literally incapable of acting because a stable majority could not be found in Parliament. Czechoslovakia is splitting up, and nobody yet knows the implications of this development. Hungary is affected by the external instability in the north and in the south, although the democractic system has proved to be robust.

On the economic side, the success of the transformation is more uncertain. The old economic planning system has been dismantled and sometimes bold reforms have been made in order to introduce market economy. Although the changes seem to be definitive in Central Europe, this is less obvious in Russia or other parts of the former Soviet Union. The results have not yet led to the promised land of prosperity and stability which was hoped for. Industrial production in all three fast-reforming countries is falling rapidly and inflation is still not checked (See Table 1). In several Eastern European countries, inflation has been brought under control, but still remains on high levels. As Table 2 documents, high rates of inflation lead to painful reductions in real wages and seem to be correlated with political instability.[1] Privatisation proves to be much more tedious than

---

[1] See Wyplosz (1992) for a theoretical model on the link between politics and economics.

anticipated and government finances are seriously constrained in rebuilding a dilapidated infrastructure.

Table 1. Former centrally planned economies: Recent output developments (annual percent change)

	1990	1991
Eastern Europe and former USSR	-1,5	-9,7
Eastern Europe	-7.1	-13.7
Albania	-10.0	-29.9
Bulgaria	-10.6	-23.0
Czech and Slovak Fed.Rep.	-0.4	-15.9
Hungary	-4.1	-11.0
Poland	-11.6	-7.0
Romania	-7.4	-13.0
Yugoslavia	-7.5	-17.0
Former USSR	-0.4	-0.9
Armenia	-8.5	-11.8
Azerbaijan	-11.7	-0.7
Belarus	-3.0	-3.0
Estonia	-3.6	-13.4
Georgia	-12.4	-23.0
Kazakhstan	-1.5	-10.0
Kyrghyzstan	4.0	-2.0
Latvia	-0.2	-3.5
Lithuania	-0.5	-13.6
Moldova	-1.5	-11.9
Russian Federation	1.2	-9.0
Tajikistan	-0.6	-8.7
Turkmenistan	1.5	-5.9
Ukraine	-3.4	-11.2
Uzbekistan	4.3	-0.5
Mongolia	-2.5	-16.2
Memorandum		
Former German Democratic Rep.	-15.0	-21.9

Source: IMF

Given the instability in the East, Western European countries have sought to strengthen their internal cohesion by agreeing the Maastricht Treaty on 'ever closer union'. But the Danish referendum in June 1992 and the narrowness of the French referendum in September, together with the crisis in the European Monetary System have left doubt in the minds of many observers as to whether such union can and will actually be realised. In the meantime, massive immigration from Eastern Europe has provoked a nasty reaction against foreigners in Germany, being the country primarily affected.

Table 2.

	Poland			Hungary			Czechoslovakia		
	1989	1990	1991	1989	1990	1991	1989	1990	1991
RG % *	1.5	-12.0	-7.0	-0.2	-5.0	-7.0	-0.7	-3.1	-14.0
RW % *	9.0	-24.4	0.8	-1.4	-3.1	-5.0	0.9	-5.7	-29.9
UR % *	0.1	6.1	11.4	0.5	1.7	8.5	0.1	1.0	8.1
IR % *	244	585	70	17	29	32.0	1.0	10.0	58.0
BB % of GDP **	-2.6	0.4	-3.0	-1.9	-0.1	-4.6	-0.8	0.7	-2.0
BCA (bn$)									
convertible	-1.8	6.6	-1.4	-1.4	0.1	0.3	0.4	-1.1	0.4
non-conv. currencies	-0.8	0.4	0.1	0.9	0.3	0.1	0.5	-0.2	0.6
GFD in conv. curr. (bn$)	43	46	42	21	22	23	8	8	9

Source: Herr 1992

RG Real growth
RW Change in real wages
UR Unemployment rate
IR Inflation rate
BB Budget balance
BCA Balance of current accounts
GFD Gross foreign dept
* Change from previous year
** Proportion in year in question

All these uncertainties have lowered the interest in Western Europe with respect to the problems in Eastern Europe. Curiosity was high when dramatic events in the East dominated the news. Now that the nuclear threat seems to have receded and the novelty has worn off, it appears nearly impossible "to marshall the enthusiasm for a large support programme."[2] The European Community seems to be preoccupied with internal intricacies. Accommodating special interests is one way of keeping a fragile consensus in the Community alive and governments afloat. The problems at home have also prohibited the opening of the European Community's markets for imports from Central and Eastern Europe. This has become particularly obvious during the negotiations on the association agreement for Hungary, Czechoslovakia and Poland.[3]

Of course, technical assistance is given by the Community, as well as by the

[2] cf. Dornbusch (1992) p 396.
[3] See Reinicke (1992).

IMF, the World Bank, the Group of 24, the OECD and the EBRD. The PHARE program is certainly useful and has permitted many strategically important actions. But ultimately the necessary condition for growth and successful transformation of the Eastern European economies is access to the markets of the European Community and the pursuit of an export oriented strategy. However, it is clear that the fulfillment of a certain number of internal conditions on the macro and micro economic level is required if transformation to a prosperous market economy is to succeed.

2 The Economic Framework for Transformation

Money is at the heart of a modern market economy. In centrally-planned economies, money had only a very limited role as a *lubricant* for consumer transactions while resources were allocated by the plan. Accounting units were *material quantity coefficients*. Real resources rather than money were used as *stores of value*. Hence the use of money was not fully developed.[4]

If money is used as a unit of account, and simultaneously as a store of value, it fulfils a function as a means of deferred payment. This effectively means that the promise to pay later establishes credit contracts between economic agents, in exchange for which a title of ownership is issued. Thus, with the phenomenon of credit, there is a counterpart created which is capital, that is, the right of ownership over resources. Communism therefore had to cut out some of the essential functions of money in abolishing capitalism and setting up centrally-planned economies.

The consequences of this amputation of money functions have been important, because money as a means of exchange was always readily available and never scarce. Consequently, in the planned economy, resources were scarce and therefore served as a store of value. This in turn contributed to the shortage of goods in these economies.[5]

From these considerations it follows that if money is to be the store of value, it has to be made scarce. This is the essence of the systemic transformation of formerly centrally planned economies into modern market economies.

The three prime tasks of systemic transformation are, therefore, the creation of so-called legal property rights, which lie at the root of ownership titles and are necessary to provide collateral for credit; adequate control of money supply in order to make it scarce and valuable so that agents will always agree to exchange their goods against it; full convertibility after money has become scarce. Convertibility into commodities is a first step, but the true litmus-test of successful reforms is external convertibility. These tasks establish three policy

---

[4] Riese (1990).
[5] Riese (1990).

axes.

First, *privatisation* represents the systemic change in property rights and economic decision making. The central motivation is to make managers accountable to owners who have a clear interest in maximising the value of their enterprise.[6] This necessitates a reliable legal framework and, ultimately, the purpose is to make the supply side of the economy more elastic and efficient so that it may respond flexibly to the price signals of the markets.

Second, *price liberalisation* is to give companies the autonomy to manage resources and production in accordance with monetary market signals, subject to a hard budget constraint.[7]

Third, *currency convertibility* in internal and external markets requires a coherent and stable macroeconomic environment, so that microeconomic price signals can operate as a rational incentive structure. Without trade liberalisation and external currency convertibility, integration into world markets is incomplete and resources are not used in the most efficient way. The success of privatisation is therefore partly dependent on this macroeconomic framework.

Control of inflation is fundamental to the creation of a properly functioning monetary economy. This is because without price stability money will not correctly fulfil its function as a store of value which makes it a universally accepted means of payment.[8] Inflation leads to a flight into either foreign currencies or tangible assets which can then be used as reserve values. The reduced utility of money prevents the creation of a workable domestic asset market (banking system, capital markets, interbank money markets etc.) when money holders seek to substitute local currencies for higher forms of liquidity. That this is still happening to a significant degree in the fast-reforming countries of Central Europe, despite stabilisation programmes, is evidenced by Table 3. (Illegal transfers are not taken into account.) Ultimately inflation erodes the monetary system and stimulates barter and self-subsistence economies. Signs of such return to mediaeval practices have recently been witnessed, not only in what used to be the Soviet Union but also in international trade relations amongst former Comecon countries.

---

[6] See IMF (1992).

[7] See Blanchard, Dornbusch, Kongman, Layard, Summers (1991).

[8] Dornbusch (1992), p 410 recounts the experience of the first Hungarian soviet Government in 1919: "Issue of money in the name of the Soviet Government did not succeed, even when death penalty was threatened for people who refused acceptance."

Table 3. Domestic foreign currency deposits in Poland, Hungary and CSFR (in per cent)

	CSFR		POLAND		HUNGARY	
	1990	1991	1990	1991	1990	1991
Share of foreign currency in total household deposits	3.5	8.0	57.7	47.2	17.3	26.9
Share of foreign currency in corporate deposits	9.3	7.1	7.4	4.1	17.8	20.7
Share of foreign currencys in total deposits	5.9	7.6	39.3	31.4	17.5	24.4

Source: Herr, Westphal (1993)

In order to control inflation it is obviously necessary to stabilise public finance. The budget deficit is to be reduced to manageable size and a modern and efficient tax system needs to be built up. The budget balance to GDP in the three fast-reforming countries of Central Europe is certainly within tolerable limits. (See Table 2). But this achievement is obtained at the price of low expenditure at a time when public investment (transport, communication etc.) is needed to set up the infrastructure for new development. In Russia the deficit in 1991 and 1992 was pushing 15% of GDP.[9] In the Ukraine the public deficit even attains 47% of GDP and monthly inflation in December 92 100%.[10] Without tax and fiscal reforms, privatisation of public companies which used to be the prime sources of state finance will undermine the fundaments of the market economy itself, as governments are then forced to use the printing press to finance the revenue shortfall.[11] The monetary crisis of Russia, with monthly inflation of 33% in 1992, is an instructive demonstration in this respect.

A further aspect of bringing inflation under control is appropriate income policies. i.e. effective policies of collective bargaining which maintain the prospect of workers' standards of living improving through future growth. It is interesting in this respect that among the three fast-transforming countries of Central Europe, Czechoslovakia has been quite successful in containing inflation by obtaining social acceptance of a significant fall in real wages, but the resulting social discontent has been regionally unequally distributed, with the consequence that the country is splitting up.

[9] Financial Times, Dec 16, 1992.
[10] Courier International no 10, Dec 10, 1992.
[11] See McKinnon (1991), chapter 11.

Controlling inflation is a necessary condition of economic development, but insufficient by itself. An additional element in stimulating growth and transformation in the Central and Eastern European economies is appropriate exchange rate policies. A stable and slightly undervalued currency gives a natural incentive to economic growth and development, provided it is maintained over a long period of time. Post-war performances of Germany[12] and Japan are classic cases, and the example of the newly-industrialised countries in East Asia[13] or the experience of Chile in the 1980's[14] are additional recent references for this thesis. A stable undervalued currency creates a bias to export promotion and thereby facilitates integration into the world market. But as long as inflation is not under control, local currencies run the risk of being overvalued in real terms and normally exchange rate devaluations are necessary to correct the distortions. However, frequent exchange rate devaluation undermine the confidence in local asset markets and are therefore counter-productive in stimulating local accummulation. This is why a stable undervaluation of exchange rates is to be the aim, in order to stimulate growth in Central and Eastern Europe.[15]

3 Micro Economic Level

On the micro economic level, privatisations of public companies have proven to be more difficult than expected.[16] The logic behind privatising industry and agriculture is to improve the private incentive structure by making people personally responsible and thereby increasing efficiency. However, given the lack of political and social stability, people refrain from taking risks. Particularly in countries where the legal framework does not yet guarantee the certainty of property rights, it is unlikely that privatisation will have the desired effect. Property rights have to establish the full transferability of property titles so that they can also be used as collateral in credit markets.

It is therefore not surprising that privatisations have primarily succeeded in the small business sector (trade, services, crafts, etc.). Not one country has yet achieved large scale privatisation of large and medium-sized firms.[17] Consequently, markets for property titles are slow to develop.

All this leads to the conclusion that the creation of workable asset markets

---

[12] See Riese (1990b).

[13] Measured in terms of free trade regimes, the currencies of Korea and Taiwan were actually overvalued (Urban 1992). But the sophisticated system of export incentives was effectively a substitute of currency devaluations and realistic exchange rates. (See Lanzarotti, 1992, p 157).

[14] See Edwards, Edwards (1987), McKinnon (1991), chapter 6.

[15] As Dornbusch (1992) points out, overvaluation 'invariably leads to real and financial crisis' (p 418). This can also be the result of overly zealous stabilisation policies. They need to be remedies as well, but of course relaxing policies is easier than tightening.

[16] For an assessment of recent experiences, see IMF (1992).

[17] See Herr (1992).

needs to be at the center of the process of economic transformation in Central and Eastern Europe. The question I would like to raise now is : How could the European Community help in this process?

4 The Integration of Central and Eastern Europe into the European Community

Systemic transformation and economic stabilisation require external support. Joseph Schumpeter, having failed the Austrian stabilisation as Finance Minister in 1919 came to the conclusion: "Without external assets there cannot be a stabilisation of currency and hence no order in the public finances. The reverse sequence, first to establish internal order and then to seek external credit is a path of desperate dissipation (Verblutung) which has been taken all too often in financial history. The fateful vicious circle: no external credit, no internal order but without internal order no external credit, must be solved."[18]

Numerous governments and politicians in Central and Eastern Europe have declared their intention to solve this dilemma by joining the European Community. But such integration requires time in order to make the joining economies compatible with the delicate balance of interests that mark the Community. Full integration should therefore be the strategic long-term target, while intermediate steps help to reach this goal. A short-term response can be the strengthening of the Association Agreements; a medium-term support structure could be the creation of an Ecu Zone.

4.1 The Association Agreements

A first important step to integrate Poland, Hungary and Czechoslovakia more extensively into the European Community has been the formulation of the Association Agreements which were concluded in early 1992. Although they are different in the specifics applicable to each of the three countries they have a common structure which is based on six components:[19]

(i) Political dialog between the Community and the respective countries
(ii) The four freedoms of movement of goods, services, capital and labour
(iii) Economic cooperation
(iv) Cultural cooperation
(v) Financial cooperation
(vi) Institutional cooperation between the Association Council, the Commission and the European Parliament.

---

[18] Quoted by Dornbusch (1992), p 406.
[19] See Reinicke (1992) for details.

Useful as these provisions may be, they do not go far enough in helping these countries of Central Europe to find their way into the family of the West European Countries. Clearly, one of the most important contributions the EC could make at this stage would be the opening of its markets to the East. But this remains insufficient in the Agreements. For example, in the case of Poland, the Community will open itself over the next 5-6 years, while Poland will only start in 1995. This should enable Poland to increase its exports of industrial goods by just 20% over the period. On a similar line, Czechoslovakia hopes to increase EC exports by $300 mio over the 1990s.[20]

The deficiency in the Association Agreements is threefold. First of all, the asymmetric opening of the markets which is promised and envisaged by the Association Agreements does not apply to agriculture,[21] which is an important factor for these Central European Countries. In 1991 agricultural exports to the Community amounted to 21% of total Polish exports, 24% in Hungary and 7% in the CSFR.[22] Secondly, protectionism played a large part in the negotiations. The Association Agreement negotiations nearly broke down several times, as when France, supported by Belgium, Greece and Ireland, refused to accept an increase of 10% in meat imports over the next five years or when Germany and Portugal objected to increases in coal and textile imports.[23] This prevents the countries of the Troika from benefitting fully from their specific comparative advantages, and to solve the problems of restructuring sectors such as agriculture or the textile and steel industry.[24] Thirdly, capital liberalisation is not yet complete and this prevents the functioning of asset markets. This is obviously a handicap resulting from the insufficient stabilisation of the Eastern Economies[25] and here, outside support is crucial.

4.2 The Creation of an Ecu Zone

In order to create such an Ecu Zone the participating countries would have to pool part of their reserves into an Eastern European Stabilisation Fund. In exchange they would receive a supporting convertibility stand-by facility by the European Community and those funds together could be used for stabilising exchange rates. Thus the Ecu Zone resembles in some ways the European Monetary System, but several of its features are more suitable to Eastern Europe and allow far greater flexibility.

Three instruments of cooperation form the institutional foundation of the Ecu Zone: the Ecu Zone Surveillance Board, the Reserve Pool & Stabilisation Fund

---

[20] Reinicke (1992), p 92.

[21] In agriculture the process of liberalisation is based on reciprocity. As one Polish negotiator commented 'We cannot agree to the Community offering us concessions for commodities that we do not produce, for example bananas, pineapples or oranges.' Reinicke (1992), p 99.

[22] Reinicke (1991), p 101.

[23] Reinicke (1992), p 94.

[24] For an analysis of comparative advantages see Hare, Hughes (1991).

[25] See Collignon (1992).

and the Exchange Rate Mechanism for the Ecu Zone.

In view of some of these difficulties, the Association for the Monetary Union of Europe has made a proposal[26] for the creation of an Ecu Zone. The aim is to assist the integration of the economies of Central and Eastern Europe with those of Western Europe, on the basis of a properly functioning monetary economy. Only if the reforming countries converge over time to the stability standards of the European Union, outlined in the Maastricht Treaty, will it be possible for them to join the Community. The proposal is meant to create a legal and institutional framework which allows the coordination of policies and the improvement of free trade between the related countries. The proposal also wishes to stimulate trade not only between East and West, but also between the fast transforming economies themselves. Finally, the creation of an Ecu Zone would help to strengthen the quality of local currencies by approving the credibility committments to greater macro economic stability. In this way the creation of an Ecu Zone would establish a kind of antechamber for full EC membership in the future. It is an instrument which would permit a managed adjustment of the economic and political convergence of Central and Eastern Europe to the standards of the European Community.

4.2.1 The Ecu Zone Surveillance Board (EZSB)

The purpose of such a Board is to ensure that economic policies in the participating countries converge to the stability norms of the European Community. It assumes the management of the pooled foreign exchange reserves of the participating countries and of the stand-by facility from the European Community. The board would also coordinate the Ecu Zone Exchange Rate Mechanism and monitor the macro economic compatibilities of the monetary and economic policies pursued. The EZSB would also contribute to the creation of new institutions that will be adapted to a future membership in the European Union. The EZSB would thereby permit a gradual integration of the fast-reforming economies into the European Community by providing an institutional framework of cooperation and coordination of policies. At the same time it would provide a mechanism which would allow the controlled opening of markets for products, services and capital, which are necessary if a full membership of these countries in the European Community is ultimately intended.

The decision-making body of the Surveillance Board would consist of representatives from the participating Central and Eastern European governments and Central Banks (these banks should be made independent of political influences, similar to the European Central Bank), the European Community Institutions as well as the IMF and EBRD. This would ensure that recommendations and implementations of the Board would be based on the braodest possile consensus.[27] It would also give a clear signal to wage

---

[26] For details of the suggestion see Collignon (1991) and (1992).

[27] The actions of the EZSB might therefore have greater democratic legitimacy than the commissioners

bargaining parties (trade unions, management of firms and governments) what kind of income policies are compatible with the long term objective of joining the exclusive club of the rich EC-countries. This should increase the political and social acceptability of the measures suggested by the EZSB.

4.2.2 The Ecu Zone Stabilisation Fund

At the heart of the proposal is the Stabilisation Fund, into which the participating Central and Eastern European countries would transfer a significant part of their reserves. On the other side, the European Community would establish a stand-by facility on which the Ecu Zone Stabilisation Fund could draw when necessary, within the guide lines set by the Ecu Zone Surveillance Board. The standby facility would be unlimited for very short-term requirements, and subjet to strong conditionality for medium and long-term borrowing. The purpose of this fund is to strengthen convertibility of local currencies and to stabilise foreign exchange transactions on a day to day basis for the fast-reforming economies of Central and Eastern Europe, without locking them into detrimental rigidites. At the same time the fund would help to increase the credibility of monetary and economic policies in those countries so that private investors rather than governments can take the lead in creating investment and growth. The final objective of the Ecu Zone Stabilisation Fund is to provide the means for exchange rate interventions.

4.2.3 The Ecu Zone Exchange Rate Mechanism

As we have pointed out above, a stable, slightly undervalued currency is a useful device in order to stimulate exports and growth. Rather than allowing savage 'beggar-your-neighbour' policies and wild devaluations, a manged exchange rate policy with respect to the European Community could be a useful stabilising anchor for the fast-reforming economies. It is therefore suggested, that the countries participating in the Ecu Zone would peg their exchange rates to the Ecu. The Ecu in its present form as a basket of EC currencies already represents the best weighted average of different interests in Western European economies. Furthermore, as the Ecu is intended to become the single European currency of the Community, using the basket Ecu today is a useful means of anticipating future relations with the post-Maastricht European Union, which is committed to having a single currency.

The importance of exchange rate policy is obvious from the structure of trade flows. 75% of East-West (OECD) trade between CSFR, Hungary, Poland, Bulgaria and Romania is oriented to the European Community and 13% to the EFTA states.[28] Intra-industry trade between the first 3 Central European countries and the EC is also rather important and likely to expand rapidly without

installed by the League of Nations in the States of the ex-Austrian Empire. See Dornbusch (1992).
[28] See Baldwin (1992).

much political resistance.[29]

Within the Ecu Zone Exchange Rate Mechanism several different regimes are possible. They need to be chosen with respect to the different stages of economic development in the respective countries. In view of the different economic comparative advantages and difficulties in individual countries, a large degree of flexibility is required. Countries beginning the economic transformation process under the constraint of sticky wages and an insufficient tax system, aiming to restructure their production potential in order to give it greater export orientation, may wish to establish at first a crawling peg, compensating for high rates of inflation. To the degree that stabilisation policies become effective the crawling peg may be reduced, according to a pre-announced schedule, and ultimately the exchange rate regime could be transformed into a fixed but adjustable exchange rate peg. The objective of such an exchange rate mechanism is to allow gradual convergence towards the stability standards of the European Community and to tie the participating Ecu Zone countries to the discipline that goes with this. However, given the structural rigidities, the nominal exchange rate has to maintain for some considerable period of time a degree of flexibility that is necessarily larger than within the European Monetary System of the European Community, or even a full Monetary Union.[30]

Table 4. Intra-industry trade with the EC: CSFR, Hungary and Poland engage in more intra-industry trade with the EC than Portugal and Norway.
(100 indicates 100% of trade with EC is two-way trade in similar products)

F	UK	NL	CH	BL	D	E	S	A	I
82	77	77	77	76	75	73	70	68	63

DK	IRL	H	CS	PL	P	SF	N	GR	IS
63	59	50	46	42	42	39	36	29	4

Source: Baldwin 1992

Note: F=France, UK=United Kingdom; NL=Netherlands, CH=Switzerland, BL=Belgium-Lux., D=Germany, E=Spain, S=Sweden, A=Austria, I=Italy, DK=Denmark, IR=Ireland, H=Hungary, CS=Czechoslovakia, PL=Poland, P=Portugal, SF=Finland, N=Norway, GR=Greece, IS=Iceland.

[29] See Table 4.
[30] For the viability of such solutions for Eastern Europe, see Bofinger (1991).

4.2.4 Qualification and Participation

The institutional arrangement of the suggested Ecu Zone is naturally linked to the perspective of joining the European Community at some future stage. It is also clear that only those countries could participate that have already achieved a substantial degree of systemic reform, as otherwise the instruments of policy correction of the Ecu Zone would be insufficient. At present, Hungary, Czechoslovakia and Poland seem the most likely candidates, although one has to wait for the monetary consequences of the CSFR break-up. Possibly Bulgaria and Romania will soon make the necessary progress in economic transformation.

As for some of the smaller newly-emerging countries in Eastern Europe, it may be recommendable to base their monetary system on some kind of a currency board scheme and then link this arrangement to the Ecu Zone. The first example of such reform was provided by Estonia in June 1992, although the Kroon was linked to the DM and not to the Ecu.[31] Linking the currency board to the Ecu Zone arrangement could provide additional credibility which would allow relaxing capital controls.[32] It would also have the advantage of maintaining and even strengthening traditional trade links between countries which are regionally close and whose productive structures are still to a large degree interdependent. This issue will gain additional urgency after the break-up of the rouble zone.

5 Conclusion

The creation of an Ecu Zone for Central and Eastern Europe would allow participating countries to reap some significant benefits in the course of the transformation of their internal economies. It would allow the Central and Eastern European economies to stabilise their macro economic policies less harshly, as the external support from the Community would provide greater confidence in the measures envisaged and would encourage private investors to seize the opportunities in the new markets. It would also help to make the hardships of economic transformation more acceptable for the public at large, as they would see the possibilities of full EC membership at the end of the road. The greater stability in the system would contribute to the formation of workable asset markets, which are ultimately the precondition for economic development. However, the Ecu Zone would also benefit Western Europe. It would guarantee greater stability in the East and could thereby help to slow down the migration flows, not to mention military instability. It would provide new investment opportunities and last but not least, enlargen the use and credibility of the Ecu as an attractive currency, even before it has become Europe's single currency. In this way the Ecu would truly become a unifier, not only within the European

[31] IMF (1992), p 52.

[32] See Bofinger (1991) on some of the difficulties of currency boards in Eastern Europe.

Community, but also between East and West.

References

Baldwin R (1992) An Eastern Enlargement of EFTA: Why the East Europeans should join and the EFTANS should want them. CEPR Occasional Paper, No 10 London, November

Blanchard O, Dornbusch R, Krugman P, Layard R, Summers L (199 , Reform in Eastern Europe; Cambridge, Mass

Bofinger P (1991) Options for the Payments and Exchange Rate System in Eastern Europe; CEPR Discussion Paper No 545 London, April

Collignon S (1992a) An Ecu Zone for Central and Eastern Europe: a Supportive Framework for Convergence. In: Barrell R, Economic Convergence and Monetary Union in Europe. London

Collignon S (1992b) A Proposal to Create an Ecu Zone to Assist Eastern Europe's Transition to a Market Economy. In: De Pecunia Vol III, No 3, Dec. In Italian: Una zona Ecu per l'Europa dell'est. In: Revista di Politica Economica, Marzo

Collignon S (1992c) Intégrer les pays de l'est à l'Europe: une zone Ecu. Dans: Revue d'Economie Financière. No Special, Septembre

Dornbush R (1992) Monetary Problems of Post-Communism: Lessons from the End of the Austro-Hungarian Empire; Weltwirtschaftliches Archiv, Bd 128, Heft 3

Edwards S and Edwards AC (1987) Monetarism and Liberalisation: The Chilean Experiment. Cambridge, Mass

Hare P, Hughes G (1991) Competitiveness and Industrial Restructuring in Czechoslovakia, Hungary and Poland; CEPR Discussion Paper No 543 London, April

Herr H (1992) Eastern European Transformation Problems, Taking Poland, Hungary and Czechoslovakia as Examples. From: Employment Observatory East Germany, EC Commission, No 3/4 September

Herr H, Westphal A (Hg)(1993) Makroökonomische Probleme der Transformation; forthcoming

IMF - World Outlook (1992), Washington DC, October

Lanzarotti M (1992) La Corée du Sud: une sortie du sous-développement, Paris

McKinnon R (1991) The Order of Economic Liberalisation. Financial Control in the Transition to a Market Economy; Baltimore

Reinicke WH (1992) Building a New Europe. The Challenge of System Transformation and Systemic Reform; Bookings Occasional Paper, Washington DC

Riese H (1990) Geld im Sozialismus. Zur theoretischen Fundierung von Konzeptionen des Sozialismus. Regensburg

Riese H (1990b) Das Forschungsprojekt 'Geldpolitik als Grundlage der ökonomischen Entwicklung der Bundesrepublik Deutschland'. In: Riese H, Spahn HP. Geldpolitik und Ökonomische Entwicklung - Ein Symposium. Regensburg

Urban W (1992) Economic Lessons for the East European Countries from Two Newly Industrialising Countries in the Far East? Wiener Institut für Internationale Wirtschaftsvergleiche, Forschungsbericht No 182, April

Wyplosz C (1992) After the Honeymoon. On the Economics and the Politics of Economic Transformation; CEPR Discussion Paper No 734, London November

Convertibility in Eastern Europe*

Åkos Valentinyi
Institute for Economic and Market Research, Budapest

1 Introduction

The political changes in Eastern Europe[1] took place very rapidly, causing great surprise to the world. Yet, the transition from a centraly planned economy to a market economy needs much more time than a political revolution. This paper aims to analyze the issue of currency convertibility in Eastern Europe as it relates to liberalization of international transactions and to its macroeconomic consequences.

At the outset, the different definitions of currency convertibility are described. Next the conditions for convertibility and the possible scenarios for its introduction are analyzed. After explaining how convertibility can be introduced, its costs and benefits are examined. Such costs and benefits depend on the manner of introduction.

It is easier to implement convertibility than to sustain it. The latter part of the paper includes an explanation of the conditions of sustainable convertibility. The paper tries to show the possible conditions at given institutions and in a given macroeconomic situation in Eastern Europe. In addition, the effects of a possible payments union among Eastern European countries are analyzed prior to the summary.

2 Concepts of Convertibility

The most general and simplest definition of convertibility is the following: a currency is convertible if it can be exchanged for any foreign currency at a certain exchange rate. Obviously, different international transactions can be restricted differently. From this point of view, there are several levels of currency convertibility. The convertibility or inconvertibility of a currency may be analyzed in four dimensions:[2]

---

* I would like to thank Wolfgang Gebauer, Ursula Hauser, Gábor Oblath, Michael Thiel and Andreas Worms for comments on an earlier draft. Of course, any errors and omissions are my responsibility.

[1] For the purpose of this paper, Eastern Europe does not encompass the countries of the former Soviet Union.

[2] Oblath (1992) pp 2-7, and Williamson (1991a) pp 252-254.

(i) for whom the currency is convertible,
(ii) for what kind of transactions the currency is convertible,
(iii) whether there are some restrictions on real transactions that require foreign currency,
(iv) whether the country announces the convertibility of its currency or convertibility is introduced without announcement.

If domestic agents can exchange their currency into foreign currency in order to carry out international transactions, there is *internal convertibility*. In this case, a distinction may be made depending on whether households and enterprises have the same right to carry out international transactions. If foreigners can conduct transactions in domestic currency, there is *external convertibility*.[3]

According to the characteristics of international transactions, a distinction is to be made between *current account convertibility* and *capital account convertibility*. The Articles of Agreement of the International Monetary Fund prescribe that "no member shall, without approval of Fund, impose restrictions on making payments and transfers for current international transactions" (Article VIII).[4] This requirement means that households may exchange freely their currency for foreign currency in order to cover their travel expenses abroad. If restrictions on capital movements are canceled in a manner not required by the IMF, *full or unrestricted convertibility* comes into being.

Currency convertibility relates strongly to the liberalization of real international transactions. If several restrictions exist on *real* transactions, the domestic currency for non-residents, and the foreign currency for residents, cannot fulfill the function of money because they cannot operate as medium of exchange. Let us assume that enterprises are able to make payments in foreign currency carried out through foreign exchange reserves of the central bank. If enterprises need a permission from the authorities to transport goods into the country, then convertibility does not exist. If transactions on commodities and services are liberalized, there is *commodity convertibility*. *Financial convertibility* will exist only after the removal of restrictions on capital movements.

There is difference between *de facto convertibility* and *de jure convertibility*. If the government has removed restrictions on international transactions, but convertibility has not been declared, the currency is de facto convertible. However, an announcement of convertibility does not necessarily mean that the government ensures the free exchange of currency or the sustainability of such exchange.

The concepts above show that introduction of currency convertibility may have several meanings. Costs and benefits of convertibility can be interpreted only in the context of particular meaning.

---

[3] The enterprises established by non-residents in the country are regarded as residents.

[4] Many members of the IMF cannot fulfill this requirement. They have the opportunity to meet the requirement of Article IV, which requires members to endeavor to introduce currency convertibility.

3 Introduction of Convertibility in Eastern Europe

Currency convertibility has become a myth for the people in Eastern Europe. It represents welfare and belonging to Europe. Nevertheless, people do not know exactly what convertibility means, what conditions should be met for its implementation, how it can be introduced, and what kind of costs and benefits it has.

3.1 Preconditions of Convertibility

It is difficult to specify general conditions for the implementation of currency convertibility. Of course, the central bank must have appropriate and stable amount of foreign exchange reserves to finance convertibility. However, in Eastern Europe there are some additional preconditions which should be fulfilled before, or simultaneously with the introduction of convertibility.[5]

The accumulation of household savings in the region was forced by commodity shortages in the centrally planned economies. At a given fixed price level, the stock of forced savings caused excess demand on the commodity market. This *stock disequilibrium*, the monetary overhang, should be eliminated before the introduction of convertibility. Otherwise excess demand for foreign exchange reserves appears with any kind of convertibility. This leads to decreasing foreign exchange reserves and/or increasing external debt. In general, there are two opportunities to solve this problem. The government can lower the real value of the money stock by decreasing the nominal value of the money stock at a given price level, or by increasing the price level. The first case can be carried out through currency reform where the households are permitted to exchange only a part of their old money into new money, or where certain notes are declared invalid. Because of the difficulties of implementation of such measures, governments try to decrease the real money stock through price liberalization. Open inflation replaces repressed inflation. The two methods achieve the same result: the real money stock decreases.

Another macroeconomic problem is *flow disequilibrium*. The Eastern European countries have large budget deficits financed by money creation. Moreover, the central banks exercise weak control over the credit supply to the enterprises. The increasing money supply causes inflation and a permanent increasing demand for foreign exchange reserves at given interest and exchange rates. Foreign exchange reserves can decrease rapidly through this demand pressure and the currency convertibility cannot be sustained. Money growth must be slowed either before the introduction of convertibility or at the same time with it.

---

[5] Cochrame, Ickes (1991) pp 103-104, Fischer, Gelb (1991) pp 94-96, and Lipton, Sachs (1990) pp 90-99.

The sustainability of convertibility depends strongly on the credibility of the government. If economic agents are sceptical that the government will maintain the measure in the short run or doubt the longer-term sustainability of convertibility in the longer run, they will exhaust the foreign exchange reserves of the central bank. The government must have credibility to be able to introduce currency convertibility successfully. From this point of view, it must be emphasized that the government should try to introduce convertibility only if it is sure that it can sustain it. An unsuccessful attempt induces credibility loss and raises the cost of future introduction of convertibility (e. g., through a greater exchange rate depreciation to avoid the exhaustion of foreign exchange reserves).

3.2 Possible Scenarios

The implementation of convertibility as described above can be carried out in several ways. In the following paragraphs, we describe different possibilities, and analyze the costs and benefits of individual means.

Convertibility can be introduced at a particular time with one policy package as a part of a stabilization program.[6] This is the so called *big bang approach or shock therapy.*[7] According to IMF-conditions this convertibility is valid for current account items. At a given time, restrictions on imports and exports of commodities and services are abolished for domestic agents, and payments on factor income are liberalized for residents and non-residents. Thus, a foreign exchange market is created. The timing of liberalization of capital movements depends on the success of stabilization and on the future macroeconomic situation.

Convertibility also can be implemented through *gradual import liberalization*. Imports of commodities and services are liberalized step-by-step. First, certain commodity groups may be imported by domestic enterprises without permission of the authorities. The group of freely importable goods is enlarged over a certain period until all goods are free for import. Payments on factor income are liberalized only for foreign investors. If these reform steps are not accompanied by current account disturbances, further measures are taken to provide a foundation for the foreign exchange market, and initiation of liberalized capital movements.

Both approaches share the same principle. If residents have domestic currency or non-residents have foreign currency, the central bank will exchange the currencies into the currency which makes it possible to conduct the planned transaction (or economic agents are allowed to buy or sell foreign exchange on the market directly or indirectly through commercial banks). Convertibility means free access to foreign currency at any

[6] See Dornbusch (1991) pp 177-178, and Lipton, Sachs (1990) pp 112-119.

[7] Convertibility through monetary union is an example of this approach.

time so that economic agents can carry out international transactions. Convertibility does not mean the simple possession of foreign currency (unless it is for conducting international transactions). However, it is theoretically possible to implement convertibility in such a way that enterprises receive permission to retain some proportion of their export revenue. This is the *currency retention system*. In this case, enterprises must sell a part of their foreign currency to the commercial banks at an exchange rate given by the central bank. However, they may hold a part of their export revenue in foreign exchange accounts as well. There are two possibilities for importers to obtain foreign currency. The first one is buying it from other enterprises on the free foreign exchange market. The exchange rate is determined on this market by demand and supply. The second possibility is buying at the central bank at a given exchange rate at which the foreign currency is rationed among enterprises.

The Eastern European countries have achieved different levels of convertibility in several ways.[8] After the retention system collapsed, internal current account convertibility had been implemented as a part of the stabilization program in the former Yugoslavia at the end of 1989. Households could buy foreign currency in order to conduct capital account transactions as well. In Poland, internal current account convertibility for households and the business sector was introduced within the scope of a stabilization program on January 1st 1990. Hungary gradually liberalized its import regime between 1989 and 1991. Since 1991 practically all goods may be imported without a license. In 1992, an interbank foreign exchange market began to operate. The access of households to foreign currency remains restricted, however. In Bulgaria, implementation of a stabilization program was initiated at the beginning of 1990. Internal current account convertibility for enterprises has been introduced. A currency retention system operates for enterprises in Rumania. Households can buy foreign currency on a free foreign exchange market. Czechoslovakia implemented internal current account convertibility for enterprises in 1991 as a part of a stabilization program. However, there are still several restrictions on international transactions of households.

All Eastern European countries have introduced *de facto internal current account convertibility for the business sector*. Some countries have made it possible for households to access foreign currency. All countries in this region have abolished some restrictions on transactions of non-residents in order to encourage capital inflows. Therefore, certain transactions on capital account items can be considered liberalized.

---

[8] Marer (1991) pp 329-333, and Williamson (1991b) pp 55-86.

3.3 Costs, Benefits and Risks

The introduction of currency convertibility affects the economy in a fundamental way. It can be shown that costs, benefits and risks of introduction depend on how convertibility is implemented.

Currency convertibility leads to the following consequences:[9]

(i) competition on the domestic market is enhanced by the increasing demand for imported goods,
(ii) development of a price system based on relative scarcities of commodities takes place more rapidly,
(iii) efficiency of the external trade improves because of the increasing number of enterprises practicing external trade, and
(iv) investment by non-residents increases.

In addition, overall efficiency of the economy improves through these factors.

Most of the expected benefits described above already occur if a de facto internal current account convertibility is adopted. However, it is doubtful whether this liberalizing step can encourage capital inflows without liberalization of capital movements. The Eastern European experiences have shown that the extent to which capital enters the country depends on the level of general liberalization, on investment possibilities and on political stability.

Benefits are accompanied by costs. Any form of introduction of convertibility requires *exchange rate depreciation* since the central bank does not have certain information about the level of the exchange rate prior to liberalization which could prevent exhaustion of foreign exchange reserves. There is not enough information about the state of excess demand for foreign exchange reserves. Moreover, economic agents are much more likely to believe in the sustainability of convertibility if introduction is accompanied by an exchange rate depreciation. On the one hand, exchange rate depreciation causes a cost-push in a small open economy with liberalized imports. On the other hand, the current account surplus which is necessary for debt service leads to higher money growth after depreciation. These factors generate, ceteris paribus, *higher inflation*. Because there is no information about the extent of excess demand for foreign exchange reserves, a greater depreciation than may be necessary must take place. This will be clear only after liberalization as in the case of Poland. Gradual import liberalization needs smaller depreciation. In this case the adjustment process is slow and the effects of liberalization on foreign exchange reserves are slow as well. If depreciation is smaller than necessary to ensure a sufficient level of foreign exchange reserves, central banks have time to correct it due

---

[9] Blanchard, Dornbusch, Krugman, Layard, Lawrence (1991) pp 15-20, Ellman (1991) pp 483-485, Lipton, Sachs (1990) pp 118-119, and Williamson (1991a) pp 254-256.

to the slow adjustment.

Rapid liberalization allows little time for domestic economic agents to adjust to new conditions. The *shorter period for adjustment* leads to a *deeper recession* than that would have been in the case of slower liberalization.

The cost of convertibility seems to be smaller with gradual import liberalization but there are dangers that the benefits of convertibility will not appear, or that the positive effects of convertibility are weaker than with the big bang approach. These perils can be avoided or diminished if any liberalization step achieves a *critical mass*. If only a few commodity groups are liberalized, or only noncompetitive goods are importable after the first step, the positive effects of liberalization are scarce.

Convertibility through a currency retention system carries perhaps the greatest danger. If the public doubts the success of stabilization, currency substitution can take place very rapidly through the foreign exchange accounts. This has an accelerating effect on inflation.

Eastern European convertibility has a special problem.[10] In several countries households can hold *foreign exchange accounts*. Some years ago, the former governments introduced this measure in order to draw the foreign currency stock of households traded on the black market into the foreign exchange reserves of the central bank. In some countries, households dispose of significant amounts of foreign currency on foreign exchange accounts and there are practically no restrictions on the use of these accounts. This process can be used de facto for carrying out capital account transactions. If current account convertibility for households is introduced, deposits accounted in domestic currency can be changed into deposits accounted in foreign currency. Therefore, the monetary base decreases, the velocity of money circulation increases, and inflation increases as well.[11] Furthermore, current account convertibility means capital account convertibility in this case because there is de facto no restriction on foreign exchange accounts. The introduction of current account convertibility for households requires a substantial depreciation, or restrictions on foreign exchange accounts of households.

4 Sustainable Convertibility in Eastern Europe

It is easy to introduce or declare currency convertibility. However, it is much more difficult to sustain it. To this point, the conditions of introduction of convertibility has been analyzed. In this chapter some conditions of sustainable convertibility are

[10] Oblath (1992) pp 14-15, and Szegvári (1991) pp 37-38.

[11] For empirical evidence in case of Israel, see Dornbusch, Fischer (1986) pp 27-28.

explained.

4.1 Fiscal Policy

Obviously currency convertibility needs *fiscal discipline*. However, it is difficult to define exactly what fiscal discipline means. It does not merely depend on the size of the fiscal deficit. Fiscal discipline means that the government has no doubt about the macroeconomic consequences of the deficit and the type of deficit financing. It also means avoiding the inflationary effects of the deficit through targeting the size of the deficit, as well as the type of financing.[12] It is difficult for Eastern European countries to practice a disciplined fiscal policy. In the traditionally centrally planned economies, there was no explicit tax system. Enterprise revenues were simply revenues of the state from the fiscal point of view. Further, prices fixed by the government made some spending unnecessary (e.g. household received the benefit of prices fixed at a low level). This *implicit tax system* causes problems during the liberalization of economic activities. If price liberalization takes place, households lay claim to more government spending. The higher the proportion of private enterprises to GDP, or the more independent the state-owned enterprises, the less are the revenues of the government.[13]

The fiscal deficit must increase until a new efficient tax system begins to operate. An explicit tax system existed in some reforming centrally planned economies. However, these systems are very unstable. The creation of a stable tax system could not ensure stable tax revenue. For example, experience from Hungary, where a new tax system was implemented in 1987, shows that liberalization and privatization brings about decreasing tax revenues even though the new tax system has been operating for several years.

It would be possible for governments to cut the budget. However, it is more likely that revenues would decrease faster than spending could be cut. Relatively *large budget deficits* are to be expected in Eastern Europe.

So how could governments finance budget deficits during liberalization? The *issuance of government bonds* has some problems. High interest rates have to be payed on government bonds because of mistrust in the governments. High interest rates can lead to a high total deficit (including interest). The dynamics of debt are affected by the difference between real interest rates and real economic growth. If the real interest rate on government bonds exceeds the real growth rate, and if the primary deficit is larger than revenue from money creation, the debt-to-output ratio will continue rising without limit.[14] At some point, the government cannot sell its bonds. Then, either

---

[12] Cooper (1991) pp 78-81.

[13] McKinnon (1991b) pp 110-113.

[14] Haliassos, Tobin (1990) pp 901-904.

the deficit must be cut or the government must finance the deficit by printing money. This theoretical relation means that the bond-financed deficit can induce inflationary pressure in the future, and if the public expects inflation in the future, it can increase the current inflation rate as well.[15] The deep recession in Eastern Europe encompassing negative real growth, indicates a great positive wedge between the real interest rate on government bonds and real economic growth. Therefore, sooner or later, *monetisation of the budget deficit* must occur.

A budget deficit financed by money creation generates inflation. If money growth is needed by the government to stabilize seigniorage, it can lead to a steady state of inflation. Monetisation of the budget deficit creates further problems. If money demand function is Cagan-type, the following relation is valid in a steady state: money growth - real growth of GDP = inflation. Decreasing GDP results in an increasing inflation rate if the government needs an unchanged rate of money growth to finance the budget deficit.[16]

Eastern European governments cannot renounce revenue from money creation in order to slow down inflation. This kind of budget deficit financing leads to higher inflation than in Western Europe, and probably not only in the short run. Restrictive fiscal policy cannot be expected and therefore other instruments have to assure sustainable convertibility.

4.2 Monetary Policy

Let us assume that a two-tier banking system exists. Such is the case in Poland and Hungary. In other Eastern European countries, such reforms are in progress. A possible central bank policy in a one-tier banking system is not analyzed here.

In Eastern Europe, the money supply process is influenced by budget deficits financed by money creation, by the surplus of the non-interest current account required for the debt service, and by capital inflows encouraged by economic liberalization. Money supply shocks brought about by an increase in net foreign assets have to be sterilized.

How can central banks in Eastern Europe sterilize money supply shocks? The stock of government bonds is too small to effectively influence money supply through open market operations. The central bank has at least two opportunities to sterilize money supply shocks: by changing the (i) refinancing credit limits of commercial banks, and (ii) reserve requirements ratios.

If the government seeks to sterilize the money supply by decreasing refinancing credits, after a time this tool is no longer available (i.e., credits reach zero limits). The

---

[15] Sargent, Wallace (1981) pp 2-7, and Bruno, Fischer (1990) pp 364-372.

[16] For empirical evidence, see Melnik, Sokoler (1984) pp 233-235.

change of reserve requirements has become more and more important for monetary authorities in Eastern Europe as well as in developing countries. Reserve requirements also can be treated from the point of view of fiscal policy. Increasing reserve requirements means increasing tax base for the inflation tax collected by the central bank for the government. The graph of inflation tax revenue on reserve requirements against the reserve ratio has the Laffer curve property. If the central bank does not pay market rates on reserves, commercial banks will suffer relative losses which they will try to shift on to someone else. They pay lower deposit interest rates and demand higher loan interest rates. If the decline in deposit interest rates is caused by an increase in the reserve ratio, then the real value of deposits must decrease at a given income. Adjustment takes place through inflation which produces lower real deposits and a lower real monetary base. If commercial banks can increase loan rates without a decrease of deposit interest rates (adopted to avoid losses generated by the higher reserve ratio), then the inflationary effect of this monetary policy instrument does not take place. The more elastic the demand for real deposits and for real loans with respect to a fall in the deposit interest rate and rise in loan rate, the lower is the limit for the reserve ratio above which a single unit increase in the reserve ratio induces inflation and a lower real monetary base.[17] The increase in the reserve ratio does not cause inflation at a low reserve ratio. If the reserve ratio is high enough, the central bank cannot sterilize money supply shock with an increase in the reserve ratio without causing inflation.

The consequence of this argument is that the central banks can sterilize money supply shocks in Eastern Europe only weakly, which results in *higher inflation rates* than in Western Europe. Inflation rates must be different in Western European countries because of the different development of monetary policy instruments and different initial macroeconomic situations in the Eastern European countries.

4.3 Exchange Rate Policy

Generally, Eastern European countries can choose a fixed or floating exchange rate regime, or something in between, such as a kind of crawling peg regime.

There is a strong argument *against the floating exchange rate regime*.[18] It is impossible to obtain the necessary information for an efficient exchange rate and monetary policy with a floating exchange rate regime during liberalization. The money demand function is not stable or the saving propensity of households is unpredictable, because of rapid institutional changes which would be needed for a monetary and exchange rate policy backing steady growth of the money supply. Additionally, the

---

[17] Blanchard, Fischer (1989) pp 513-516, Brock (1989) pp 112-118, and McKinnon (1991) pp 55-64.

[18] Williamson (1991b) pp 41-43.

floating exchange rate can function effectively if portfolios of economic agents also can adjust to shocks. This would be needed to develop capital markets which hardly exist in Eastern Europe. Moreover, there is a high risk that the great uncertainty, the rapid institutional changes during liberalization, and many other factors will generate irrational and speculative bubbles among economic agents leading to an unstable exchange rate, and unstable changes in the exchange rate as well.

The countries which have introduced convertibility as a part of a stabilization program have used the exchange rate as a nominal anchor in standard stabilization scenarios.[19] Moreover, the fixed exchange rate has provided the anchor for the new price system imported by liberalized external trade.

Some Eastern European countries have tried to control inflation by a *fixed exchange rate* over the last few years. A fixed exchange rate regime can be sustained only in the short run if the difference between domestic and foreign inflation is greater than zero. In this case, the central bank must depreciate sooner or later in order to ensure a stable amount of foreign exchange reserves. When depreciation does take place, it is no longer possible to slow down inflation through an exchange rate policy. Nevertheless, it is possible to continue real exchange rate appreciation under certain conditions. If capital inflows are high enough to compensate for a non-interest current account deficit brought about a *real appreciation*, inflation can slow down with the appropriate exchange rate policy. The capital inflow is high because liberalization involves increasing profit expectations. However, a strong real appreciation generates declining investments into the export sector, and those that must compete with imports. Moreover, sharpening import competition further deepens recession. Foreign capital may flow out because of deepening recession, leading to an exchange rate collapse and increased inflation.[20]

Eastern European countries can maintain fixed exchange rates only in the short run. Analyses of fiscal and monetary policy indicate that the inflation rate must be higher in Eastern than in Western Europe. In this case, a floating or *crawling peg regime* can be chosen. Because of the problems of a floating regime in Eastern Europe analyzed above, a crawling peg regime seems to be less risky than a floating regime. An ordinary crawling peg regime is continued only in Poland. There is a fixed exchange rate with occasional nominal adjustment in Hungary and Czechoslovakia. A floating exchange rate exists in Bulgaria. This country had no other choice because it did not have appropriate foreign exchange reserves to support any exchange rate. An uniform exchange rate exists in these countries. Three different exchange rates exist in Romania: the first one exists on the foreign exchange market for households; the second one exists on the market among the enterprises; and the third one exists on the foreign exchange market of the central bank.

---

[19] Dornbusch, Struzenegger, Wolf (1990) pp 57-59, and Aghelvi, Khan, Montiel (1991) pp 13-19.

[20] Cooper (1991) pp 76-78, Aghevli, Khan, Montiel (1991) pp 17-19, and Edwards, Montiel(1989) pp 890-900.

5 Payments Union Proposal

After the Second World War the European Payments Union (EPU) played an important role in the development of Western European economies, and in promoting stronger economic relations among these countries. Now, many experts propose that convertibility in Eastern Europe should be implemented through a payments union.[21] Some conditions necessary for such a payments union need examination. A payments union can operate efficiently if

(i) the trade volume between and among member countries amounts to a large part of the whole trade volume and both the governments and the economic agents are interested in increasing trade volume among the member countries,

(ii) the macroeconomic situation of the member countries is similar or can be made similar in the short run,

(iii) convertibility for all member countries is a step forward relative to the previous system.

In the aftermath of the collapse of the CMEA-trade one has witnessed a rapid decline in trade between and among the Eastern European countries. The most important problem, which has generated an enormous supply shock, has been the loss of markets in the former Soviet Union. The trade volume between the Eastern European countries was much lower than the trade volume with the former Soviet Union. Yet the benefit to be gained from a payments union is *very small* for several reasons. The old trade structure adjusted to the demand of the former Soviet Union could not be maintained. While the trade between Eastern European countries is relatively light, trade between any Eastern European country and Western Europe is large and increasing. The Eastern European countries are interested in increasing trade with Western Europe and with the rest of the world because of the non-interest current account surplus required by external debt service. If several restrictions on trade with non-member countries were introduced as in Western Europe after the Second World War in order to increase the trade volume between the member countries, it would be a step back for many Eastern European countries. They would be introducing restrictions which already have been eliminated.

All Eastern European countries are in a similar macroeconomic situation in the sense that inflation rates in these countries are higher than in Western Europe. But there are some important *dissimilarities* as well. The burden of debt service, international liquidity, the inflation rate, the depth of recession and the development of the market institutions, are dissimilar. In light of these factors, it is questionable

---

[21] For a summary see, Wiliamson (1991b) pp 32-35.

whether a payments union is sustainable.

Eastern Europe's countries have taken their *own path* in liberalizing the economy and introducing convertibility. The problems of these countries relate to that what kind of liberalization steps should be taken in the future in order to achieve unrestricted convertibility. They must take measures conforming with previous measures.[22]

The question may arise whether a payments union established with the assistance of the European Community could provide special advantages.[23] Such a measure could ensure *additional credibility* for convertibility which could not be offered by previous measures and cannot be offered by other measures. Economic agents would have more faith in the sustainablity of convertibility if the European Community supported it. This payments union requires exchange rates of member countries to ECU for a fixed but adjustable peg. From the conclusion of this paper on the differences in inflation rates between Eastern and Western Europe, it follows that such an exchange rate regime cannot be sustained. If stable exchange rates cannot be sustained, the additional credibility may be very small.

The foregoing analysis does not suggest any reason for the Eastern European countries to change the strategy on convertibility they have pursued until now.

6 Summary

One of the most important elements of the reform programs in Eastern Europe is the liberalization of international transactions. Such measures are identical to the introduction of currency convertibility. There are several definitions of convertibility both from the theoretical and the practical point of view. A currency can be convertible for residents and/or for non-residents, for households and/or for enterprises. A currency can be convertible for different items in the balance of payments, meaning that the currency is convertible only for certain transactions.

Any kind of convertibility can be achieved in different ways. The costs and benefits of convertibility depend on the strategy of implementation. The more rapid the introduction of convertibility, the higher are the costs of convertibility. However, the slower the introduction of convertibility, the higher is the probability that benefits do not arise. In this case any reform step should achieve a critical mass. There are examples for both rapid and slow introduction of various levels of convertibility. Most

---

[22] For instance, the experts of the Joint Hungarian Blue Ribbon Commission have proposed further measures for implementing unrestricted convertibility from this perspective.

[23] See Collignion (1992).

Eastern European countries have achieved de facto internal current account convertibility for enterprises. Some countries have abolished the restrictions on current account transactions of households as well. Non-residents may carry out certain kinds of current account and capital account transactions.

The experiences with currency convertibility in Eastern Europe today confirm the theoretical assumption that most benefits of convertibility - namely sharper competition on the domestic market, rapid development of the new price system expressing relative scarcities, increase in investment propensity of non-residents, better adjustment capability of the economy - have arisen as a consequence of the level of convertibility introduced thus far.

Whether or not convertibility once introduced can be sustained depends on fiscal, monetary and exchange rate policies adopted. Because of the lack of efficient tax systems, the money supply is strongly influenced by the fiscal deficit. With underdeveloped monetary instruments, money supply shocks can be sterilized only to a limited degree. Therefore, it is to be expected that inflation rates in Eastern Europe will be higher than in the European Community. In this case, the Eastern European countries can only sustain the real exchange rate. If they tried to maintain the nominal exchange rate in the longer run, the exchange rate would collapse and convertibility would have to be withdrawn.

It is difficult to give general conditions for unrestricted convertibility. It seems certain, however, that stronger control of the money supply, and a stable amount of foreign exchange reserves are necessary. Further, liberalization of international transactions should be carried out carefully because the lack of information on the expected behavior of economic agents during transition can cause many surprises which cannot be handled with the existing underdeveloped economic policy instruments.

References

Aghevli BB, Khan MS, Montiel PJ (1991) Exchange Rate Policy in Developing Countries: Some Analytical Issues. Occasional Paper 78, International Monetary Fund, Wasington DC

Blanchard O, Dornbusch R, Krugman R, Layard R, Lawrence S (1991) Reform in Eastern Europe. Cambridge, Mass: The MIT Press

Blanchard OJ, Fischer S (1989) Lectures on Macroeconomics. Cambridge: The MIT Press

Brock PL (1989) Reserve Requirements and the Inflation Tax. In: Journal of Money Credit and Banking 21, (February): pp 107-121

Bruno M, Fischer S (1990) Seigniorage, Operating Rules, and the High Inflation Trap. In: The Quarterly Journal of Economics 104, (May): 353-374

Cochrane SH, Ickes BW (1991) Inflation Stabilization in Reforming Socialist Economies: The Myth of the Monetary Overhang, Comparative Economic Studies 33, (Summer), pp 97-122

Collignon S (1992) An ECU zone for Central and Eastern Europe: a supportive framework for convergence. In: Barrel R (ed) Economic Convergence and Monetary Union in Europe, Paris: Association for the Monetary Union of Europe, pp 191-211

Cooper RN (1991) Economic Stabilization in Developing Countries. San Francisco: ICS Press, OECD

Dornbusch R, Fischer S (1986) Stopping Hyperinflations Past and Present. Weltwirtschaftliches Archiv 122, (Heft 1): pp 1-48

Dornbusch R, Sturzenegger F, Wolf H (1990) Extreme Inflation: Dynamics and Stabilization. Brookings Paper on Economic Activity, 2:1990, pp 1-84

Dornbusch R (1991) Strategies and Priorities for Reform. In: ed. Marer P, Zeccini S (1991) The Transition to a Market Economy, Paris: OECD

Edwards S, Montiel (1989) Devaluation Crises and the Macroeconomic Consequences of Postponed Adjustment in Developing Countries. IMF Staff Papers 36, (December), pp 875-903

Ellman M (1991) Convertibility of the Rouble. Cambridge Journal of Economics 15, pp 481-497

Fischer S, Gelb A (1991) The Process of Socialist Economic Transformation. Journal of Economic Perspectives 5, (Fall), pp 91-105

Haliassos M, Tobin J (1990) The Macroeconomics of Government Finance. In: ed Friedman BM, Hahn FH (1990) Handbook of Monetary Economics, Amsterdam, North Holland

The Joint Hungarian International Blue Ribbon Commission (1992): Sustainable Forint Convertibility for Hungary: What Type, and When and How to Introduce It, Policy Study #1, Hudson Institute

Lipton D, Sachs J (1990) Creating a Market Economy in Eastern Europe: The Case of Poland. Brookings Papers on Economic Activity: 1, pp 75-147

Marer P (1991) Foreign Economic Reform in Hungary and Poland. American Economic Review Papers and Proceedings 81, (May), pp 329-333

McKinnon RI (1991a) The Order of Economic Liberalization: Financial Control in the Transition to Market Economy, New York: John Hopkins University Press

McKinnon RI (1991b) Financial Control in the Transition from Classical Socialism to a Market Economy. Journal of Economic Perspectives 5, (Fall), pp 107-122

Melnick R, Sokoler M (1984) The Government Revenue from Money Creation and the Inflationary Effects of a Decline in the Rate of Growth of GNP. Journal of Monetary Economics 13, pp 225-236

Oblath G (1992) Convertibility in Eastern Europe: Concepts, Issues and Strategies. Paper presented at the AIECE meeting 'Monetary Reform in Eastern Europe', May 6-8, 1992 Copenhagen

Sargent TJ, Wallace N (1981) Some Unpleasent Monetarist Aritmethic. Federal Reserve Bank of Minneapolis Quarterly Review 5, (Fall), pp 1-17

Szegvari I (1991) Systemic Change and Convertibility: a Comparison of Poland, Hungary and Yugoslavia. In: ed. Csaba L (1991) Systemic Change and Stabilization in Eastern Europe. Brookfield: Dartmouth

Williamson J (1991a) Convertibility. In: ed. Marer P, Zeccini S (1991) The Transition to a Market Economy, Paris: OECD

Williamson J (1991b) The Economic Opening of Eastern Europe, Washington, D.C.: Institute of International Economics

Exchange Rate Pegging to the Ecu in Northern Europe: The Nordic Experience

Sinimaaria Ranki
Swedish School for Economics and Business Administration, Helsinki
Gothenburg School for Economics and Commercial Law

1 Background

The choice of exchange rate arrangement has been actively discussed within the Nordic countries.[1] A policy question that has been raised is, under what exchange rate regime the Nordics most likely would achieve their macroeconomic policy goals of high levels of employment and high levels of economic growth, and with stable prices. In general, the policy of keeping the exchange rate fixed in the Nordic countries has been an accepted practice, because it has been assumed that stable exchange rates would reduce the uncertainty related to international trade.

In the 1980s the Nordic countries practiced an active exchange rate policy as an instrument of external adjustment, to restore competitiveness or to preserve inflation. However, recently they have attempted to establish a more stable nominal effective exchange rate. The authorities clearly recognize the value of this objective for the credibility of their general stabilization effects. As a sign of their true will and engagement to reach the goal of stable economic growth, Finland, Norway and Sweden have during the last two years, one after the other, pegged their national currencies to the Ecu.[2]

Economically, it is also in the EC's interest to extend the zone of monetary stability to other European countries. At the time being there is no room for formal associations, as the members are totally engaged in formulating the EMU in greater detail.[3] Hence, the Nordic countries, willing to follow the EMS

[1] Throughout the text the notion "Nordic countries" will refer to the non-EC countries Finland, Norway and Sweden. Iceland, the fourth non-EC Nordic country, has been left out because an exchange rate pegging to the Ecu is, for economic reasons, excluded at the moment.

[2] The European Currency Unit (Ecu), a basket currency consisting of the currencies of the member countries in the European Communities (EC), is one of the elements of the European Monetary System(EMS), established in 1979 as an attempt to create a zone of relative monetary stability in Europe. It is one of the steps of the states in the EC towards a monetary union. Every member currency has a fixed Ecu related central rate, over which bilateral parities are calculated. These parities must be kept within given margins; no individual country can unilaterally decide to shift this fluctuation band. For a description of the EMS see e.g. Louis (1990), Svensson (1990) or Bulletin der Europäischen Gemeinschaften (1991: Beilage 2).

[3] In the beginning of May 1992, the Ministers of Finance discussed in their meeting in Portugal the

discipline, must stick to unilateral solutions.

1.1 Increasing Integration

Economic integration, both real and financial, increases the need of a credible exchange rate policy. The Nordic countries have a particular interest in a high degree of stability in the foreign exchange markets, because their economies are dependent on international trade to a very large extent. The trade has shifted more and more towards the EC.

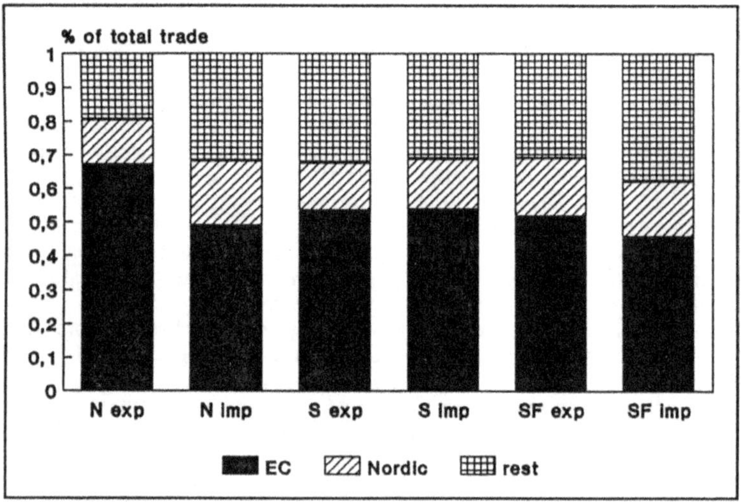

Figure 1.The share of EC trade and the trade with the other Nordic countries of the total USD value of the trade in the Nordics, third quarter 1991.
Source: International Monetary Fund

Figure 1 shows the share of the EC countries and the other Nordic countries in the foreign trade of Finland, Norway and Sweden in 1991. The integration of the Nordic countries' foreign trade and factor markets with the EC will cause pressure to adjust their exchange rate regimes to changing conditions.

The increased liberalization has concerned even the financial markets. On July 1, 1990, all restrictions to capital movements were lifted within the EC area. Even

---

formal association of non-EC currencies to the EMS. No decisions were made but the issue will be investigated. The impression was that no decision can be expected in the near future either.

the Nordic countries have since mid-1980s little by little removed regulations. The liberalization of capital markets implies that capital is crossing borders faster and easier than before. This puts an extra constrain on the credibility of the domestic economic policy. On foreign exchange markets expectations play a crucial role, and along the liberalization capital movements have become more sensitive with respect to both interest rate differentials and exchange rate expectations.

As the economic integration in Europe proceeds, and as general financial market liberalization takes place, one can ask whether it is still possible for the Nordic countries to pursue independent interest rate policies and to also set strategic monetary policy variables independent of what happens in the EC. Because of the very different construction of the old, trade-weighted currency baskets and the Ecu basket, the old baskets could have forced the Nordic countries to manage their interest rates in the opposite direction as EC interest rate movements, resulting in remarkable capital flows and negative effects on the trade flows. The more integrated the markets, the larger such destabilizing effects would have grown making a reliable exchange rate policy even more difficult than hitherto.

1.2 Political Atmosphere

The EMS is by no means only an economic instrument; the political dimension is of at least equal importance. Monetary integration is a close complement to the real and financial integration. One could say that close cooperation in monetary and foreign exchange policy is the most intimate form of economic cooperation one can have. Therefore it is important that the political atmosphere is favorable. Previously, the main argument for Sweden and Finland to remain outside the EC cooperation was the neutrality issue. However, the change in the global political setting has removed the grounds for this argument to be an obstacle.

Also the UK's participation in the ERM facilitates a closer association by the Scandinavian countries. The UK is an important trading partner for the Nordics, which was reflected in the currency baskets of these countries. In the Norwegian and Finnish baskets, the EMS currencies took a share of 59%, and in the Swedish one of 54% - of those shares the GBP counted for, on average, 7.5%.

1.3 EC Membership

The Nordic countries seem to have realized that in a future world with a tightly integrated EC, perhaps even EMU, staying outside that powerful block could become fatal for small countries who are largely dependent on international trade, like Sweden, Norway and Finland are. The real integration of the EC alone is enough to provoke comparative disadvantages that can be expected to shrink the trade with the EC. As we saw above, trade with EC accounts for more than half of the total Nordic trade. In addition, outside the EC the Nordics could not enjoy the monetary and exchange rate stability provided by the EMS to the same extent as EMS members. As non-EC members the most we perhaps could reach is an eventual future association with the EMS. The practical consequence of not operating within the EMS framework would be higher risk premia for the Nordic currencies and hence, higher financing costs in the international capital markets and higher real interest rates in the domestic markets.

It has been argued amongst the EC opposition that the present European Economic Area (EEA) agreement[4] guarantees quite enough benefits, and that the free movement of capital and financial services puts a strict strain on the conduct of independent monetary policies. If one country diverges from the policy path, it will lead to counter-reactions by others. Hence, in practice the EEA will mean a very close monetary connection between the Nordic countries and the EC, even if there is no formal agreement on it.

The truth is, however, that the EEA must be seen as a waiting room for EC membership. In the meantime, the Ecu pegs can be seen as a technical approach to the EC. The peg, if credible, will restrict the possibilities of the Nordic authorities to pursue, in the long and medium term, economic policies much different from the one predominantly followed within the EMS.

2 General Aspects

There is one major aspect that is common for all of the Nordic decisions to peg their currency to the Ecu. (A country by country analysis of the consequences of the new peg follows in section 3). All of them have suffered from high inflation rates (see figure 2), a consequently worsening competitiveness of the export goods, and a thereof resulting current account deficit. As to compensate for these losses all Nordic countries used devaluations (listed in table 1), whose long-term outcomes always were unfavorable. The economies were experiencing rapid growth, and as in growing economies generally, especially the public sector boomed. The effect of rising domestic prices was strengthened by the large wage costs, which the powerful labor unions managed to bargain. Hence, it was difficult to cut the wage-inflation circle, especially as the exchange rate arrangements did not provide the desired constraint on the economic actors that a fixed exchange rate in theory is supposed to provide. However, a continued low inflation is necessary as the source for sustained and balanced growth. A solution to the situation was seen in pegging to the Ecu and the discipline of the EMS, which was expected to have an impact on inflationary expectations. If this component of

---

[4] The EEA is an agreement between the EC and EFTA countries that shall introduce the "four freedoms", i.e. to guarantee free movement of goods, capital, services and labor between the 18 European participants. The main differencies between the EEA and an EC membership are that the EEA does not contain any monetary or political obligations. The agreement has been planned to become effective at the same time as the internal market program of the EC, i.e. from the beginning of 1993.

the inflation could be diminished, it would be easier to get control over the actual inflation, too.

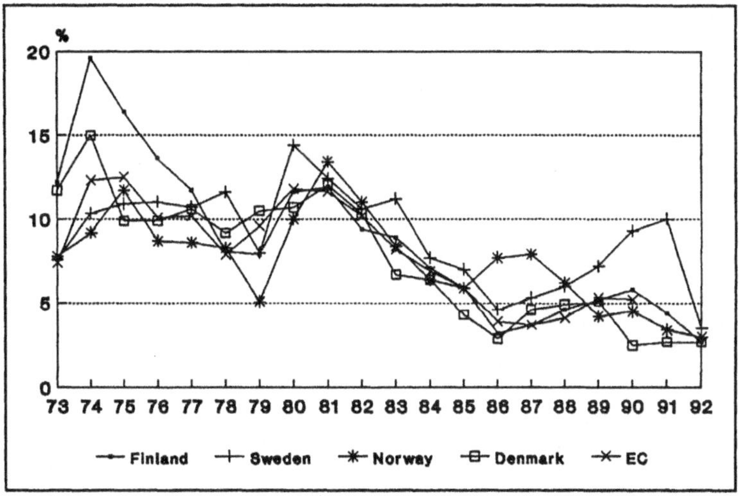

Figure 2. Private consumer deflators in the Nordic countries, as compared to the average EC rate.
Source: OECD

Table 1. The devaluations of the Nordic countries in the 1980s, as change of the parity.

1981	September	Sweden	11.0 %
1982	August	Norway	3.5 %
	September	Norway	3.1 %
	October	Finland	8.0 %
		Sweden	19.0 %
1984	July	Norway	2.0 %
1986	May	Norway	12.0 %

Source: The Central Bank in the respective country

For those countries whose currencies participate in the Exchange Rate Mechanism (ERM)[5], there is a certain restriction of national sovereignity to the

[5] The ERM is also one of the elements in the EMS. It forms the parity grid for bilateral exchange rate (see footnote 1). The notations ERM and EMS are often used interchangeably when referring to the

extent that as changes of central rates can no longer be decided unilaterally, but are subject to the consensus of all participants. Since participation in the EMS is at the present possible only for EC member countries, to which the Nordic countries do not belong, there are no binding obligations between the EC and the Nordic monetary authorities. The Nordics can therefore only pretend as if the constraints of the EMS were valid for them, too. Therefore, whether reaching the gains from the disciplinary effect or not depends solely on the determination of the domestic authorities.

2.1 Central Bank Credibility

The theoretical background behind the disciplinary effect of the EMS runs as follows:[6] In the long run, a country with a fixed exchange rate regime has to keep its inflation rate at a level low enough to guarantee the competitiveness of its exports on the international markets. Otherwise, since the exchange rate policy tool is missing, it experiences a real appreciation which dampens the foreign component in the aggregate demand and lessens the pressure on the domestic goods markets. Within the EMS, the real appreciation experienced is not compensated for in the realignments. Hence, EMS membership brings potentially large credibility gains to policy makers in high-inflation countries because it not only attaches an extra penalty to inflation in terms of losses in competitiveness but makes the public aware that the policy maker is faced with such a penalty, and thus helps to overcome the inefficiency stemming from the public's mistrust for the authorities.

A special problem in the Nordic countries has been the labor markets. Therefore, the first goal of the Ecu pegs is to discipline the domestic price and wage formation. It shall hand over the power and responsibility for profitability and employment from the authorities to the parties of the labormarket. The inflationary wage settlements, typical for the Nordic countries, would be held back, since both employers and trade unions would know in advance that they would face as opponents of inflationary wage settlements not only their own government and their own central bank, but also the governments and central banks of the EMS countries. However, this division of the roles can be expected to exert considerable effects on the wage formation only if the authorities do not mitigate or eliminate the negative effects of irresponsible wage contracts. Otherwise, there is no mechanism driving the negotiating parties in the labor markets to bear the responsibility for the economy. Accommodating policies like devaluations and expansive monetary policy, in order to offset the profitability

---

restrictions on the exchange rate movements. At the present, of the EMS currencies only the Greek Drachma and Potuguese Escudo are not participating in the ERM.

[6] The general opinion is that the arrangements of the EMS have provided especially the inflation-prone member countries monetary discipline. As a result, the inflation rates within the EMS have converged, and towards lower rates. The disciplinary aspect of the EMS is studied in e.g.Giavazzi & Giovannini (1988), Welfens (1991) or Alesina, Grilli (1991).

and employment effects of poor competitiveness, are strictly forbidden. Instead, it is necessary to activate structural reforms that bring the economy towards more efficiency.

To attain the credibility gains requires a relatively better performance of the economic policies of the Nordic countries because the decisions to peg their currencies to the Ecu were unilateral decisions. The exchange rate arrangement is based purely on national law, and implies no international legal obligations. This means that the Nordic countries can untie from the Ecu whenever they want. It, hence, remains a task of the domestic authorities to prove that they are seriously struggling towards the goals of the EMS, i.e. to satisfy the criteria of having

- a sound economy, characterized by the avoidance of major external disequilibria and, in particular, a price performance which should be close to that of the best performers of the EC
- the readiness and ability to follow a stability-oriented policy, in particular, in respect of inflation, as a necessary pre-condition for maintaining stable exchange rates without the need for massive or frequent interventions
- essentially free capital movements.

2.2 The Technical Procedure: A Change of the Currency Basket

In Finland, Norway and Sweden the international competitive position of the economy has been the chief consideration when choosing the currency composition of the official currency basket. This is justified against the background that maintaining an exchange rate which is fixed on average in relation to the most important trading partners, ensures that the competition environment remains as stable as possible. The external value of the Nordic currencies FIM, NOK and SEK, was defined in terms of an index reflecting a weighted average of the exchange rates of the convertible currencies most important for the respective country's foreign trade. The value of the index was then maintained by the domestic central bank. Figures 3-6 show the percentage composition of the old baskets and the Ecu basket.

The difference between the previous and the present arrangements was not very large, since both are basket arrangements. Replacing the currency index with an exchange rate arrangement based on a fixed central rate in relation to the Ecu was therefore a purely technical measure.

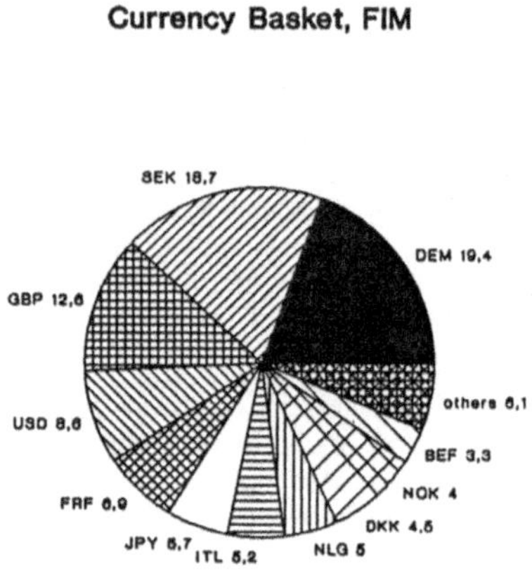

Figure 3. The old trade-weighted basket of the FIM. The arrangement was changed on June 7, 1991. Source: Bank of Finland

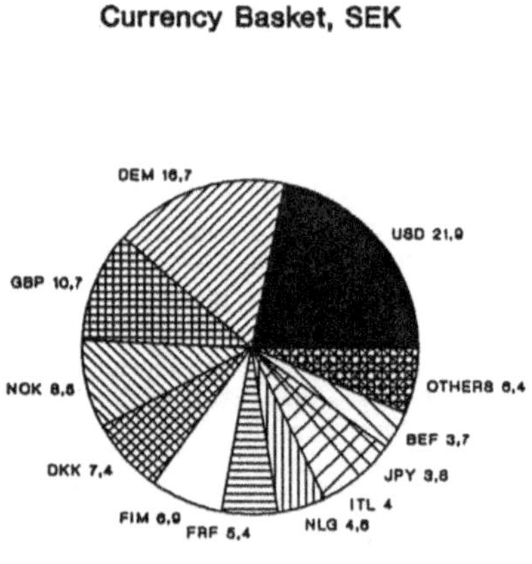

Figure 4. The old trade-weighted basket of the SEK. The arrangement was changed on May 17, 1991. Source: Bank of Sweden

Currency Basket, NOK

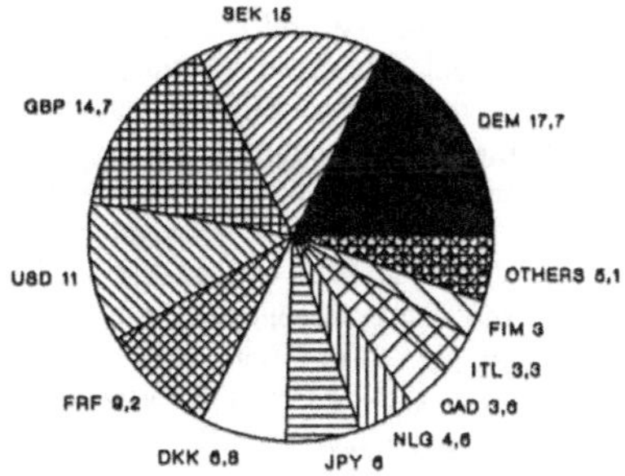

Figure 5. The old trade-weighted basket of the NOK. The arrangement was changed on October 22, 1990; Source: Bank of Norway

Ecu Basket

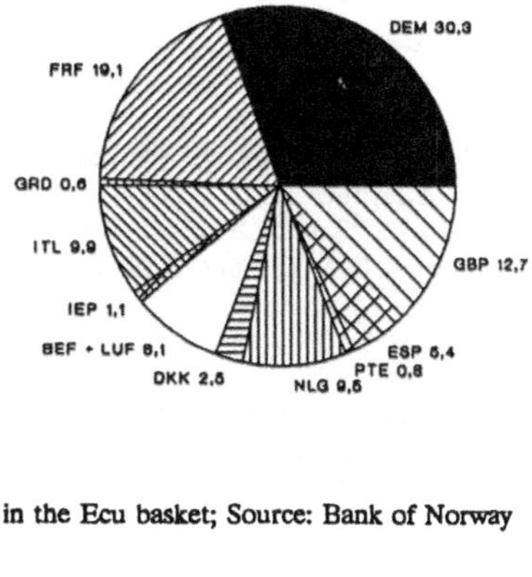

Figure 6. The weights in the Ecu basket; Source: Bank of Norway

The main counter-argument for the Ecu-peggings was that the Ecu basket is not an optimal basket for any of the Nordic countries. Each country has its own optimal basket, depending on the size and structure of the economy, the nature of international disturbances and the target variables. If it is assumed that the goal of a country is to stabilize its exchange rate in terms of a basket of currencies that will minimize fluctuations in the real exchange rate, then the Ecu basket differs from the optimal basket calculated for the Nordic countries. The Ecu basket is weighted according to the economic importance of each EMS country, whereas the baskets of the Nordic countries are designed to stabilize the competitiveness of the open sector and foreign trade prices. The major concern was therefore that the USD that had a large weight in each of the previous baskets, would now be excluded. A float against the USD is expected to imply undesired fluctuations in the competitiveness of the exports producing sector. Hence, it was argued that pegging to the Ecu would not contribute to stabilizing competitiveness in non-EC markets and consequently yield only small gains. To prove that argument remains a long-run empirical question.

3 The Nordic Countries after the Peg

This section analyzes the short-run effects of the Ecu pegs for each country and tries to find indications of whether the credibility has increased or not.

3.1 Norway

Norway was the first non-EC country to peg its currency to the Ecu. An association to the EMS has perhaps been discussed more in Norway than in the other Nordic countries, and hence, the entry into the EMS was rather a question of timing. On October 22, 1990, the Norwegian government decided to peg the NOK to the (theoretical)[7] Ecu, thus unilaterally associating the NOK with the ERM. The new parity was set at 8.01 NOK/Ecu, with an unchanged fluctuation band of +/-2.25%, or between NOK 7.83 and NOK 8.19.

3.1.1 Reasons

The Norwegian opinion was that one should first solve domestic problems before choosing to enter the EMS. In 1990, the time was seen to be ripe for joining the EMS: Norway had succeeded in bringing down its inflation from almost 10% in

[7] The difference between the theoretical Ecu and the private Ecu is that the value on the former is calculated according to the formal definition of the Ecu basket, wheras the value for the latter is determined on the foreign exchange markets according to demand and supply conditions.

1987 to around 4%, wage increases in 1989 were pretty much in line with developments in the EMS countries, and the external deficit had been turned into a surplus. Hence, the Ecu peg was only a confirmation to new, anti-inflationary economic policy.

The decision to peg the NOK to the Ecu was made in order to seek support for an economic policy of balancing the Norwegian economy. The decision strengthened the ties between the NOK and the EMS currencies. The political implication of the decision was clear: it was a signal of a commitment to align economic and monetary policies in Norway towards prudent and anti-inflationary policy aims pursued within the EC. The change in the currency system underlined the importance of a credible, fixed exchange rate policy and the interest of Norway in contributing to extending the zone of monetary and economic stability in Europe.

3.1.2 Present Arrangements

The decision to peg the NOK to the Ecu was a unilateral decision. However, two bilateral elements are included in the Norwegian participation in the EMS. Firstly, the arrangements of annual meetings between the Norwegian Minister of Finance and the President of Ecofin has been agreed upon. Secondly, the Bank of Norway has obtained a credit support for intervention purposes. This extended bilateral cooperation is based on the Norwegian decision. The EC central banks and the Bank of Norway have concluded bilateral swap arrangements governed by uniform terms and conditions. These swap agreements will give the Bank of Norway access to the short-term funds for intervention purposes up to the equivalent of a total of Ecu two billion. Norway further has the status of "other holders" of the Ecu. The Bank of Norway undertakes to take due account of the EMS agreements and exchange rate policies, and to cooperate with EC central banks intervention policies vis-à-vis third currencies. These arrangements are supportive of Norway's determination to conduct stability-oriented policies in a way which is in general accordance with the stability objectives of the EMS and extended beyond the exchange rate mechanism itself the zone of exchange rate stability combined with freedom of capital movements and non-inflationary monetary policies.

3.1.3 Empirical Evidence

The contractive economic policies have succeeded in pushing down the inflation rate (see figure 2). This, in turn, has resulted in smaller inflation expectations, and as a consequence, the authorities have been able to lower the nominal interest rates (see figure 7), without suffering from capital outflows. The interest rate differential against the (average of the) EMS countries has successively decreased during the last years, and has now settled to about 0.5% -points above the Ecu level. From time to time, the difference has been even non-existing.

The fact that the Norwegian interest rates, as well short-term as long-term, have been declining ever since 1988, is a sign of an increased credibility of the NOK.

The Bank of Norway has kept the exchange rate very stable, and only in late summer 1991 there was little confusion on the markets, stemming from the uncertainty about the Norwegian attitude towards an eventual future EC membership.

3.2 Sweden

On May 17, 1991 the Bank of Sweden decided to tie the SEK to the (theoretical) Ecu. The value of the SEK was not changed but the tying was made at the actual prevailing market exchange rate, which was SEK 7.40054 at that hour. The fluctuation band for the exchange rate was kept at the same interval as in the old currency basket, i.e. ±1,5%, meaning that the Ecu may take values between SEK 7.28953 and SEK 7.51155.

3.2.1 Reasons

The Swedish decision to apply for an EC membership was the main reason for the Ecu peg. Accordingly, the peg can be seen as the first step in the adjustment of the exchange rate system to the conditions prevailing in the EC. The Bank of Sweden states that the second step will be to apply for an association with the EMS (as soon as possible), and the final step will be full participation in the EC monetary cooperation.

In Sweden particularly, the basket policy has been an instrument for an aggressive devaluation policy. Since the establishment of the basket in 1977, Sweden has exerted three big devaluations. The Swedish exchange rate policy has not so far had a very disciplinary effect on the increase in costs, and the offensive devaluation policy (in 1982) does not give credibility to the stabilization efforts. Therefore, there are now forces which see participation in the EMS not only as acceptable in order to be able to conduct a strict monetary policy with the focus on inflation combating, but even as necessary. The pegging can be seen as a political sign of the fact that the strategy of devaluations has come to an end; to stay outside the EMS would have been taken as a sign that Sweden wants to maintain the right to devalue. This would have created speculations about devaluations and hence, stressed the domestic interest rates and the foreign exchange reserves of the Bank of Sweden. The Ecu peg was intended to make the announced anti-inflationary policy more credible, and also to enhance the credibility of the Swedish undertaking in 1982 never to devalue again.

3.2.2 Present Arrangements

The Swedish Ecu decision is based on a unilateral act. This means that the Bank of Sweden is solely responsible for keeping the SEK within its margins. The EC central banks have no obligations to intervene in order to maintain the SEK exchange rate within the target zone.

3.2.3 Empirical Evidence

The desired outcome of the decision is that the credibility increases, the inflation decreases, the interest rates go down, and, hence, the costs decline, and the Swedish competitiveness improves. The choice of maintaining the very narrow fluctuation corridor should show the true determination of the Swedish authorities to proceed towards prolonged economic stability, and, first of all, price stability even in a long-run perspective.

In Sweden, as in Norway, the new strict course of the monetary policy has been fruitful. The contractionary course was taken first in autumn 1990, as the conservatives won the election, and the goal of an EC membership was confirmed. The inflation rate has fallen dramatically from over 10% to below 3%, being one of the lowest in Europe. As a consequence, the nominal interest rates have been falling since late 1990. The clearly formulated Swedish aim to become a member in the EC by the end of the decade has been in the background for the interest rate development.

In the financial markets, the immediate reaction to the Ecu peg were remarkable capital inflows, both as short-term deposits and as direct investments. Consequently, the interest rates continued to fall: during the first week after the peg they went down with 0.7%-points. The effect was so clear because before the peg, quite many unpredictable factors had influenced the future course of the Swedish economic policy.

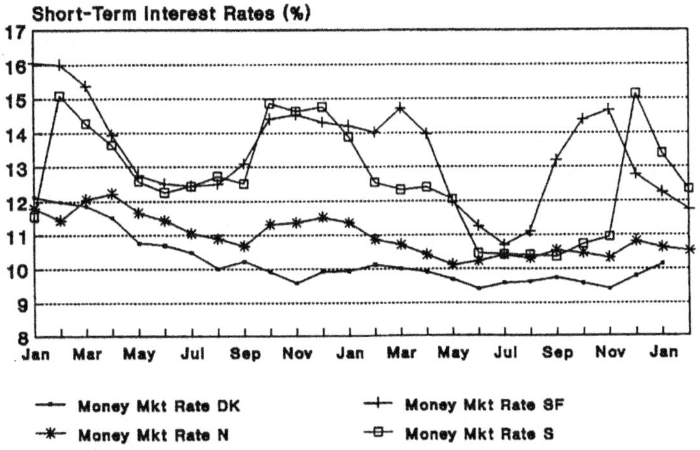

Figure 7. The development of the short-term (3M) money market interest rates in the Nordic countries after the Ecu pegs.
Source: International Monetary Fund

But the Ecu peg established an exchange rate and monetary policy whose meaning is commonly wellknown. Later, after the fall the interest rates rose again, but this was merely a reaction of the actors to find a new equilibrium interest rate level. During the first half of 1992, one year after the regime change, the Swedish interest rates have stabilized at a level about 1.5%-points above the Ecu interest rate.

It seems to be that in the financial markets, the Nordic countries are treated as a currency area where all countries have their currencies pegged to the Ecu. Hence, any economic development in one of the Nordics will affect the others. Therefore, one could expect that as long as there is uncertainty about the course of the economic developments in any of them, even the two others will have to pay a higher premium for "suspicious" investors. This has already been experienced twice in the Swedish financial markets, where the downwards course of the interest rates has (for the short maturities) been disturbed by some uncertainty stemming from the actions in the neighbour countries Finland and Denmark. In autumn 1991, the Swedes suffered from the "Finnish disease": the devaluation of the FIM arose speculations about the fate of the SEK, too. To assure the markets about the true purpose to keep the new Ecu peg literally fixed, the Bank of Sweden shock raised the interest rates to as high as 17%. After that the interest rates have not fallen to the same level as in the first enthusiastic months after the peg. It seems to be as if the Finnish devaluation made the market aware of the fact that there still is a possibility of a devaluation despite the peg. In April 1992, the Swedish money markets were suffering again, this time by the "Danish disease": the surprising voting result concerning their future participation in the EMU[8] implied uncertainty about the Swedish will to really join the EC if that should become possible. Even this time the interest rates jumped as investors escaped Nordic currencies.

In general, despite of the "infection threat" from the neighbour Nordics, the Swedish interest rates have declined from the level before the peg, though they are not at their lowest post-peg level any more. The decrease, made possible by the remarkable capital flows after the peg, indicates that the credibility in the Swedish (exchange rate) policy has increased. Before the peg the market was characterized by uncertainty about the future design of the fixed rate system as well as whether a change of the fixed exchange regime would imply a change in the exchange rate of the SEK. The Ecu peg removed these uncertainties.

3.3 Finland

The Swedish peg created a pressure on Finland to follow. However, the Swedish peg was by no means the reason for the Finnish Ecu peg; Finland had started its own preparations before the Swedes decided to peg to the Ecu. But obviously, the Swedish peg determined the timing of the Finnish action, and the procedure was

---

[8] See the appendix for a brief comment on that subject.

hurried up as rumours about an eventual devaluation of the FIM started to wake the interest of foreign exchange dealers. Hence, Finland followed the Swedish initiative taken a few weeks earlier by pegging the FIM at the prevailing market rate to the Ecu on June 7, 1991.

As a consequence of the economic developments in Finland, the Bank of Finland was forced to devalue the FIM only five months after the Ecu peg: on November 14, the FIM was set to float freely as the central bank could not defend the peg for the massive speculative flows any more. One day later the markets had found a new equilibrium exchange rate, and the new peg was set 12.3% above the initial Ecu peg, i.e. at 5.55841 FIM/Ecu. The fluctuation band was set at ±SEK 7.28953 and SEK 7.51155.

3.3.1 Reasons

The reasons for the Finnish peg hardly differ from the reasons for the Swedish peg. Even in the Finnish economy, major changes have occurred. Due to the collapse of the Sovjet economy, the Sovjet trade has fallen to about a quarter from what it used to be. Finland naturally started to search for new export channels in the western markets, and the importance of the EC consequently grew remarkably. In addition, capital movements have been liberalized as well in the domestic money markets as in the foreign exchange markets. As a result, the sensitivity of capital flows to interest rate and exchange rate changes, and perhaps first of all, exchange rate expectations have increased. Further, the integration of Finland's foreign trade and factor markets with the EC, as will be implied by the EEA agreement, gathers pressure to adjust the exchange rate regime to the changing environment.

3.3.2 Present Arrangements

The Finnish Ecu decision is, as is the Swedish one, based purely on a unilateral act. Hence, no bilateral elements are agreed upon between the EC central banks and the Bank of Finland. Though as speculations against the FIM arose again in mid-April 1992, the German central bank gave a promise to provide the Bank of Finland with intervention aid, in order to prevent a new devaluation. However, the support is only of short term, and definitely of temporary nature; Finland must restructure the economy to avoid long-run devaluation expectations based on weak economic performance rather than momentual speculative attacks.

3.3.3 Empirical Evidence

The Finnish economy is going through an extremely deep recession, largely due to the collapse of the foreign trade. The staggering foreign demand has depressed the aggregate demand and led to decreasing prices. The deflation has resulted in very high real interest rates, which in turn has crucially depressed domestic demand. As a consequence of this depression, the Finnish inflation rate is at a record low level.

Pegging the FIM unilaterally to the Ecu basket, even with the possibility to borrow from the EMS central banks for interventions, has not substantially increased credibility. The Finnish authorities have retained their decision-making power in exchange rate policy. As we have seen, an increase in credibility was only of short-term and psychological nature, and it soon vanished in front of the economic imbalances that forced the Bank of Finland to devalue. In the prevailing economic circumstances, a devaluation was seen as the best solution. Still, there is a major weakness: the devaluation and the Ecu peg fit badly together. Hence, only if we succeed in maintaining the present, devalued Ecu exchange rate, the peg could be seen as a political signal to the markets that the economic policy will be improved.

4 Conclusion

The economic advantages the Nordics expect to attain from the new exchange rate regime will not accrue painlessly or automatically, simply as a consequence of participation in the ERM. They have to be worked for through disciplined policy actions, whether inside or outside the exchange rate framework. If the exchange rate commitment is to be credible, it has to be absolutely and unequivocally clear that the policy would be continuously directed to the counter-inflationary discipline required to sustain it. All the Nordic countries have now announced that they have directed their policies towards reaching a stable and sound ground for the economy. The interest rates and inflation rates have declined; though the price has been an increasing unemployment in all of the Nordic countries. However, the real trial will be faced when the cycle turns, and capacity utilization increases: it is necessary to be able to keep the inflation rate down even under such circumstances. Equally necessary is to solve the structural problems within the public sector, which have been temporarily hidden under the prevailing recession.

The peggings to the Ecu can be seen as a part of a broader EC approach, where a membership of the EC is the natural final achievement. Sweden and Finland have already applied for membership; in Norway, the subject is still being discussed. However, at the very moment, the accomplishment of the EEA and the pegging of the currencies to the Ecu is the closest the Nordic countries can come to the EC before the EC will accept new members. Even if the peg cannot be considered as economically optimal, in political terms, the Nordic Ecu pegs can be seen as optimal, however. Pegging to the Ecu is like overcoming one obstacle, even if a small one, on the way towards EC membership.

This paper is based on the developments up till June 1992. However, in autumn 1992 the European foreign exchange rate markets were very turbulent, and quite many things have changed. At the moment, Finland has a floating exchange rate regime, which shall last until the economic situation settles. The expenditure cutting programs of the government have not been able to convince the investors of a change in the economic situation towards more stability. Hence, on September 8, 1992, the Bank of Finland was forced to let the Finnish Markka float. This event raised the interest rates in the neighbour countries to extreme heights. Norway has experienced interest rates close to 20%, whereas the Bank of Sweden, in its attempts to convince the markets of the true determination to stick to the Ecu peg, chose to use an interest rate weapon of 500%. If Sweden is able to keep the SEK fixed to the Ecu at the initial rate depends on the extent of speculative attacks - not on domestic economic conditions.

At the same time, the ESP was devalued by 5.5%, and the GBP and the ITL had to leave the ERM. These changes were due to speculations arised by the French referendum concerning an EMU membership. The voting result turned out to be "yes", which was a relief to the weak currencies in the ERM. Both the GBP and the ITL are expected to rejoin the ERM as soon as possible.

Appendix: The Danish Surprise

Another interesting and still hot potato is the Danish electoral result as they voted about a future particiaption in the EMU. With a marginal majority of +0.8% the result was negative, or as the Danes put it: "Yes to Europe but no to EMU". For the EC this was cetrainly a surprise. If the Danish result remains "within the borders", i.e. does not lead to similar changes in opinion in other member countries, it will be of no importance for the EC and the EMU negotiations. The rest of the EC can - and will - proceed towards the EMU even without the small Denmark. More important implications the "no" has for the Nordics applying for an EC membership. We were counting on the support and help from the Danes. Assuming that the application procedure will not be suspended because of the Danes, the only effect on the Nordics will be that we will have to manage the situation by ourselves; we did loose a small but important supporter. However, it has been said that the Danish result will lead to a suspenison of any application procedures. In that case, we will have to wait longer to eventually become a part of the EC.

If one wants to speculate very long in the future and assume that there is going to be an EMU and that the Nordics are going to be EC members and are willing to take part in the EMU, the situation will become quite strange. Finland, Sweden and Norway in the North, the Danes in between, and the rest of the EC in the South. Another possibility is that the Nordics become EC members and that there is going to be an EMU, but none of the Nordic countries is willing to take part in the EMU. Hence, we would have a divided EC with a unified Central Europe and a non-EMU Northern Europe. Such a situation would resemble the present EC-EFTA-positioning, but be at an integration level with more depth.

One could speculate forever with the consequences of the Danish result. The Danish decision is certainly going to affect the approaching of the Nordics to the EC in a way or another. Yet there is not much to say to it. Our Ecu pegs will remain as they are. The question becomes relevant first when we start to discuss an EC membership, and after that, an eventual participation in the EMU. The Danish voting result cannot prevent our attempts to approach the economic performance of the EC countries; it could, at most, have helped us in the application procedure.

References

Agell J, Vredin A (1991) Normer eller diskretion i stabiliseringspolitiken. Ekonomisk Debatt, no 4, pp 336-350

Alesina A, Grilli V (1991) The European Central Bank: Reshaping Monetary Politics in Europe. Discussion Paper No 563, CEPR

Anckar P (1991) EFTA and the European Monetary System. Meddelanden fråan ekonomisk-statsvetenskapliga fakulteten vid Åbo Akademi, Ser A:339

Anckar P (1992) EC Monetary Integration and Its Ramifications for Non-Member Countries - A Nordic Perspective. Meddelanden fraån ekonomisk -statsvetenskapliga fakulteten vid Åbo Akademi, Ser A:361

Bergqvist R, Johansson L (1991) Den internationella valutamarknaden 1990 och 1991 - EMS-blocket expanderar. Penning-och valutapolitik, 4, pp 5-15

Branson W (1991) Exchange Rate Policies for the Nordic Countries in the 1990s. Discussion Paper no 586, CEPR

Giavazzi F, Giovannini A (1988) The Advantage of Tying Ones Hands. EMS Discipline and Central Bank Credibility. European Economic Review, 32, pp 1055-1082

Kommission der Europäischen Gemeinschaften: Regierungskonferenzen: Beiträge der Kommission, Bulletin der Europäischen Gemeinschaften, Beilage 2/91

Korkman S (1992) Finland och EG. Ekonomiska Samfundets Tidskrift, Vol 45, no 1, pp 25-30

Lindberg H, Lindenius C (1991) Den svenska kronans koppling till ecu. Penning- och valutapolitik, no 3, pp 15-23

Louis JV (1990) From EMS to Monetary Union. Document, Commission of the European Communities

Nilsson C (1992) Den europeiska monetära unionen - konvergenskrav och anpassningsbehov. Penning- och valutapolitik, no 1, pp 26-31

Ranki S (1991a) Sverige, Norge och Danmark i makrofokus. Forum för ekonomi och teknik, 10, pp 8-11

Ranki S (1991) Ecu-magik. Forum för ekonomi och teknik, 10, pp 10-11

Svensson LE (1990) Finansiell integration, resursfördelning och penningpolitik. Avvecklad valutareglering och medlemskap i EMS. Svensk ekonomi och Europaintegrationen, Bilaga 5 till LU 90

Sveriges Riksbank (1992) Penning- och valutapolitiken 1991. Penning- och valutapolitik, 1

Welfens P (1991) Creating a European Central Bank after 1992: Issues of EC Monetary Integration and Problems of Industrial Innovation. In: Welfens P (ed) European Monetary Integration. From German Dominance to an EC Central Bank?, Springer Verlag, Berlin

Studies in Contemporary Economics

B. Hamminga, Neoclassical Theory Structure and Theory Development. IX, 174 pages. 1983.

J. Dermine, Pricing Policies of Financial Intermediaries. VII, 174 pages. 1984.

Economic Consequences of Population Change in Industrialized Countries. Proceedings. 1983. Edited by G. Steinmann. X, 415 pages. 1984.

Problems of Advanced Economics. Proceedings, 1982. Edited by N. Miyawaki. VI, 319 pages. 1984.

Studies in Labor Market Dynamics. Proceedings, 1982. Edited by G. R. Neumann and N. C. Westergard-Nielsen. X, 285 pages. 1985.

A. Pfingsten. The Measurement of Tax Progression. VI, 131 pages. 1986.

Causes of Contemporary Stagnation. Proceedings, 1984. Edited by H. Frisch and B. Gahlen. IX, 216 pages. 1986.

O. Flaaten, The Economics of Multispecies Harvesting. VII, 162 pages. 1988.

D. Laussel, W. Marois, A. Soubeyran, (Eds.), Monetary Theory and Policy. Proceedings, 1987. XVIII, 383 pages. 1988.

G. Rubel, Factors Determining External Debt. VI, 264 pages. 1988.

B. C. J. van Velthoven, The Endogenization of Government Behaviour in Macroeconomic Models. XI, 367 pages. 1989.

A. Wenig, K. F. Zimmermann (Eds.), Demographic Change and Economic Development. XII, 325 pages. 1989.

J. K. Brunner, Theory of Equitable Taxation. VIII, 217 pages. 1989.

E. van Imhoff, Optimal Economic Growth and Non-Stable Population. IX, 218 pages. 1989.

P. S. A. Renaud, Applied Political Economic Modelling. XII, 242 pages. 1989.

H. König (Ed.), Economics of Wage Determination. XI, 373 pages. 1990.

C. Dagum, M. Zenga (Eds.) Income and Wealth Distribution, Inequality and Poverty. Proceedings, XIII, 415 pages. 1990.

A. J. H. C. Schram, Voter Behavior in Economic Perspective. X, 274 pages. 1991.

J. B. Woittiez, Modelling and Empirical Evaluation of Labour Supply Behaviour. VI, 232 pages. 1991.

R. Arnason, T. Bjorndal (Eds.), Essays on the Economics of Migratory Fish Stocks. VIII, 197 pages. 1991.

Ch. Czerkawski, Theoretical and Policy-Oriented Aspects of the External Debt Economics. VII, 150 pages. 1991.

D. Stern, J. M. M. Ritzen (Eds.), Market Failure in Training? VII, 233 pages. 1991.

M. Savioz, New Issues in the Theory of Investment. XVI, 216 pages. 1992.

W. Franz, (Ed.) Structural Unemployment. X, 132 pages. 1992.

N. Blattner, H. Genberg, A. Swoboda, (Eds.), Competitiveness in Banking. VIII, 315 pages. 1992.

M. Carlberg, Monetary and Fiscal Dynamics. VIII, 194 pages. 1992.

H.-J. Wagener, On the Theory and Policy of Systemic Change. VIII, 234 pages. 1993.

E. Wurzel, An Econometric Analysis of Individual Unemployment Duration in West Germany. X, 244 pages. 1993.

W. Gebauer, Foundations of European Central Bank Policy. VI, 258 pages. 1993.